CRISIS
OF
CONSCIENCE

CRISIS OF CONSCIENCE
Perspectives on Journalism Ethics

CARL HAUSMAN
New York University

HarperCollinsPublishers

Sponsoring/Executive/Senior Editor: Melissa A. Rosati
Project Editor: Thomas A. Farrell
Design Supervisor/Cover Design: Stacey Agin
Production Administrator: Paula Keller
Compositor: Publishing Synthesis, Ltd.
Printer and Binder: R. R. Donnelley & Sons Company
Cover Printer: The Lehigh Press, Inc.

For permission to use copyrighted material, grateful acknowledgment is made to the copyright holders on page 205, which is hereby made part of this copyright page.

Crisis of Conscience: Perspectives on Journalism Ethics

Copyright © 1992 by HarperCollins Publishers Inc.

All rights reserved. Printed in the United States of America. No part of this book may be used or reproduced in any manner whatsoever without written permission, except in the case of brief quotations embodied in critical articles and reviews. For information address HarperCollins Publishers Inc., 10 East 53rd Street, New York, NY 10022.

Library of Congress Cataloging-in-Publication Data

Hausman, Carl, (date)-
   Crisis of conscience : perspectives on journalism ethics / Carl Hausman.
     p. cm.
   Includes bibliographical references.
   ISBN 0-06-500365-9
    1. Journalistic ethics. 2. Journalism—Objectivity. I. Title.
PN4756.H38 1992
174'.9097—dc20   91-28064
                                                       CIP

91 92 93 94 9 8 7 6 5 4 3 2 1

Contents

Preface vii

PART ONE THE PREMISE 1

Chapter 1
Evolution of Modern Journalism 3

Chapter 2
On Reflection: Ethics and Its Relevance to Modern Society 13

PART TWO PRINCIPLES 25

Chapter 3
Accuracy and Objectivity 27

Chapter 4
Social Responsibility 42

Chapter 5
Fairness 54

Chapter 6
Professional Conduct 67

PART THREE PRINCIPLES IN CONFLICT 75

Chapter 7
The Right to Privacy Versus the Public's Right to Know 77

Chapter 8
Ends Versus Means 93

Chapter 9
Profit Versus Responsibility 104

Chapter 10
The Medium Versus the Message 113

<u>*PART FOUR   TOWARD RESOLUTION*</u>

Chapter 11
Codes of Ethics 125

Chapter 12
Methods of Review 133

Chapter 13
Critical Self-Examination 145

Conclusion 153

Appendix A   Notes on Further Readings in Philosophy and Ethics 159

Appendix B   Further Readings in Journalism Ethics and Related Subjects: A Critical Annotated Bibliography 173

Appendix C   Methodology of the Pilot Study 195

References 199
Credits 205
Index 207

Preface

The State of Journalism Ethics

The study of journalism ethics has become something of a growth industry. Whereas only a decade ago there was just a handful of books on the topic, today there are dozens. Several nationally distributed periodicals devote themselves entirely to the subject, and scores of other publications include regular articles and studies about *journalism ethics*, a discipline that more than one observer has contended—only half in jest—is a contradiction in terms.

Is there really a need for another book about journalism ethics? I wrote this work partly out of frustration—not at the quality of other works in the genre, because most are excellent in their own specific ways—but because few observers have attempted to knit together all the offerings from various fields, leaving us very much like the blind people clinging to assorted parts of the elephant's anatomy. We all seem to have grabbed a piece of something and assumed that what we have is all there is: that the tail is a rope, the trunk is a snake, and the leg is a tree.

Perhaps you've noticed this phenomenon in your own reading, or by viewing seminars at which experts from various fields debate whether the news media have acted "ethically" or "unethically." Usually, the constituency of these panels includes practicing journalists, former journalists who now teach and/or write about the profession (the category into which I fall), and a variety of academics from disciplines outside of journalism.

On paper, these presentations usually promise to be lively and intriguing; in actuality, they often fall flat, and do so in a predictable pattern. The journalists parade their horror stories. The communications researchers hand out their papers and statistical analyses. The historians lecture about original intent in the Constitution. The lawyers recite their libel law. The philosophers quote some Aristotle. And then we pack up our briefcases and leave *without making any real attempt to draw interconnections among the ideas presented.*

Goal of the Book

If you are using this book as a text in a course about journalism ethics, you probably share some of the same frustrations. Is the field of "ethics" about law, philosophy, communications theory, or just commonsense applications of what you learned in Reporting I? I believe it is about all these things—and more. There is a spiderweb of connections among all of these disciplines, and taking a step back and appreciating the pattern of that web is the goal of this book. *Crisis of Conscience: Perspectives on Journalism Ethics* dissects the case histories of alleged media biases, insensitivity, lack of objectivity, irresponsible and unfair reporting, and "unprofessional" journalistic conduct. But the book also traces the sometimes spectacular historical struggle for freedom of expression, and clarifies some of the arguments which—once they are translated from the often obscure technical language of philosophy—shed a blinding, crisp light on ethical problems that have confronted men and women for centuries. Note, too, that what we term "philosophy" also digs into some rocky ground for the student of journalism ethics. We'll study logic—a branch of philosophy—and see how unwarranted leaps of logic can distort the facts as we see them. And we'll even dig a little more deeply into the concept of how we "see" those facts by occasionally examining a branch of philosophy known as *epistemology*—the study of how we know what we think we know.

Above and beyond the fact that the study of journalism ethics involves an enormous linkage to other eras and other disciplines, the field itself is *fascinating*. Once we take the time to fit all the interdisciplinary pieces together, we find that the factors that have intermingled to form the doctrines under which American journalism now functions crackle with the excitement of a good novel. A host of characters advance the plot—in ways that may surprise you.

For example, we'll explore the fact that Christopher Columbus, a consummate public relations practitioner, was probably as important a player in the early development of mass communications as was Johannes Gutenberg, the inventor of movable type. We'll examine why the U.S. Civil War forever changed the way news was gathered and presented and also transformed our ideas about "objectivity." And we can travel back just about a hundred years to discover that many of our fundamental concepts about privacy stem not from abstract legal doctrine but from the anger felt by a young attorney named Brandeis, who went into a huff when reporters crashed a social gathering at his law partner's home.

In addition, this book makes an effort to *define* some of the terms we use to debate journalism ethics. For instance, we consistently batter each other with charges that we have not been "fair" or "objective," but we do so without *really* coming to grips with what those terms mean. As we will see, concepts such as fairness are often in the eye of the beholder—or, as another example, in the artificial eye of the camera lens, which can be used by an operator skilled in artifice to paint entirely different pictures from the same set of circumstances. Even such seemingly self-evident concepts as "truth" will be dissected, thrust under our microscope, and reassembled in such a way that we can at least do battle with a common vocabulary. In Chapter 5, for instance, we reprint two completely "true" stories—stories that evoked entirely different "realities" and, in a strange type of verbal reversal, eventually backfired, producing reader reactions exactly opposite from the author's and editors' original intent.

Finally, we will, at appropriate points, consider journalism ethics as an *individual* responsibility, evaluating whether ethical questions are a matter of groupthink and collective puzzle solving, or if they begin and end with the virtue of one man or woman—a man or woman who may have to make an individual decision and pay the resulting individual price.

These approaches in and of themselves are not entirely new, of course. Historians—good ones—are usually quick to point out that history is a web of interconnections, not a series of dates, battles and revolutions unique entirely unto themselves and unrelated to the rest of society. Many philosophers, including the Britisher A. J. Ayer, noted that most arguments are a waste of time until we get down to the business of defining exactly what it is we're talking about—sort of an intellectual "garbage-in–garbage-out" theory of reasoning. And the concept of individual virtue as an ethical yardstick was hardly foreign to such thinkers as Socrates, Plato and Aristotle, the first of whom learned and taught a particularly difficult lesson about paying a price, the ultimate price (via a goblet of forcibly ingested poison) for standing by an individual decision.

But taken together and applied to journalism, I hope that these frameworks will provide an original approach to the issues involved. Here is how it will be approached:

Organization of the Book

This book is divided into four parts:

Part One of *Crisis of Conscience: Perspectives in Journalism Ethics* examines some of the premises on which our concepts of journalism and journalistic ethics are based.

Part Two focuses on some of the principles we commonly associate with journalism, principles such as accuracy, objectivity, responsibility and fairness; the chapters in Part Two unravel the fabric of those ideas and search for the common thread with which we can reliably trace an ethical conflict.

The chapters in Part Three probe how principles of journalism come into conflict with the day-to-day realities of news and news gathering.

Part Four examines the successes and failures of various attempts to resolve the problems, and proposes a concluding personal viewpoint on journalism ethics and a defense of that view.

There Are No Easy Answers

Every journalist learns, at some point in his or her career, that when you cannot come up with an articulate summary for an article, chapter or, in this case, a book introduction, you can always fall back on the stock phrase, "There are no easy answers." That cliché is intoxicatingly compelling because it is almost always true. But there *are* answers to some of the questions that confront journalism; I truly believe that. And the answers don't elude us because we are inept at finding answers.

We just haven't been asking the right *questions*.

Acknowledgments

I should like to thank the professionals who reviewed the manuscript: Lawrence Budner, Rhode Island College; Henry Schulte, Syracuse University; and Herbert Strentz, Drake University. Stan Searl, Hal Karshbaum, and Lewis O'Donnell also provided advice and insight. All errors of commission and omission, though, are mine alone. Much of the work was made possible through the support of the Department of Journalism and Mass Communication at New York University and the Mellon Fellowship in the Humanities.

CARL HAUSMAN

PART
One
THE PREMISE

Chapter 1
Evolution of Modern Journalism

If I loosened the reins on the press, I would not stay in power three months.

—Napoleon, explaining why he would control the newspapers of Paris and appoint himself editor in chief of his own house organ, the Moniteur.

*I*n 1579, an independent-minded journalist named John Stubbs was among the first in his profession to discover, in a painful and convincing manner, the predicament that underlies many decisions about what makes the news and what does not. Stubbs, whom historian and journalist Nat Hentoff (1988, p. 57) termed "a critic of certain royal policies," found his freedom of expression compromised by Queen Elizabeth. She was (they were?) not at all amused by an attack Stubbs had written concerning the proposed marriage between the Queen and the Duke of Anjou.

To prevent him from promulgating further sedition, Stubbs's right hand was severed. Then more acutely aware of where his best interests lay, Stubbs raised his remaining hand and uttered a simple and direct oath: "God save the Queen."

The co-opting of Mr. Stubbs is one example of the long series of conflicts that affect the journalist: What do journalists have a right to say, and by whose authority can they be forced not to say it? By what mechanisms are journalists, including the unfortunate Mr. Stubbs, restrained from disseminating information that is inflammatory, biased, an invasion of privacy, obtained illicitly, in violation of a personal or professional ethical standard, or simply false?

These and other frictions will, of course, be discussed at length in the following chapters. But first, it may be worthwhile to take a closer look at several of the deep, underlying fossils that chronicle the evolution of present-day concerns over the practices and scruples of journalists.

The modern mass media began, appropriately enough, as a commercial venture. It is unlikely that Johannes Gansfleisch, later to adopt his mother's surname of Gutenberg, harbored particularly lofty ambitions when he set about perfecting a machine that used movable type, an innovation that made mass production of written material possible and eliminated the need for the cumbersome process of copying any manuscript by hand. Rather, in true entrepreneurial fashion, he reacted to supply and demand factors: The Black Death had devastated the literate community and the surviving scribes commanded outrageous salaries.

Some sort of automated writing was, for those weary of being gouged by the surviving scribes, a dire necessity. The technology, though, proved hideously difficult to perfect. The Chinese had tried—for centuries—but their clumsy porcelain-block technology and huge inventory of alphabetic symbols made their efforts hopelessly cumbersome. But Gutenberg, a goldsmith from Mainz, Germany, had two major advantages over the Chinese: a knowledge of metalworking and an alphabet of only 23 characters.

While the precise technological origins of automated printing and movable type are in dispute (many inventors lay claim to portions of the process) the historical effect is quite clear. Knowledge, in the words of journalist and historian James Burke (1978, p. 105) was "democratized." Provided you could "pay and read," Burke wrote, "what was on the shelves in the new bookshops was yours for the taking. The speed with which printing presses and their operators fanned out across Europe is extraordinary. From the single Mainz press of 1457, it took only twenty-three years to establish presses in 110 towns: 50 in Italy, 30 in Germany, 9 in France, 8 in Spain, 8 in Holland, 4 in England, and so on."

While a product recognizable as a newspaper would not surface for another two centuries, the printing press almost immediately became a powerful medium of spreading information about events which recently happened—or, for lack of a better definition—*news*. And, as became the case with this new commodity of easily spread *news*, the relationship between the medium and the event was symbiotic. In the case of the Gutenberg machine, the power of the press was linked to the discovery of the New World. The power of the event was fed by the reach of the media; the power of the media was fed by the excitement over Columbus's discovery.

Christopher Columbus was keenly aware of the benefits of good public relations. He did, after all, rely on the largess of notables and nobility, and from historical accounts (Stephens, 1988, pp. 82–83) Columbus was active on the banquet circuit and spread news of his discoveries with the zeal of an accomplished press agent. The new printing press, which had virtually just arrived in Spain, was put to work spreading word of the New World. Hundreds of copies of Columbus's version of his exploits were in circulation when the explorer's tour returned to Barcelona, and other such materials were translated and printed in Rome, Paris, Antwerp, and Florence.

The net effect? As Mitchell Stephens described in *A History of News: From Drum to Satellite* (p. 83):

> Thus the letter press Gutenberg had developed—the invention of the century—was able to circulate a firsthand account of Columbus's voyage—the story of the century—to a significant portion of literate Europe within months of his return. Columbus's voyage helped demonstrate the power of Gutenberg's press as a method for moving news. And the letter press arrived in a Europe whose geographical, philosophical and economic frontiers were about to race outward, a Europe ready for a news medium equipped to give chase.

But the Europe so ready to expand its borders was not so eager to expand the freedom to use this new device. The British monarchy, as Mr. Stubbs would learn fifty years later, quite naturally viewed the "democratization" of information as a threat to the established order.

How the British and eventually the Americans dealt with this threat is the main path of our narrative, but it is worth a side trip to note that the Columbus/Gutenberg connection would be but one example of the symbiotic relationship between advances in media technology and events that propelled that new medium to greater importance. When Morse refined his telegraph, for example, he not only put the Pony Express out of business but also made it possible for a group of newspapers to pool their resources and form the Associated Press, the first nationwide electronic news service. This service was a totally new type of business, and it would foster a totally new type of information exchange—for the AP would soon become the principal source of information about the American Civil War. Since the AP served customers of all political persuasions, the coverage had to be neutral in tone. As a result, a new mass communications technology melded with an event of staggering proportions in a new symbiosis that produced not only the news service but the principle of journalistic *objectivity*.

When wires became cumbersome for certain communications applications (ship-to-shore transmissions being an obvious case in point) the "wireless" would mature, expand, and enjoy its great moments—again, in a symbiotic relationship with a major event. In this case, the event shook the world and radio brought the earthshaking news into living rooms half a world away. As Edward R. Murrow, the pioneer of broadcast journalism, intoned his famous "This . . . is London," Americans felt the immediacy of a distant war. They vicariously experienced the hardships of Londoners during World War II, and heard with their own ears the cacophony of the Nazi blitz. Moreover, they felt the *drama*. Murrow's pregnant pause after "This . . ." heightened the intensity. (Indeed, the pause had been incorporated into his reports at the suggestion of his one-time speech teacher.) Radio became the medium that brought great events into the living room, and with it brought elements of the dramatic, the theatrical, and the *sensational*.

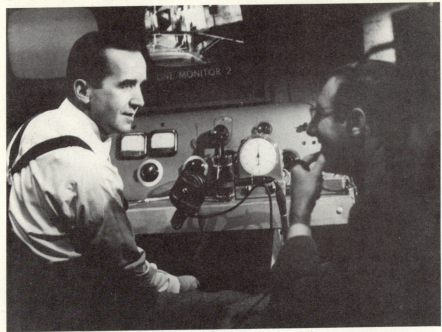

Figure 1.1 Edward R. Murrow and Fred Friendly, pioneers in television journalism, were also pioneers in confronting ethical dilemmas. Their documentaries prodded the powerful and caused consternation and controversy at CBS.

Television, regarded in the years after the war as something of a clumsy stepchild to radio, would eventually create a sense of drama and immediacy equaling and in some ways surpassing radio. TV, though, lacked two prerequisites: technical feasibility and a symbiotic event to propel it to its great moment.

From a mechanical standpoint, early TV was a technical disaster. It was studio-bound and hopelessly cumbersome. Film crews could provide pictures for TV, but the technology still offered a minimum of portability; as a result, TV was a novelty but not a practical method for disseminating news. Former CBS News President Fred Friendly remarked (interview, 1987) that covering the Korean War for television was like being forced to carry "a two thousand pound pencil."

Even studio operations were clumsy. Newscasters had very little alternative but to read their copy to the camera, blinking through the blinding lights that were needed by primitive cameras. There were no TelePrompTers, of course, so a newscast usually involved little eye contact and a great deal of paper shuffling, and the static shot of the announcer simply reading the news was not particularly evocative. Alternatives were tried. Douglas Edwards's producer (Don Hewitt, now executive producer of "60 Minutes") tried to convince Edwards to learn how to read Braille; Edwards refused. Some newscasters prerecorded their scripts into an audio tape recorder before airtime, and played it back through an earpiece as they repeated the script while holding eye contact with the camera. While a novel approach, this was not something everyone could master.

And what could a newscaster show, given the constraints of early TV? Newsreel footage was available, but it was hardly a timely way to relay information; the two-thousand-pound pencil still could not instantly be pressed into use to cover breaking news. Personalities such as John Cameron Swayze tried diligently to inject visuals, sometimes pointing to hand-drawn maps. The effect was, if not ludicrous, rather ungainly.

But as technology evolved, television would now have its great moments. The innovators who refined this laughingstock of a medium knew that the impact of actually *seeing* events would someday be stunning—and surely enough, viewers marveled at the famous moment when Murrow would show live shots from the West and East Coasts. As television became "respectable," viewers would soon number in the *millions*; they would be marshaled into what might be described as a manufactured national experience.

The year 1955 produced such an experience, a milestone of sorts: On March 7, one out of every two Americans was watching Mary Martin play Peter Pan on television. Media analyst Leo Bogart (1972, p. 1) asserted that, "Never before in history had any single person been seen and heard by so many others at the same time. The vast size of the audience was a phenomenon in itself as fantastic as any fairy tale."

But the phenomena of size and power had, by this time, become painfully evident to Joseph McCarthy, the junior senator from Wisconsin who resurrected the witch-hunt as a political tool. McCarthy enjoyed enormous power as a result of his fanatical inquisitions into the lives of supposed Communist infiltrators. But in 1954 McCarthy had seen his career scuttled when millions watched the evolving medium and did not like what they saw. It was, perhaps, the first great TV moment, the event that was finally able to capitalize on the evolving technology and use that new technology to its ultimate. Murrow assumed a role of objectivity and used film, film shot on the Senate floor under reasonably ideal and static conditions, conditions that did not reduce television images to a cumbersome two-thousand-pound pencil, to lay bare the sinister tactics used by McCarthy. Murrow simply played back portions of McCarthy's speeches, and McCarthy's tactics were reflected—warts and all—to the public, reflected by the medium that had been dubbed "the mirror with a memory."

Television, then, had added another element to the media arsenal: spectacle. The mass spectacle could not only galvanize millions who marveled at Mary Martin but also could *mobilize mass opinion* among those who had been repelled by their unfiltered reflection of the junior senator from Wisconsin.

The abilities of the media to reach large audiences, to provide immediacy and spectacle, and to provide an audience with ostensibly objective (and therefore believable) news are, of course, at the core of any debate over journalistic practices. If the media had no power, no audience, no immediacy or impact, it is doubtful that anyone would care to ponder questions of right and wrong, good and evil.

And those questions might, indeed, be moot, were it not for the peculiar set of circumstances that date back to that unfortunate left-handed publisher, John Stubbs.

In the face of absolute power there is little opportunity for the powerless to judge the powerful, a factor that would weigh heavily on individual freedoms and the parallel development of press freedoms.

Systems of distinguishing right from wrong, and mechanisms for expressing those distinctions, serve little practical purpose during times of total repression. During much of the Middle Ages, for example, there essentially was no need for a codified Anglo-Saxon system of justice because torture proved so expedient. In the event of a crime, likely culprits (perhaps "the usual suspects") were rounded up, tortured, and either confessed or implicated another party. In either event, the matter was, in the eyes of those who controlled the rack and the hot irons, conveniently settled.

England, though, would eventually carve out an environment that dealt concretely with individual rights. While far from perfect—far, far, from perfect, on occasion—the British system would evolve into a model that would shape the American system of laws and, as a related factor, press practices.

What would become the American democratic experience was unique in that it evolved from the British democratic experience, which also was unique. While France had an embodiment of an assembly in its Three Estates, and Spain had a similar structure in the Cortes, England had not only an assembly but *a document upholding certain rights of the individual.* That, of course, was the Magna Charta, a document pried out of King John. This "Great Charter" made England, in the words of H. G. Wells (1949), "a legal and not a regal state."

While power would shift relentlessly and sometimes violently between the elected assembly and the monarchy, British merchants and peers would usually find ways to keep the throne from regaining total autocracy, and from the thirteenth to the seventeenth centuries they made life particularly difficult for their monarchy. From that struggle emerged another precedent-setting document, a *document that extrapolated the rights of a previously existing charter.* It was the 1628 "Petition of Right," a text that cited the Magna Charta, reiterated its provisions, and called on the king not to tax, punish, or quarter soldiers without due process of law.

Vestiges of the Magna Charta and the Petition of Right would surface again. That reincarnation would have a profound impact on journalism as it is today practiced in the United States, a connection discussed presently.

First, though, the fate of the Petition of Right: The document set forth a lofty goal, one that would not be fully realized for some time, but during the resulting three-pronged battle among the monarchy, the owners of private property, and that nebulous group Wells called "the quite common people," the power of the crown began a gradual decline and continued to dwindle.

This is not to imply, though, that during the waning years of its autocracy the Crown did not keep a powerful hand in the affairs of the press at home and in the Colonies. In fact, one tradition imported to American shores was the European practice of licensing the press and imposing strong sanctions against those who would criticize the monarchy or other extensions of the government.

Licensing began in England soon after the introduction of Gutenberg's press, and in 1538 the Star Chamber (the governing body of a sort of royal secret police) not only required printers to have a license, but mandated that any book to be printed be approved in advance by the king's minions. The penalty for failing to comply could, if the offense were particularly heinous or repeated often enough, be the ultimate penalty; and twenty years later, the sanction of immediate execution was expanded and imposed on people who read "wicked and seditious" books *and* on those who found such books and failed to burn them immediately (Hentoff, p. 59).

American colonists, although separated by an ocean, knew all too well of the British penchant for censorship: The first newspaper printed in the United States managed to produce exactly one issue before being shut down. Benjamin Harris (who had encountered similar difficulties with censors back in England), produced an issue of *Publick Occurrences Both Foreign and Domestick* in 1690. Harris failed to mend his ways in the Colonies; he dared to publish without first seeking a license from the governor of Massachusetts.

Censorship would continue to cloud the Colonies, and about thirty years later, the issue would thrust one of America's Founding Fathers into the publishing business. James Franklin was an unlicensed publisher, but had managed regularly to produce his *New England Courant*—until he published an article particularly critical of the government. His views landed him in jail and afforded his 16-year-old brother Benjamin entry into the world of journalism.

Both James and Benjamin continued publishing the *Courant*, albeit a slightly toned-down version, without authority. In point of fact, England had actually ended its practice of licensing and prior restraint in 1695, but old traditions die hard and Colonial authorities had continued to bully printers into seeking government authorization to publish. In addition, rulers on both sides of the ocean were now armed with powerful sedition laws, sanctions which imposed heavy penalties *after* publication and which would, for all practical purposes, prove highly successful in suppressing the press for years to come. Legal historians (Gillmor et al., 1990, p. 3) note that prosecution for seditious libel gradually supplanted licensing as the instrument for governmental restraint.

The most celebrated journalist to be prosecuted with that instrument of restraint was a German immigrant by the name of John Peter Zenger. Zenger, editor of the *New York Weekly Journal*, had been sharply critical of New York Colonial Governor William Cosby. As a result, Zenger was jailed in 1734 and tried the following year for the crime of seditious libel.

Zenger's attorney, the elderly, white-maned Andrew Hamilton, argued that since the criticisms of Cosby were *true*, they did not constitute libel. The prosecution, though, contended that the truth of the comments only exacerbated the crime. Veracity, under the seditious libel law in effect during pre-Revolutionary days, only served to make the statements more inflammatory.

But Hamilton argued his case brilliantly, actually convincing the jury to ignore the judge's instructions and find Zenger innocent. His tactic? Hamilton circumvented the abstract issue of a "free press" and concentrated instead on the right of average citizens to complain about an incompetent administration.

And so a major precedent had been set: Truth was a *defense* against libel, and seditious libel was therefore weakened as a tool of restraint.

British control would, of course, soon be overthrown, and a new framework of law would emerge from the Constitution and the Bill of Rights. And while some would argue against portions of the Bill of Rights, there was comparatively little opposition to a *general statement* affirming the general concept of a free press during the Constitutional Convention of 1787 or the drafting of the Bill of Rights in 1789. *Specifics*, though, were another story. Klaidman and Beauchamp (1987, p. 7) in their insightful study *The Virtuous Journalist*, provided a historical sketch of the climate of the times:

> Virtually everyone accepted the principle of press freedom, as a rejection of precensorship and licensing. However, the context of the principle was unsettled. The idea that there should be no prior restraints on publication was supported almost unanimously, but so was the principle that there should be legal recourse for anyone damaged by licentious publication.

While the "context of the principle"—the precise rights granted by the First Amendment—remains unsettled to this day, the die had been cast. The American press, while not allowed absolute freedom, had been granted specific and fundamental legal protections by a government which, in the process of its creation, had granted *itself* only limited powers. While, as Jimmy Carter once pointed out, the United States certainly did not *invent* freedom or human rights, it could rightly be said that the quest for freedom and human rights invented the United States.

Control of mass communications is the first and most fundamental conflict in what is, when viewed from a historical perspective, a relatively new phenomenon. The democratization of information gave birth to an entirely new set of practical dilemmas.

As one example, before the advent of mass communication, little if any sustained thought was given to invasion of privacy (a topic discussed in depth in Chapter 7). Sedition was certainly a less onerous threat to the ruling class when the flames of rebellion were spread only by word of mouth; the evolution of mass communications media changed that completely and permanently.

Communications media would encounter entirely new dilemmas. The immediacy of the new technological wonder called radio could convey not only the drama of the blitz on London, but also had the power to cause a nationwide panic among naive listeners who could not distinguish between the drama of a real war and the drama of a fictional Martian invasion. The spectacle and mass audience appeal of television could bring down a demagogue, but could also be used for far less noble and evenhanded enterprises. As a result, the practitioners of journalism faced dilemmas involving *ethics*.

What, exactly, is ethics, and how does one reason ethically?[1] Consideration of those questions must wait until the following chapter, but at this point it might be worth noting that many of the journalists who pioneered the practice of judging right from wrong—and as John Dewey (edition 1969, p. 1) noted, it is the business of ethics to judge—did so on a very personal level. Stubbs, Harris, and Franklin faced a risk to their persons. Later practitioners risked their personal reputations and careers. And in a field where so much ethical firmament was carved out of personal risk, a case can and will be made that ethics must remain largely a matter of *personal judgment*.

While it is undeniable that news reporting has become a bureaucracy, bureaucracies have never been known for sharing a collective ethic. Codes of ethics have been employed, certainly, and management of all media has handed down ethical edicts and intricate procedures governing professional conduct. But can virtue be passed down by edict? To paraphrase Aristotle, it is doubtful that a person of bad character will be reformed by lectures.

Consider, also, the role that *personal* ethics played in the development of modern journalism, as news outlets continued their evolution away from government control and, as recounted by former *Columbia Journalism Review* Editor James Boylan (1986, p. 32), moved away from institutional and bureaucratic control as well.

> In general, these new managements [of newspapers which in the 1960s began to shift away from centralized institutional control] shifted toward greater emphasis on reporting, less on editing, allowing reporters to look at themselves as true

---

1 Some scholars of ethics and philosophy draw a distinction between "reason" and "ethics," maintaining that reasoning and ethics are different things, and therefore "reasoning ethically" is difficult or impossible. For example, D. A. J. Richards in his book *A Theory for Reasons and Actions* (Oxford: Clarendon Press, 1971) makes this distinction, claiming it is inaccurate to confuse "rationality" and "reasonableness." The rational is governed by the principles of logical choice, but what is reasonable is what is required by moral principles that specify duty and obligation, and, to sum up the argument in my own words, never the twain shall meet. However, such a view is not universally held. If you are interested in a rebuttal, see Ronald D. Milo's *Immorality* (Princeton, NJ: Princeton University Press, 1984), in which he argues that morality can indeed be a source of reasoning.

professionals, overcoming at last the petty standards imposed by the desk. Being a pro came to mean more than being a good soldier; it meant *allegiance to standards considered superior to those of the organization and its parochial limitations.* (Emphasis mine.)

That personal ethic reflects what has been termed the "professionalism" of reporters. While the word "profession" has many connotations not necessarily relevant to this discussion, many, including columnist and author Walter Lippmann, saw the professionalism of reporters as the most striking change in journalism since the British and Colonial governments abolished press licensing.

In an address to the International Press Institute in 1965 (cited by Boylan, p. 34), Lippmann maintained that:

This growing professionalism is, I believe, the most radical innovation since the press became free of government control and censorship. For it introduces into the conscience of the work of the journalist a commitment to seek the truth which is [again, emphasis mine] *independent of and superior to all his other commitments*—his commitment to publish newspapers that will sell, his commitment to his political party, his commitment even to promote the policies of his government.

Lippmann would later live up to his personal ethic when he refused to be co-opted by Lyndon Johnson, who—stung by Lippmann's refusal to toe the party line on Vietnam policy—made Lippmann something of a pariah in the Washington press corps. As Lippmann packed up and left Washington, he warned his colleagues to "put not your trust in princes."

The practitioners of the personal ethic of virtue have, historically, seemed equally reluctant to invest unquestioned trust in princes, in elected officials, in news bureaucracies or even the people themselves. Murrow and his colleague Fred Friendly bucked an unsupportive CBS corporate structure and a timid, apathetic press corps when they sought to illuminate the tactics of Senator McCarthy. In fact, Murrow and Friendly faced such corporate trepidation that they were forced to invest money from their own pockets to produce and promote the program.

Murrow summed up what might be the core of the personal ethic at the conclusion of his "See It Now" program on March 9, 1954. After letting viewers see McCarthy tactics with their own eyes, Murrow pointed out (Murrow collected broadcasts, 1957, p. 355) that McCarthy did not create the climate of fear, but "he merely exploited it and rather successfully."

"Cassius was right," Murrow concluded. "'The fault, dear Brutus, is not in our stars but in ourselves.'"

Chapter 2

On Reflection: Ethics and Its Relevance to Modern Society

At least you'll have a short bibliography.
—Reaction to Professor H. E. Goodwin when he told friends he was writing a book on journalism ethics

While it is doubtful that editorial conferences in most newsrooms will soon involve regular analyses of Kant or Aristotle, a case can be made that the works of so-called classical philosophers are having an impact on the way decisions are made; and that a demystification of philosophical reasoning could at the very least provide an individual an insight into his or her ways of thinking and decision making.

As examples, consider the context of these two remarks:

During the PBS series "Ethics in America," former CBS News President Fred Friendly spoke of the need for a "categorical imperative" when evaluating newsroom ethics. Act, Friendly advised, as though your principles would be followed by everyone.

A newspaper editor interviewed by this author once decided to proceed with publication of a controversial investigative article concerning a Colorado judge—an article that apparently was the cause of the judge's suicide. The editor, Jay Whearley, who at the time of the incident worked for the *Denver Post*, maintained that he was guided by utility, the principle of "producing the greatest good for the greatest number." It was regrettable that the subject of the exposé had killed himself, but this was a legitimate story about a public official. In the long run, more people were helped than hurt by the discovery of the scandal.

It would appear that there is something of a junction developing between the disciplines of journalism and philosophy. Witness the examples cited above: Terms such as "categorical imperative" and "utilitarianism" were once the sole domain of the ethicist, but are gradually moving into the newsroom's lexicon. At the same time, highly publicized journalistic dilemmas are becoming the subjects of debate and analysis by scholars trained in philosophy.

But decisions regarding ethics, by their very nature, are rarely clear-cut. Since the issues are generally intertwined with a series of problems and dilemmas, the decision maker must recognize those ideologies and thought processes that contribute to the issue at hand—recognizing that the typical "ethical" dilemma does not emerge from a vacuum and unfold with mathematical precision.

Second, there is a danger of slinging charges involving the term "ethics" when it is unclear exactly what that term means. Similarly, how do we define "moral" or "immoral" behavior, and how do ethics differ from morals?

For the sake of simplicity, let's examine the second question first: How, exactly, do we define *ethics*?

Ethics is often defined as the branch of philosophy that deals with questions of right and wrong, and good and evil. By extension, the term "ethical" is often taken to mean behavior that conforms to the basic principles of right and good. John Dewey (1969 edition, p. 1) noted that ethics is a science dealing with human action, but while other such sciences—such as anthropology and psychology—encompass human action, too, those branches of knowledge *describe*. "It is the business of ethics," he wrote, "to *judge*."

Morality usually refers not to the philosophy of right and wrong, as such, but to prevailing customs. In common usage, however, the terms are roughly synonymous, although we can easily observe our tendency to ascribe the term "moral" to matters dealing primarily with customs and not fundamental philosophy. For example, we would be far more likely to describe marital infidelity as "immoral" as opposed to "unethical." Another point of usage: "Ethics," when used to refer to the branch of philosophy, is usually treated as a singular noun, thus, "Ethics is a controversial subject." When referring to individual collections of ethical principles—"My personal ethics are quite flexible"—the word takes a plural form.

The differentiation between "ethics" and "morals" is not always a clear cleavage, but a different perspective on the word "ethics" might ease some of the confusion. As philospher Antony Flew noted (1979, pp. 112-113) there is a reasonably clear definition of ethics among philosophers, but a more generalized "lay" definition which suggests a "standard by which a particular group or community decides to regulate its behavior." So if we assume that there are least two meanings of ethics—the study of right and wrong within philosophy *and* the more common understanding that identifies "ethical" behavior with good behavior—we can eliminate the problem of trying to differentiate between "ethics" and "morals." The more informal definition of ethics, according to many scholars, including Flew, generally corresponds with the concept used by academicians; this is a long way of saying that from this point forward we can deal with "ethical" behavior using the most commonly understood sense of the term without being inaccurate.

In any event, tightening the definition of ethical and/or moral behavior is difficult for any research in any field. One investigator, Raymond Baumhart (1968, pp. 11, 12), asked 100 businesspeople for their definition of "ethical." While most responses centered on a vague idea of "what my feelings tell me is right," some were astonishingly honest. One said:

> Before coming to the interview, to make sure that I knew what we would talk about, I looked up ethics in my dictionary. I read it and can't understand it. I don't know what the concept means.

While certainly among the more candid responses, the above answer just might be among the more cogent. Few of us can completely articulate our concept of ethical behavior, and even those who have written volumes on the subject cannot always completely clarify their thoughts; in fact, the precise reason they have taken volumes to define those concepts is that the general concept of ethical behavior is difficult to define narrowly. In addition, philosophers who examine such issues tend to create intricate definitions of ethical standards, qualifications of those definitions, and qualifications of the qualifications.

This, of course, is the nature of philosophical discourse. That discourse sometimes appears impenetrable to the layperson because it is couched in the precise language necessary for detailed evaluation. To the uninitiated, Aristotle can be as bewildering as an article in the *Journal of the American Medical Association*.

But as is often the case, when the technical verbiage is stripped away, the concepts are quite clear. While much of communications ethics is, by nature and necessity, related to examinations of recent case histories, many educators have reached back into the literature of philosophy and incorporated classical thoughts into their texts and curricula. One of the more influential books on media ethics education, *Media Ethics: Cases and Moral Reasoning* by Christians, Rotzoll, and Fackler (1987, pp. 9–17), for example, employed Aristotle's *golden mean*, Kant's *categorical imperative*, Mill's *principle of utility*, Rawl's *veil of ignorance*, and the fundamental *Judeo-Christian* ethic as models to link classical thought to modern newsroom dilemmas.

To simplify the discussion, we can at this point utilize very basic definitions of those concepts. (More extensive discussion follows later.) The golden mean, of course, refers to what Aristotle thought was the ideal course of action and thought, a middle path between two extremes. Kant urged a categorical imperative that would dictate that you act as though your individual action would be applied in every case, and would become a universal constant. The veil of ignorance is a mental device whereby one tries to screen out preformed opinions and concepts. Among the precepts of the Judeo-Christian ethic are tolerance, compassion, and the resolve to do unto others as you would have them do unto you.

A trio of highly influential mass communications scholars named Siebert, Peterson, and Schramm (1964) utilized the classical literature in their landmark *Four Theories of the Press*, a book which analyzed press workings within the framework of cultural influences. The authors identified four constructs:

- The authoritarian theory, under which a powerful government controlled the press either by censorship or punishment after publication.
- The libertarian theory, which held that an educated public would choose wisely among information in a free marketplace, and should be allowed that privilege.
- The Soviet Communist theory, under which the government not only controls but produces the news.
- The social responsibility theory, which contends that the media owe a duty to the public and must be held accountable in some way should they be derelict in that duty.

In their analysis, Siebert, Peterson, and Schramm linked those theories to influential writings and ideas of the past. The authoritarian theory (pp. 12, 13) was compared to the philosophies of Plato, Machiavelli, and Hobbes. Early Christian philosophies, as well as writings of Locke and Milton, were cited as foundations of the libertarian theory (pp. 41–45). The Soviet Communist theory was, of course, related to the philosophies and social sciences of Marx (pp. 106–107). The social responsibility theory was linked with modern extensions (primarily since World War II) of the libertarian theory (pp. 75–81), and was further extended by writers such as Peterson (1966, pp. 33–49), who argued that the philosophical climate of the twentieth century created conditions where social responsibility extends to the *public*, which is obligated to be well informed and soundly evaluate information from the media.

Even the decisions of the U.S. Supreme Court have relied on philosophical musings, and have gone so far as to *cite* Milton and Mill, among others. The English poet John Milton (1608–1674), who began his career in poetry, wandered into political polemics, and eventually returned to poetry, penning *Paradise Lost* and *Paradise Regained*. While *Paradise Lost* was arguably Milton's most familiar work, an essay titled *Areopagitica*—a defense of free speech— was probably his most influential work. Milton's argument for the importance of free speech was cited by the Supreme Court in the famous *Times* v. *Sullivan* case, in which the right to criticize public figures was expanded.

John Stuart Mill (1806–1873) was also cited in the *Times* v. *Sullivan* case. Mill, like Milton, wrote on a wide variety of subjects, but many legal scholars feel that his essay "On Liberty of Thought and Discussion" was "his most lasting contribution to political thought" (Gillmor et al., 1990, p. 4). For Mill, freedom of thought and expression were precious commodities.

So it seems apparent that the thoughts of these philosophers were not interred with their bones, although those ideas did at times have to wait on the shelf for a few centuries or so before their full value could be fully exploited. As one example, consider the fact that Mill was rarely applied to First Amendment ethical issues until the 1920s—the era following a clash between governmental censorship and press freedom in World War I. It was only after this confrontation that First Amendment law was given any extended or serious attention by the Supreme Court (Gillmor et al., p. 5). And when that consideration was given, the justices reached back a century for the ideas of Mill and blew almost three centuries' worth of dust from the works of Milton.

While applying philosophical reasoning to journalism ethics is hardly a new idea, it is a fairly recent innovation in the classrooms of journalism and communications schools. Educators in the field, such as Emerson College's Thomas W. Cooper (1986, p. 76), frequently contend that an understanding of some of the more fundamental questions involving ethical choices can be more illuminating than a simple recitation of case histories. "For a student to ask how a local editor might handle a conflict of interest may prove educational," Cooper writes, "but to ask how Thomas Hobbes or David Hume would resolve an ethical dilemma may lead to both a broader and deeper set of discoveries."

However, developing an understanding of those "broader and deeper" discoveries can be daunting; it is difficult indeed for someone who may or may not have had extensive training in the field of formal philosophy to mesh the somewhat arcane world of ethics with the often mundane realm of newsroom operations. The development of various strains of philosophy and ethics is far beyond the scope of this chapter, although the recommended reading list in Appendix A does provide a brief time line of ethical thought that might prove helpful.

But a simpler method to illustrate that interrelationship involves using the most fundamental dividing point of ethical analysis to demonstrate the ways in which terms such as "categorical imperative" and "principle of utility" have a palpable impact on understanding journalistic decision making.

In the very simplest (and admittedly simplistic) analysis, philosophers who address the subject of ethics fall into two camps: those who judge the ethical implications of their actions by the expected consequences, and those who evaluate an ethical choice by categorically applying pre-evaluated rules, rather than anticipating the outcome of the decision.

Merrill and Odell (1983), who married the fields of philosophy and journalism in an unusual and possibly unique book of precisely that title, made that distinction, holding that analyzing the differences between ethicists who deal in consequences and those who do not is the logical first step in examining theories and approaches to ethics. In defining the dichotomy, they use the terms *teleological* and *deontological*.

A *teleological* theory, as defined by Merrill and Odell, is "any theory which measures the rightness or wrongness of an action or set of actions in terms of its/their consequences" (p. 79). A *deontological* theory is exactly the opposite; it ignores consequences and grounds ethical judgments on categorical reasoning, or God's will, or the conventions of society (p. 79). A simpler and more linguistically intuitive method of expressing this concept is to utilize the more common synonymous terms *consequentialist* and *non-consequentialist*. A teleological theory is a consequentialist theory; a deontological theory is non-consequentialist.

To augment the consequentialist versus non-consequentialist scenario, we can assume that some people confronted with an ethical decision will stay roughly in the middle, advocating an approach that adds up the pluses and minuses and takes the central path, a *mean*, that balances two extremes.

Figure 2.1 shows a continuum which illustrates the concept of *consequentialism*, *non-consequentialism*, and the *mean*.

Consequentialists essentially hold that instead of attempting to judge whether an act itself is right or wrong, the judgment should be predicated on the *outcome* of the act. John Stuart Mill and Jeremy Bentham were noted consequentialists. They advocated a type of consequentialism called "utilitarianism," the course of action which produces the greatest good for the greatest number, or, as Mill put it, "the greatest happiness." (Note that while Mill and Bentham share the same basic ideas, there are differences in their philosophies.) In short, consequentialists will argue that the ends justify the means, and that motives are not a particularly important factor in the analysis. If someone saves you from drowning, Mill might argue, it does not

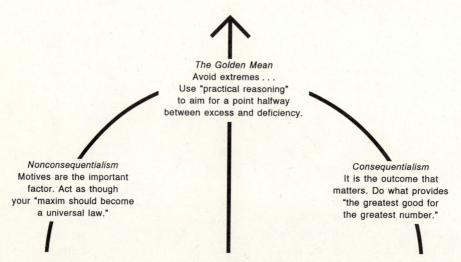

Figure 2.1 An ethical continuum that can be used to visualize the distinctions among non-consequentialism, consequentialism, and golden mean reasoning.

matter if he saved you out of the goodness of his heart or to get his name in the paper: You were saved, and that is all that counts.

Non-consequentialists contend that results are not the standard by which we judge an action. Motives are the critical aspects in the decision. Immanuel Kant is probably history's most prominent non-consequentialist, and his philosophies still guide those who believe in his "categorical imperative." Basically, Kant held that people live in a sort of moral democracy in which double standards have no place. What applies to one person, he felt, applies to all. The categorical imperative means that each person should act as though his or her "maxim should become a universal law." Kant might argue, for instance, that you have no right to steal food even if you are lost and starving. Stealing—even under apparently justifiable circumstances—condones dishonesty and violates the categorical imperative.

Philosophers who have taken the middle ground essentially put trust in the individual's judgment. In other words, a person trying to evaluate a situation must aim for a point halfway between excess and deficiency. Aristotle called this the "golden mean," the quickest path to excellence. Aristotle contended, for example, that moral virtue is the mean between extremes, a mean that can be determined not by blind adherence to only the consequences, or only the motives, but to "rational principle . . . that principle by which the man of practical reason would [make a decision]."

Another middle path was pointed out by W. D. Ross, who offered a consequentialist footnote to Kant's theory: Keep the principles and maxims as having prima facie validity ("stealing is always wrong"), but make a rule for exceptions under certain tragic circumstances, when adhering to the maxim would produce serious and substantial damage ("do no harm"). In this way Ross mediates the ethical principles of justice (treat all equally according to moral law) and of benevolence (do good, not harm, to people).

The concepts of consequentialism, non-consequentialism, and the golden mean are easily adapted to discussions of typical journalistic decisions. Here is a hypothetical situation (based loosely on a recurrent real-life situation regularly faced by reporters and editors), followed by examples of how the situation can be analyzed via consequentialism, non-consequentialism, and the golden mean.

> SITUATION: A teenager, the captain of the local football team and the president of his high school senior class, commits suicide by hanging himself inside a school building. It is the unwritten policy of the *Hypothetical Herald* not to publish the names of suicide victims who are essentially private people (as opposed to public figures or officials). However, there is no law prohibiting the publication of the name and details of the suicide, and three editors are considering the possibility of publishing full details of the incident.
>
> Editor A is a consequentialist. His argument: "You know, for years we've swept teenage suicide under the rug. We've pretended that it doesn't happen, or maybe it just happens to really messed-up kids who are runaways or strung out on

drugs. But here's a kid who had everything going for him, and he still killed himself. I'm sorry—I know it will cause his family terrible pain—but think of all the lives we might save if we give this full coverage! Let's hammer home the idea that even a kid who seems happy and successful can be a suicide victim. Let's use his name. Everybody in town knows him. This might wake a few people up. And to be honest, we can't let the other papers in town kill us on this. You know they're going to run the whole story, and they're going to run it page one. We're under the gun from marketing already, and if we blow off this story we're going to be buried."

Editor B is a non-consequentialist. Her argument: "We can't just apply the rules to the easy cases. Sure, it's tempting to run his name—the word will probably get around, anyway—but we've had a policy of withholding names for years. Why should we violate our own rules now, just because we *think* we can do some good and maybe boost circulation? Aren't we exploiting this poor kid? Look, we don't know that we're going to save any lives. All we know is that we're going to put the family through hell. That's why we have the rule in the first place. Let's stick to our own policy. If we don't, what's the point of having a policy?"

Editor C wants to follow the golden mean. Editor C's determination is largely an individualistic judgment that represents, in his or her mind, the *virtuous* decision—the decision which is neither irresponsible nor exploitative, the decision that does not cater to an extreme position but balances the two positions. Indeed, a golden mean decision, for reasons explained at the conclusion of this chapter, can be every bit as painful as a consequentialist or non-consequentialist decision. But ideally, the golden mean decision, the virtue judgment, will balance the consequentialist and non-consequentialist reasoning and take into account *why* that reasoning has taken place; again, more on that will come in the final section.

Note that a golden mean decision does not necessarily translate to a *compromise*. An editor who believes only in compromise for the sake of avoiding the hard choices on either end of the consequentialist–non-consequentialist spectrum could produce what we might colloquially call a no-pain-no-gain statement. Let's assume Editor D, a strong proponent of compromise, wanders into the room and proposes just such a settlement:

Editor D: "Can't we compromise on this? We've got an untenable situation either way. We really can't ignore the suicide; we're committing a disservice to our readers. But we shouldn't violate our own policy and run the name. Why should we suddenly pick this kid to make an example? I think we should run the story but not use the name. Give the basic information, enough information to make the point about the prevalence of teenage suicide, but withhold identification."

Note that the scenarios proposed by editors A, B, and D have particular drawbacks, and these are the same categories of problems articulated by critics who debate the premises of classical ethics. Our consequentialist,

Editor A, can be faulted for ignoring motives, and for advocating a theory that cannot be proved workable.

If you read his response closely, you can infer that one of his main concerns is not being outdone by competing media. While this is not, per se, an immoral position, it can certainly be construed as rather insensitive.

His argument about deterrence seems to make sense, but how do we *really know* what the outcome will be? Critics of consequentialist reasoning point out that we never really can judge by consequences because we very rarely know what those consequences will be. Will the story deter teenage suicide? Possibly, but possibly not. Doesn't it make more sense to base the decision on the premises of which we are sure: Our policy that, for good reason, protects the privacy of the families of terribly disturbed people who take their own lives? We do this simply because it is the right thing to do.

Non-consequentialists, like Editor B, come in for their share of criticism in classical ethical analysis, too, primarily because critics contend that blind adherence to a categorical imperative is an unrealistic ideal. Second, critics contend that this type of thinking is inherently inconsistent.

As an example of the tendency to follow an unrealistic ideal, our non-consequentialist editor might be accused of blocking a possible act of good by prohibiting full coverage of the suicide. It is arguable (and some respectable authorities *have* in fact so argued) that teenagers who are considering suicide often exhibit an initial symptom: They talk about suicide to family and friends. But if family and friends are not aware that seemingly happy and well-adjusted youngsters *do* commit suicide, and are not made intimately aware of such real-life scenarios, aren't we doing them a disservice by the imposition of this unattainable ideal of "protecting" the family?

Also, there is a problem with logical consistency here. By imposing a rule prohibiting the use of suicide victims' names, are we not *anticipating consequences*? (Besmirching the name of the victim, invading the privacy of the family, perhaps even "glamorizing" suicide are some of the arguments made for such rules.) This makes it appear that those of us who cling to the rule book are closet consequentialists after all.

The compromise of Editor D sounds like a reasonable alternative, but can it work in practice? A no-pain compromise in this case could certainly produce no palpable gain for editors or readers. By seeking a compromise, Editor D has proposed a valueless linguistic concession which solves nothing and may, in fact, be counterproductive. First of all, running a story that reports that an unidentified young man at Hypothetical High killed himself stands to send a wave of panic through every reader who has a friend or relative who is a student at Hypothetical High. If those readers have not seen their friend or relative within the last day or so, they cannot help but wonder if the suicide victim was him. Second, reporting some but not all of the story can produce absurd results. Writing, " . . . the captain of Hypothetical High's football team, and the president of the senior class, whose name is being withheld . . . " presents the facts necessary for full understanding of the story but creates an obviously ludicrous piece of copy.

However, this example is admittedly taken to its extreme. Given the right circumstances and proper editorial judgment, a case could be made for reporting the suicide but not mentioning the name. A compromise need not necessarily be an abdication of responsibility, but care must be taken to ensure that it does not cause harm by accident.

What would Editor C, the purveyor of the golden mean, do in this situation? We do not know; all that can be conjectured is that a virtue judgment would not cater to an extreme; it would somehow balance respect for the victim with the public's need to know about the event. (Again, recognize that there are self-reference problems to the golden mean, many recognized by Aristotle himself. The golden mean assumes a certain framework, meaning that the user has already presupposed the parameters. This means that if one believes mass murder is acceptable under some circumstances, there emerges some imaginary "midpoint" between reasonable and unreasonable mass murder. That type of self-reference problem won't disappear, and to an extent limits the literal applicability of golden mean reasoning.)

In any event, we *do* know that people of goodwill and long journalistic experience can and do differ on their approaches to dilemmas such as the one described above. In fact, the case is not entirely hypothetical: A popular young man in a Minnesota high school did kill himself in this way. The *St. Paul Pioneer Press and Dispatch* chose not to run the name; across the river, the *Minneapolis Star and Tribune* ran full details. The editors who made the decisions are quoted in Chapter 7; both present compelling cases, and you can judge their ethical reasoning for yourself.

The consequentialist verus non-consequentialist distinction may not be a problem solver—that is, mere awareness of the differences in approach does not guarantee a solution to the problem of making an ethical judgment—but at the very least it provides a tool for understanding our own priorities when making ethical decisions.

Priorities, of course, vary with the situation at hand; just as a position of strength or weakness may affect our choice of consequentialist and non-consequentialist reasoning, so can time constraints. Time and deadlines are brutal taskmasters in journalism, and often cause a conflict between what might be termed a logical and a temporal priority. As an example, a television report often concludes with a "standup," the closing remarks by the reporter, who might "stand up" before the White House, State Capitol, or disaster scene. This is a convention of reporting, something we are used to seeing and therefore a practice perpetuated by television reporters.

But this is a concession to temporal priority. The actual story will usually be written once the reporter returns to the television station, sifts through his or her notes, makes some phone calls, and determines, as best as possible, what the outcome of the story has been. *Logically*, this would be the correct time to tape the standup's close. But *temporally*, it is impossible, because constructing the story this way would involve another trip back to the scene.

So one result of the conflict between temporal and logical priority is that the end of the story is written first; an odd concession can affect the accuracy of the report and add an ethical dilemma. Some reporters realize this and avoid the standup tag. Byron Harris, an investigative reporter for a Dallas television station, notes (quoted by Biagi, 1987, p. 204) that the practice is "absurd.... Print reporters never had to write the last paragraph of a story before they write the story. TV reporters do it all the time. That's what a standup is. And that's an incredible thing. It's the essence: We're going to make you decide, out in the field, after being on this story for an hour, what the final line is going to be. And you're locked into that."

We do know a little about Editor C, the virtuous journalist who relies on the golden mean. Editor C is capable of making a virtue decision because he or she fulfills a certain set of criteria, criteria explained by Dr. James Gustafson (interview, 1990), author of *The Quest for Truth: An Introduction to Philosophy*. Gustafson notes that people capable of making a virtue decision will meet these qualifications:

1. They will have a basic sense of decency and a reasonable base of knowledge. Concerning decency: The midpoint between two extremes cannot be a compromise between boiling your enemies in oil or dispatching them with a quick shot to the temple. The parameters must be reasonable. And for that to be the case, the virtuous journalist must also be informed of the broad range of issues that have an impact on a decision.

    "Classical philosophers through the centuries," Gustafson says, "have assumed that decisions are made by certain types of people—people who have not only absorbed the values of decency, honesty and integrity, but understand the context of society and culture. You cannot take 'formulas' from philosophers and wrench them out of context and expect anything but a shambles."
2. They will consider the consequentialist and non-consequentialist viewpoints and understand *why* they may be using those frameworks. In many cases, Gustafson notes, consequentialist reasoning is very attractive when one is dealing from a position of power, when one clearly is in control and in a position to benefit from ends that ostensibly justify the means. Non-consequentialist reasoning is often attractive when one is in a position of weakness, and seeks to appeal to a set of rules for protection or support. Neither position assumes a value judgment; it simply offers another perspective from which to evaluate *why* we are engaging in a particular type of ethical reasoning.

3. Finally, a virtuous person seeking a judgment made along the golden mean realizes that there may be a price to be paid. According to Gustafson, "One of the problems pointed up by Aristotle is that you cannot do the right thing if you never are willing to sacrifice. A person of character must be willing to stand by principles, willing to pay a personal price for virtue."

Gustafson and other virtue-oriented philosophers sometimes bristle at the notion that ethicists are sophisticated puzzle solvers, equipped with books of formulas designed to solve any and all problems. Perhaps it is more reasonable to assume that the best decision will be made not by an accomplished puzzle solver, but by an ethical person of character who realizes that the right choice may not be the most painless choice.

No, the vast majority of us will not wind up dosing ourselves with hemlock—but perhaps we *will* learn to make virtuous decisions based on the frameworks provided by thinkers of the past, and maybe we will have to suffer a little for it. But in any event, many of us who teach and write in the field of ethics recognize that virtually any exposure to an ordered and documented system of thought brings results; such exposure can only help in the development of a mature value system.

As this realization grows, more instructors of journalism, as well as teachers in business, government, and other disciplines, are attempting to drive home the point that our modern-day ethical dilemmas are not unique. Thinkers have grappled with similar dilemmas for centuries. And while they don't have the answers for all the mind-bending questions that confront journalists, they can help apply a little method to our particular brand of madness.

PART
Two
PRINCIPLES

Chapter 3
Accuracy and Objectivity

The reverse side of a coin also has a reverse.

—Japanese proverb

On October 24, 1989, CBS News broadcast a report of a horrifying incident that had taken place the night before in Boston. The piece, according to some observers, including former CBS News President Fred Friendly (1989), "set a national agenda" for what would be a disturbing blow to the accuracy and objectivity of the news media.

The television report, prepared by CBS reporter Betsy Aaron and aired on the "CBS Evening News with Dan Rather," opened with video footage of a woman slumped across the seat of an auto, while emergency medical technicians attempted to remove her from the vehicle.

The story unfolded this way:

Video	Audio
Video of paramedics working to extract woman from auto.	CHUCK STUART: I've been shot... REPORTER: A husband calls 911 from his car phone...
Brief shot of police department emergency switchboard. Closeup of car phone.	POLICE OFFICER: Where are you now, sir? Can you indicate to me? CHUCK STUART: No, I don't know... he made us go to an abandoned area, I don't see any sights... oh, God...

Photos, side by side, of Chuck and Carol Stuart, both smiling.	REPORTER: Carol and Charles Stuart had just left a birthing class at Boston's Brigham and Women's Hospital, when a gunman forced his way into the car, robbed them of a hundred dollars and two watches, and then shot them.
Return to video of car, police and paramedics.	
Close-up of Carol in car.	Carol, with a bullet in her head, was slumped but breathing beside her husband. Charles, with a bullet in his abdomen, picked up the car phone to call for help.
	911 OPERATOR: Is your wife breathing?
	CHUCK STUART: Oh, man, aah....
Shot of Carol being unloaded from car by paramedics.	911 OPERATOR: Hang in there with me, Chuck.
Shot of Chuck being loaded into ambulance.	CHUCK STUART: Oh, man, I'm going to pass out.
	911 OPERATOR: Chuck!
	CHUCK STUART: I'm blanking out.
	911 OPERATOR: You can't blank out on me, I need you, man... I need a little better location to find you immediately. Hello, Chuck? Chuck? Can you hear me, Chuck?
	REPORTER: For thirteen minutes, Massachusetts State Police Dispatcher Gary McLaughlin kept Chuck Stuart talking.
Close-up of Dispatcher McLaughlin.	McLAUGHLIN: This is our job, that's what we do every day.
Shot of ambulance.	REPORTER: No call has ever been like this one.
Ambulance speeding down roadway.	When Chuck Stuart lost consciousness, his phone was still open. Police were able to locate the car by listening to the sound of the sirens over the phone.
Interior shot of ambulance.	Carol Stuart was rushed to Brigham and Women's Hospital, where doctors performed an emergency cesarean section, removing her son.
Ambulance pulling away.	And then she died.

Shot of Chuck Stuart being attended to by paramedics. Interior of ambulance.	Chuck Stuart is in Boston City Hospital in fair condition. He was able to give police a sketchy description of the gunman. There has been no information released on the condition of Chuck Stuart's son. Betsy Aaron, CBS News, Boston.

The Stuart case would shake the public's faith in the journalistic precepts of accuracy and objectivity—the two words which pretty much add up to "truth" in a reporter's lexicon—to the very core. Early reporting of the Stuart case had been anything but accurate. Charles Stuart had apparently fabricated the "gunman" story from whole cloth, and in January of 1990 Stuart's brother offered damning evidence to indicate that Charles Stuart had killed his wife and self-inflicted his own gunshot wound. And when the net closed, and police identified Stuart as the prime suspect in the death of his wife and infant son, Stuart killed himself, jumping into the icy waters of Boston Harbor.

Why was the evidence in the Stuart case accepted, digested, and regurgitated so uncritically by the news media? Mark Jankowitz of the *Boston Phoenix*, in a television interview (1990), noted that "page one of the manual" tells a crime reporter to "assume that the spouse is the suspect." In this case, Jankowitz admitted, "we slipped up. If there's one lesson to be learned from this [it is the need for] independent investigation."

In point of fact, many journalists *did* harbor suspicions about the case, but by and large those doubts were never aired or printed. The reason? Perhaps this exchange, which took place during a Columbia University Seminar (videotaped January 17, 1990) titled *The Other Side of the News*, helps illuminate the situation. In the exchange, Fred Friendly and Bill Kovach, the curator of Harvard's Neiman Foundation (an institute for the study of the press), discuss accuracy and objectivity in the Stuart case:

KOVACH: From the beginning of this story, every journalist covering it was skeptical of the story as it first came out.

FRIENDLY: But I've read all the papers, I've seen all the television . . . I've never heard anybody express any cynicism or skepticism. The skepticism was all in the closet. How come the newspapers and the television didn't say, "yes, *but* . . . "?

KOVACH: That's a question I have. I have talked to the journalists involved and they were skeptical. . . . I did not see the skepticism reflected in terms of "alleged," "allegations," "police say." Most of the accusations were flat, accusatory statements.

Friendly also noted that the coverage turned the Stuarts into martyrs, and the press—reflecting a need for compelling stories that reflect the good versus the bad—portrayed them as an all-American family, victims with whom *the reporters identified.*

If accuracy deteriorated during press coverage of the Stuart case, objectivity virtually disintegrated; Friendly's observation that the reporters identified with the victims—middle-class suburbanites—may explain much of the lapse. After the fact, many journalists were willing to admit that such personal identification blurred their objectivity.

The *Phoenix*'s Jankowitz, for example, pointed out that "this was a ready-made for media crime." It was a story, he alleged, that depicted ordinary people (presumably ordinary middle-class people whose circumstances bear a strong resemblance to the lives of journalists) who left an inner-city hospital "and took a right turn into hell."

From the lofty perspective provided by a postmortem, there are many processes that went wrong in the coverage of the Stuart case; among them is the way information is sanctified once it is printed or broadcast by one news organization. Other media may uncritically repeat the story, using as justification the excuse George Will burlesqued as "We accurately report real rumor." (See Chapter 7 for a discussion of sanctification of information and the rather bizarre exchange that occasioned Will's remark, which is reprinted in its entirety.)

But a deeper problem brings about lapses in accuracy and objectivity, and that is the unfortunate fact that we, as humans, are simply not capable of wielding facts per se. A "fact" is not a tangible object; it becomes a "fact" only after we have filtered it through our personal ideas, perceptions, and perspectives.

A linguist by the name of Russell F. W. Smith summed up the problem stated above this way:

> Since the concepts people live by are derived only from perceptions and from language, and since the perceptions are received and interpreted only in light of earlier concepts, man comes pretty close to living in a house that language built, located by maps that language drew, and linguistics is—or should be—one of the sciences most useful in extending the limits of human knowledge... (quoted by Postman and Wiengartner, 1966, p. 122.)

Simply stated, "knowing" is not quite as simple a quality as it might at first appear. In fact, the study of "do we really know anything and if so how?" —or epistemology— has a long historical pedigree. That heritage is too complex to address completely here, but it is worth noting that in the twentieth century, much discussion of epistemology shifted to the nature of *words*, and how they affect what we know, how we perceive what we know, and what conclusions we make about our knowledge.

Ludwig Wittgenstein, for example, tried to demonstrate that traditional problems of philosophy had usually been approached from the wrong angle. Most philosophical disputes, he maintained, stemmed from flaws in the understanding of the logic of our language. In other words, the real world is reflected by language, which in effect paints the picture of the world we see; seeming complications in the workings of that real world are merely the result of our confused descriptions of it.

A related milestone in linguistic analysis was the development of the science and philosophy of *semantics*, the study of word meanings and relations among words. Such study is a relatively new phenomenon; in fact, the word *semantics* itself is less than a century old, apparently originating (Postman & Weingartner, 1966, p. 124) in a work titled *Essay de Semantique*, published by French linguist Michel Breal in 1897. Following *Essay de Semantique*'s translation into English, the term *semantics* began to appear in publications dealing with problems of word meaning.

Much of the debate over semantics remained relatively obscure. (And, as an example of this and an excellent example of semantics in action, consider the use of the word *semantics* to connote something obscure or trivial: "That's just a matter of semantics!") However, a Polish-born engineer named Alfred Korzybski popularized (to an extent) semantic inquiry, and brought together several of the distinct branches of semantics in his book *The Manhood of Humanity*, a work inspired by the events of World War I. It was an attempt to analyze the role of language in human affairs, and to show how language was a factor in "binding" a person to his or her time. Korzybski's later work, *Science and Sanity*, dealt with what he called "general semantics," a term coined to avoid confusion among the various highly specific categories of semantic study. "General semantics" sought to combine the "binding" factor with studies of meaning, studies of language, and studies of behavior.

Semantics had thus made the leap from the study of meanings to the study of the way we *react* to words—reactions which are variously logical, illogical, or perhaps violent. Korzybski sought not only to explain words with other words, but also to explain how words are abstractions that produce reactions on high and low levels of consciousness.

In one charming example of the ways in which symbols evoke emotions, Korzybski recalled the plight of a man who had violent hay fever attacks each and every time a bouquet of roses was brought into the room. But the man also lapsed into an attack when a bouquet of *paper* roses was presented to him. At the most basic level, the man who sneezed at the paper roses had made seeing and believing a single process.

Scholars of general semantics are quick to point out that seeing and believing are never quite the same thing, because there are many levels of abstraction between the two actions. One proponent of this school of thought, S. I. Hayakawa, expanded on and popularized the works of Korzybski. Hayakawa's work on the subject, a 1941 book titled *Language in Action: A Guide to Accurate Thinking*, would bring general semantics to the attention of the general public. The work, in fact, would become a Book-of-the-Month Club selection.

Hayakawa noted that the man who sneezed at the paper roses was a victim of confusion at the lower levels of abstraction—meaning that he confused what was inside his head with what was outside. As an example of inside-outside confusion, Hayakawa (1941, p. 136) noted:

> ... we talk about the yellowness of a pencil as if the yellowness were a property of the pencil and not a product, as we have seen, of the *interaction* of something outside our skins with our nervous systems.... Properly speaking, we should not say, "the pencil is yellow," which is a statement that places the yellowness in the pencil; we should say instead, "That which has an effect on me which leads me to say 'pencil' also has an effect on me which leads me to say 'yellow.'" We don't have to be that precise, of course, in the language of everyday life, but it should be observed that the latter statement takes into consideration the part our nervous systems play in creating whatever pictures of reality we may have in our heads, while the former statement does not.

The confusion of abstractions poses no real practical problem when applied to the yellow pencil, but as Hayakawa pointed out, in other cases words become "loaded," taking on meanings deep within the listener's or reader's psyche. There is not necessarily any connection between words and what they stand for, the images they conjure up. Pictures in our heads created by leaps of abstraction can, in fact, constitute a "delusional world" (p. 147).

To simplify this idea, consider the assertion that symbols and things symbolized are independent of each other. Nevertheless, Hayakawa asserts, we have a way of feeling as though, and sometimes acting as though, there were necessary connections:

> For example, there is the vague sense that we all have that foreign languages are inherently absurd. Foreigners have "funny names" for things; why can't they call things by their "right names"? The feeling exhibits itself most strongly in those American and English tourists who seem to believe that they can make the natives of any country understand English if they shout it at them loud enough. They feel, that is, that the symbol *must necessarily* call to mind the thing being symbolized (p. 31).

While semanticists do not have a monopoly on the way knowledge is gathered, used, and interpreted,[1] their work does cut to the heart of the issue in journalism ethics controversies stemming from perceptions and word images.

---

[1] Scholars from many fields have varying ideas on how society, language, and knowledge are linked. For a useful article surveying views from the fields of education, philosophy, the basic liberal arts, literature and social sciences, see K. A. Bruffee (1986). "Social Construction, Language, and the Authority of Knowledge: A Bibliographical Essay," *College English*, 48, 5, December 1986.

The Stuart case, for example, allowed the news media to link symbols and things symbolized with abandon. Consider the reckless assumption that "a gunman" existed when such was not proved. What Friendly called "agenda-setting" is what Hayakawa would term the semantic confusion caused by *intermixing symbols and the things symbolized*. Hayakawa, himself of foreign descent, could readily appreciate the symbols and things symbolized prejudices illustrated in his quote above. The Boston community would learn how symbols-and-things-symbolized could be used as a tool to concoct an easily swallowed story: A suburban, professional couple ventured into the inner city and took that "right turn into hell."

And things only got worse. The classic semantic dilemma of linking abstractions would further inflame an already volatile situation.

Here is what happened:

Stuart had described his "assailant" as a young black man in a jogging suit. That set off a well-documented series of events that exacerbated Boston's already incendiary racial tensions. But another factor whipped the flames even higher: the discovery of alleged "suspects" and the local media's reporting about those "suspects."

In a report aired on WCVB-Boston television, and repeated for the Columbia University seminar (1990), semantic confusion produced a particularly curious leap of logic. Some background: Police, while searching an apartment in the Mission Hill section of Boston (the neighborhood where the Stuart car was found) on a unrelated incident, came across a jogging suit soaking in a sink.

The police officer who saw the jogging suit drew up an affidavit, which in the legal mechanism pertaining to search and seizure is a document brought before a judge to establish probable cause for the issuance of a search warrant. The affidavit stated that the suit seen soaking was the "same suit worn by the person who shot Carol Stuart."

That, of course, was a vast leap of logic. There is no way that the officer could have determined that it was "the same suit," but it is not atypical for affidavits to be greatly overstated because they are, in effect, "sales pieces" presented to a judge in hopes of securing a warrant.

But the WCVB-TV report took that initial leap and then dove off the cliff. "Authorities," it was reported on the eleven-o'clock newscast, "did conclude" that the black jogging suit was the one worn by Carol Stuart's killer.

Authorities? Semantically, symbols and meanings had been reconfigured to a point where truth and objectivity had been stretched to the breaking point. First, even the Suffolk County District Attorney had to admit that no police officer could possibly determine by viewing a suit in a sink that it was "the same suit" worn by the alleged killer. (Actually, the physical description of the suit given by Charles Stuart and the suit in the sink did not even match; the color of the stripe was different.) Second, the reporter had translated the affirmation of one policeman—an obviously shaky affirmation at that—into a blanket statement that "authorities had concluded."

"These," Friendly noted, "are the kinds of mistakes that rattle a lot of people . . . especially the black community, especially news observers, who say, 'How can you make a mistake like that when it distorts the whole story?'"

And that is a good question, both for journalists and semanticists.

Problems of truth and objectivity are certainly nothing new. In fact, as pointed out in Chapter 1, the concept of "objective" journalism did not really materialize until the Civil War, when economics (read: customers on both sides of the Mason-Dixon line) dictated a balanced approach.

Before that time, American newspapers were anything but objective. Media analyst W. Lance Bennett, in his book *News: The Politics of Illusion*, not only makes that contention but asserts that the lack of purported objectivity was not always a negative quality:

> Most newspapers were either funded by, or otherwise sympathetic to, particular political parties, interest organizations, or ideologies. Reporting involved the political interpretation of events. People bought a newspaper knowing what its political perspective was and knowing that political events would be filtered through that perspective. In many respects, this is a sensible way to approach the news. If one knows the biases of a reporter, it is possible to control for them in interpreting the account of events. Moreover, if reporting is explicitly politically oriented, it becomes possible for different reporters to look at the same event from different points of view (p. 123).

Lance's assertion—a common one—is that "objectivity" was born as a business practice but soon became a "value." The roots of objectivity as a market-influenced commodity are quite well documented, and some analysts, such as sociologist and media scholar Herbert J. Gans (1985, p. 32), believe that journalists value general reform more than a particular political agenda, and leave their personal beliefs "at home, not only because journalists are trained to be objective and detached, but because their credibility and their paychecks depend on their remaining detached. . . ."

But whether credibility and paychecks guarantee objectivity is in dispute. Some observers doubt that objectivity, in the strict definition of the term, is attainable. Journalism Professor Conrad Fink asserts:

> . . . true objectivity was—and is—impossible to achieve. But the *effort* to achieve it became the core philosophy of the influential Associated Press when it was reorganized in 1894 into the forerunner of today's mammoth international news agency. . . . Many individual newspapers, serving local audiences equally diverse [relating to an earlier uncited reference to "readers of all political persuasions"] and following the AP model, later developed the same business reason to strive for the ideal of objectivity.

That "ideal" evolved gradually from the time of the Civil War to the pre–World War II era. A study of newspaper objectivity by H. S. Stensaas in the *Journal of Mass Media Ethics* (1986–1987, pp. 50–60), gives some indication of this trend. The study involved the coding of stories in six major newspapers which were printed in three periods: 1865 to 1874, 1905 to 1914, and 1925 to 1934. The goal was to determine just how objective the papers were during those periods. The results indicated that nonobjective reporting appeared to be the norm from 1865 to 1874, but objectivity gained in acceptance in the 1905 to 1914 interval, and became the norm in 1925.

But evaluating objectivity with the *word* "objectivity" is really begging the question, and the question obviously is: Can journalists completely divorce themselves from their preconceptions? Further, can the "truth" always be accurately sorted from the "untruth"?

Question 1 is a softball: Obviously, no one can operate out of an emotional vacuum. Yes, journalists can try to keep personal biases out of reporting, and they can try to be fair; but not being machines, journalists cannot operate with machinelike precision—weighing this, and weighing that, and producing a product that represents an exact admixture of each and every point of view. (Fairness will be dealt with at some length in later chapters, but it is worth noting that "fair" and "objective" are not precisely the same quality, although there is considerable overlap in the concepts. We will generally think of fairness as evenhandedness and balance in handling the reporting of the story, an effort not to deliberately or accidentally distort the issue. Objectivity is often thought of as that quality of reporting the facts free from the effects of personal opinion. Some reporters—as we will explore later—think that fairness and/or objectivity are basically impossible to achieve, but some feel that one can be fair without being objective.)

Bill Moyers, a former presidential press secretary and a veteran journalist, is quick to debunk the fiction of objectivity.

> ... journalists look at ideas and events through their own eyes. There is nothing wrong with that practice: The mistake is to pass it off as something other than the pursuit of truth by men less opinionated than their peers.
>
> I learned at the White House that of all the great myths of American journalism, objectivity is the greatest. Each of us sees what his own experience leads him to see. What is happening often depends on who is looking. Depending on who is looking and writing, the White House is brisk or brusque, assured or arrogant, casual or sloppy, frank or brutal, warm or corny, cautious or timid, compassionate or condescending, reserved or callous.

Note how Moyers's list of examples could be taken directly from a semantics textbook: *assured* versus *arrogant*, *casual* versus *sloppy*, and so on. In point of fact, the underlying problem does come from a semantics textbook (Hayakawa's) and the problem is this: Words—the journalists' arsenal—have *extensional* and *intensional* meanings (Hayakawa, 1941, p. 61). The extensional meaning is generally something that can be measured or pointed to, and an extensional meaning, once asserted, leaves no basis for further dispute. If you say, "the room is ten feet long," arguments will come to a close as soon as someone shows up with a tape measure.

The *intensional* meaning is "that which is suggested inside one's head" (p. 62). (Yes, *extensional* and *intensional* have the same respective meanings as *denotative* and *connotative*, but the latter terms are borrowed from literary criticism while the former evolve from logic. *Extensional* and *intensional* are used here for the sake of consistency with previously presented material.) There is no way of measuring intensional meaning or of bringing an argument involving debate over intensional meanings to closure. Nor do intensional meanings necessarily have the same meanings when used at different times, even if they are used by the same speaker.

This, of course, is rather elementary stuff; since connotative meanings and denotative meanings are taught in grade school, what Moyers and Hayakawa say comes as no surprise. What *is* surprising, though, is the fact that this elementary principle often seems to escape readers, writers, and editors alike. Hayakawa recounts the case of a university professor who described the Gettysburg Address as a "powerful piece of propaganda." The context of the speech (p. 68) clearly showed the professor used the classic, narrowly drawn extensional meaning of propaganda—and the context also showed the professor to be a great admirer of Lincoln.

Nevertheless, the editor of the local newspaper demanded the professor's resignation, presenting an account implying that the professor had called Lincoln a liar. The editor, reacting violently to the "in-the-head" intensional meaning of "propaganda," could not be dissuaded by the actual *context* of the remark, no matter how clearly it was explained.

While this obviously was an abuse of words, an intellectual dishonesty on the part of the press, it is likely (and this is not offered as an apology, only as an amplification on the argument) that readers *could also identify with the context of the irate newspaper article*. Many readers in my community, for example, regularly are exposed to the *Boston Globe* and the *Manchester Union-Leader*. To deny that these newspapers have, to put it mildly, a different view of current events would be delusional. Yet, an intelligent reader can place varying coverage into context, and be none the worse—and perhaps a bit improved—in the process. As Hayakawa noted (p. 69):

> People in the course of argument very frequently complain about words meaning different things to different people. Instead of complaining, *they should accept it as a matter of course*. It would be startling indeed if the word "justice," for example, were to have the same meaning to the nine justices of the United States Supreme Court; we should get nothing but unanimous decisions. (Emphasis added.)

Yes, the varied viewpoints of different observers will create differing accounts; perhaps, then, we should evaluate perspectives in terms of fairness instead of the imprecise and possibly unattainable yardstick of "objectivity." (Fairness is an issue unto itself, and will be discussed in Chapter 5.)

In fact, a case can be made that we waste a great deal of energy in accusing others of intellectual dishonesty when their transgression is simply seeing things differently from the way we do—as they can hardly help doing (Hayakawa, p. 69). Bill Moyers noted that members of the news media are often charged with dishonesty when innocent discrepancy is at fault. A student, outraged that one newspaper had reported 100,000 protesters at a rally while another had estimated 300,000, told Moyers: "We might forgive journalists for not being able to write, but how can we forgive you for not being able to count?"

Virtually every journalist recognizes that it is extremely difficult to estimate the size of a crowd; and as Moyers points out, no one has yet to offer a sure way of improving our estimates. "The fact remains," Moyers contends, "that people are not willing to recognize such handicaps in judging whether we are to be believed or not. Virtue . . . can be lost quite innocently" (p. 21).

To shift gears—and disciplines—it is worth noting that semanticists are not the only scholars who grapple with the problems of objectivity, context, and truth. Historians wrestle with such problems too; but unlike most journalists, they have worked out formal, fully documented systems for evaluating information.

First, a word about truth: It is a vaunted concept in journalism—in fact, some journalists feel it is the fundamental ethic in reporting—but anyone who has worked as a journalist knows that "truth" is not an exact quantity. As an example, a certain school board candidate once maintained that his incumbent opponent had done a poor job; as proof, he proffered the fact that the reading scores of half the students in the school system were below average.

True? The facts might have been true, because an "average" is that point at which half are above and half are below, so half the scores *had* to be below average. So while the figure was true, the impression was wrong.

A similar problem confronts reporters on the police beat. Anyone who has covered the nightly carnage on the highways has received at least one tip from a citizen reporting "a horrible traffic accident," with "bodies strewn all over the place." But often the "horrible accident" turns out to be a fender-bender involving two drivers with relatively minor cuts and bruises.

In a way, the citizen's report was true: Most accidents are indeed "horrible" in some respects, and people bleeding from head cuts (head cuts are common in auto accidents, and even fairly minor cuts to the thin skin of the scalp can produce copious bleeding) are often asked to lie down while paramedics treat their injuries. It is reasonable (remember, words have different meanings to different people) to suppose they were "strewn," after a fashion.

It soon becomes apparent that depending on the source of information, and the motives of the messenger, there are many *shades* of truth. And for a journalist, the accuracy and objectivity of his or her sources often directly translates into the accuracy and objectivity of the reporter.

That dilemma, of course, is nothing new; in fact, it is quite old, and historians have confronted it . . . well, throughout history. During a period I spent working as a historical researcher, I read many works on historical method and studied under several historians, including a practicing historian now concluding a major biography of Franklin Delano Roosevelt.

I found that historians who attempted to judge truth and accuracy went about that effort in a highly organized manner. Three basic principles of historical method are particularly appropriate to the work of the journalist. They involve determining:

1. The ability of a source to tell the truth.
2. The willingness of a source to tell the truth.
3. The difference between a document and an instrument.

The ability to tell the truth. The helpful people who called the newsroom with details of "horrible" auto accidents were not trying to mislead; they simply had never seen many accidents and could not accurately gauge the severity of what they had seen. In historians' terms, they were not fully able to tell the truth.

The same situation might surface when workers in factories would call a local newsroom and claim that their plant was closing, or going on strike, or that some other calamity was looming. Such claims prove to be wrong with alarming regularity—even though the informants usually believe they are telling the truth. But, as often is the case, they cannot see the big picture. They are not privy to all the information; and as a result they jump to an inaccurate conclusion. They suffer from the same lack of perspective that caused passersby to misjudge the severity of the auto accident.

Marc Bloch, noted as a great historian and superb teacher of historical method, used *ability to tell the truth* as prime determinant in judging the veracity of the information through which a historian must sift (1964, pp. 48–78). His book, *The Historian's Craft*, is as useful to a reporter as any journalism text.[2]

Some historians term lack of overall perspective the "corporal on the battlefield" syndrome. Historians know full well that the limited perspective of a foot soldier in a battle may lead that solider into drawing some unwarranted conclusions about what really happened, how it happened, and why. That limited perspective, for example, might cause the corporal honestly to believe that his unit was the key element in winning a battle. While his tes-

---

[2] There are other useful works for the journalist. They include E. H. Carr (1977). *What Is History?* New York: Random House; and L. Gottschalk (1969). *Understanding History: A Primer of Historical Method.* New York: Knopf.

timony should not be discounted, the historian—and the journalist—must remember that he did not have access to the whole picture. At the very least, his testimony should be weighed against that of the general who was running the entire maneuver.

The willingness to tell the truth. Bloch also notes that information must always be evaluated in terms of the witness's vested interest. Does the information glorify or otherwise benefit the person who provided you with that information? If so, the historian and journalist would be wise to subject that information to closer scrutiny.

Here is a specific example of how one historian/journalist handled the problem. Richard Petrow, a professor of journalism at New York University, a former reporter for the *New York Daily News*, and the producer of the PBS "Constitution" series, wrote a book about the Nazi occupation of Scandinavia during World War II. The book was titled *The Bitter Years*. During several years of research, Petrow conducted interviews with hundreds of people who recounted their experiences with the war years—people who sometimes gave conflicting views as to what had actually happened. Petrow developed a particular standard of judgment for assessing the willingness of those people to tell the truth: *the level of the interviewee's self-interest.*

"If, when they talked about the war years, they revealed themselves as timid, cowardly, or reluctant to get involved, I tended to believe them," Petrow said (interview, 1987). "But if they portrayed themselves as heroes I tended to disbelieve them."

Petrow would also apply both the *ability* and *willingness* criteria to a fast-breaking newsroom decision. When he worked as a television journalist, Petrow received a tip from a source, informing him that a local politician was about to be indicted on criminal charges. Petrow could obtain no further confirmation, but decided to run the story.

Running an unattributed story is risky because people will often provide inaccurate facts, either accidentally or on purpose, when they know they are not going to be held publicly accountable for those statements. The journalist in the middle, then, must decide on the veracity of the item and the source.

Petrow decided to run the story. His ethical reasoning process was this:

(a) Petrow knew that the source had access to the indictment process, and had been truthful in past anonymous tips. Also, the politician had been involved in previous dealings which Petrow characterized as being on "the outskirts of legality." The source was thus *able* to tell the truth.
(b) Petrow knew the source well and felt that the informant, in Petrow's words, had "no ax to grind." In other words, the source of the information did not stand to benefit by the revelation of the

embarrassing information. The source, then, was *willing* to tell the truth.

The result: The story proved true. As an interesting sidelight, Petrow never did get clearance to run the story ("cautious lawyers," he maintains), so he gave it to a newspaper, which did run it.[3]

The difference between documents and instruments. A document is generally taken to be something which describes and *only* describes; it does not have a hidden agenda, and does not exist for any other reason than to inform. A court transcript is an example of a document. An *instrument* has a purpose other than to describe or inform. It generally exists to elicit a certain type of reaction or further a particular goal. A press release is an instrument. The press release described earlier—the one from the number-juggling school board candidate—is a particularly invidious instrument.

Procedures such as the ones above are useful, but they obviously cannot replace reasoning in the process of determining truth and objectivity. Accuracy and objectivity is as much related to individual integrity and judgment as to any particular technique of news gathering.

The journalists who bought into the scenario apparently created by Charles Stuart were not evil, stupid, or illogical. They were simply garden-variety humans who identified with the victims and let the "images in their heads" justify the confected scenario.

Often, this meant accepting and repeating information uncritically, without challenging it or submitting it to any test for logic or consistency. But this is hardly a crime unique to the press. Aristotle, known as a great logician, himself passed along unchallenged beliefs, which later proved the basis for many other unchallenged beliefs. Women, Aristotle contended, have a different number of teeth than men. (They do not.) Although he was married to several women, it apparently never occurred to Aristotle that he should verify his theory by simply asking them to let him count their teeth. Aristotle also posited that the brain serves no function in the process of thought. (We now know this to be true of only some people.) The idea—which was based on no real evidence of any sort—went unchallenged for centuries.

While Aristotle was wrong, so were the people who uncritically accepted his theories on teeth and brains. While the "facts" as portrayed by

---

[3] Petrow's thought process, as well as the reasoning of other journalists facing similiar dilemmas, was recounted in one one of the author's previous works, *The Decision-Making Process in Journalism* (Chicago: Nelson-Hall, 1990): passim. The relationship of documents to instruments was also discussed.

Charles Stuart were wrong, so were the portrayals of the critically unchallenging news media. And as semanticists assert, meanings are affected not only by the way we *use* words, but also by the way we *hear or read them.*

Truth and objectivity are a transaction. Thoreau, who liked to streamline things, put it this way: "It takes two to speak the truth," he said, "one to speak, and another to hear."

Chapter 4
Social Responsibility

You can reform yourself by dividing your newspaper into four chapters, headed: truths, probabilities, possibilities, and lies. The first chapter would be the shortest.

—Thomas Jefferson, lecturing an editor on how he could improve his product

On March 9, 1989, a fire raced through a home in the Rhode Island community of Olneyville, killing a ten-month-old boy. A photo of the victim, which might have been one of the most gruesome photos ever run on page one of a metropolitan daily newspaper, provoked a storm of outrage from readers. Many readers deplored the use of the photo, maintaining that the newspaper's action was—in the word that resurfaced many times in the running controversy—*irresponsible.*

But before passing judgment on the photo—which will be discussed and reprinted in Chapter 7—it seems incumbent to examine the root question of how a news organization acts responsibly or irresponsibly. The charge of *irresponsibility* carries with it the implication that the press has some sort of clearly mandated *responsibility.*

Defining exactly what that responsibility entails—a seeming necessity if one is going to hold the press accountable for irresponsibility—is a daunting task, and an elusive one. Scholars from any and all branches of communications and political science have never agreed on a single, unified theory of what press responsibility entails, though not for lack of trying.

With that in mind, let's delay specific discussion of the "responsibility" or "irresponsibility" of running the photo itself until Chapter 7's investigation of privacy versus the right to know, and instead *first* attempt to get a handle on that nebulous term that was wielded as a weapon in much of the criticism leveled against the newspaper. We'll also use the photo as a test case for *fairness*, the topic of the next chapter, and *professional conduct*, the subject of Chapter 6.

It might be argued that the debate over press responsibility is primarily a philosophical inquiry into the obligations of power. Arguments over obligations of power have been the cornerstone of a great deal of philosophical discourse. Plato (1981 edition, p. 126), for example, argued that the powerful have an obligation to act in the best interests of those affected by their power:

> Ought we not then to set about treatment of the state and its citizens on this principle, with the idea of making citizens themselves as good as possible? Without such a principle, as we discovered earlier, one can do no good. No other service to the state is of the slightest avail if those who acquire riches or authority over people or any kind of power are not [people] of good will.

Mass communications researcher Deni Elliott (1986, pp. 36, 37) argues, like Plato, that power brings responsibilities, and she specifically refers to the centralization of power. Since the media have, to an extent, centralized their power, she argues that John Stuart Mill (1976 edition, pp. 148, 149) might find himself in the same camp as Plato. While the following argument from Mill was leveled against government, it could presumably be extended (if we assume that the media hold "centralized power") to the press:

> To decide what opinions shall be permitted and what prohibited, is to choose opinions for the people; since they cannot adopt opinions which are not suffered to be presented to their minds. Whoever chooses opinions for the people, possesses absolute control over their actions, and may wield them for his own purposes with perfect security.

This, of course, assumes an enormous power on the part of the media—and assessing the degree of power is a question unlikely soon to be settled in these pages, or for that matter anywhere else. Yes, *to an extent* everyone agrees that the news media are powerful entities. Some observers, such as journalism professor Louis W. Hodges (1987, p. 3), director of the program on Society and Professions at Washington and Lee University, contend that journalists "have immense power" to affect the lives of others "simply by publishing ideas and information people need or want to have."

But how do we *prove* that power, and *measure* its intensity? Debates over the relative degree of power have reached no consensus. As an example, a very old jibe usually aimed at economists was recently retargeted by a weary lecturer at a mass communications seminar: If you laid all the mass communications effects researchers in the world end to end, the speaker quipped, none of them would agree. (This, of course, prompted one observer to posit that placing all communications effects researchers end to end "would be a good idea," but that is entirely another debate.)

While the issues are very complex, the controversy over media effects can be broadbrushed this way: Some researchers believe in what is often called, in a shorthand way, the weak-media-powerful-audience theory. Others suspect that the media may be more powerful than we might imagine, and take the opposite strong-media belief.

Weak-media theories often point to research into media effects conducted by researchers such as Joseph T. Klapper and Paul Lazarsfeld. The work of both Klapper and Lazarsfeld maintained, in general terms, that while the media are powerful tools for *reinforcing* ideas and concepts, they are less effective in *creating* ideas and concepts.

Klapper, who was director for social research at CBS, maintained that people select material from the mass media which is in accord with their existing views and interests, and they largely avoid material with which they disagree. Klapper also contended that when people are exposed to contradictory messages, they tend to reinterpret them in such a way as to agree with their prejudices.

Lazarsfeld's work had laid some groundwork for Klapper's thesis. During the 1940 presidential election race, researchers Lazarsfeld, Bernard Berelson, and Hazel Gaudet tracked the voting behavior of 3,000 people in a rural Ohio county; they wanted to determine how much the media influenced politics. The results? Lazarsfeld and his colleagues purported that only 8 percent of the voters in the study were *converted*. The majority of the voters, 53 percent, were, according to the study, *reinforced* by the messages.

The Lazarsfeld study, as summed up by Shirley Biagi (1988, p. 301) of California State University at Sacramento, produced these results: First, the study concluded that instead of changing beliefs, the media primarily activate people to vote. Second, family, friends, and opinion leaders had more effect on people's opinions than did the media. Third, the media had different effects on different people.

Another major study seemed to confirm the Lazarsfeld theory. Under a government grant, researchers Thomas Patterson and Robert McClure undertook 2,707 interviews prior to the 1972 presidential election. The study—an examination of the effects of political advertising—concluded that only 17 percent of those people studied placed even slight importance on ads and 7 percent predicated their voting decisions primarily on political advertising.

But the Klapper/Lazarsfeld view is not universally accepted among researchers. Sociologist S. J. Ball-Rokeach (1988, p. 319) of the University of Southern California maintains that weak-media-powerful-audience theories not only are wrong, but have handicapped media-effects research:

> Among the features of American sociology which might account for the pattern of declining attention of the last quarter-century (Ball-Rokeach, 1986) is *premature closure concerning the power of the media system.* Sociology graduate students were and are still being taught the overgeneralized and outdated "weak-media-

powerful-audience" position articulated by Klapper (1960) more than a quarter century ago. It is rarely noted that most of the research that produced this view (i.e., that spearheaded by Lazarsfeld) was conducted at the social psychological level of analysis with a limited range of questions about media effects on individuals. This position lazily hangs on. . . .

So do we have strong or weak media? Given that the jury is still out, we are probably safe in assuming that the answer lies somewhere between the extremes presented, a reasonably safe argument in any circumstance. But, again, it is reasonable to assume that the media certainly *are* powerful in various ways; we just do not know how powerful.

Modern communications theories concede this. William Rivers and Wilbur Schramm (1986) admit, "We do not fully understand at present what the media system is doing to individual behavior, much less to American culture. The media cannot simply be seen as stenciling images on a blank mind. That is too superficial a view of the communication process."

It is hoped that the foregoing discussion demonstrated that:

(a) I am not trying to evade the question of how much power the media wield, and/or
(b) If I am ducking the question, I am in good company.

So, given the fact that we all intuitively know that the media wield power—but we do not know just how much—let's move on to the next question: Does, as Plato contended, the assumption of power carry a concomitant responsibility to the people affected by that power?

Beginning at one end of the continuum, some would argue that it does not. In unguarded moments, some publishers have characterized their only responsibility as the responsibility to turn a profit. And that undoubtedly was the primary thought in the tightly focused mind of William Randolph Hearst when he rode in from the West at the turn of the century for a New York City showdown with Joseph Pulitzer. No serious reader could ascribe any underlying sense of responsibility to what Theodore Peterson (1966, p. 41) characterized as "a journalism of screaming scare-heads, faked news, pilfered pictures and cynical championship of the underdog; a jingoistic journalism which probably touched off the Spanish-American War; a journalism which faded, temporarily, only with the first World War."

Yellow journalism resurfaced after the war, and readers would be similarly hard-pressed to find any sense of responsibility to a cause other than profit in the *Graphic* (nicknamed the *Pornographic*) as it freewheeled into the depths of tabloid journalism. Peterson recounts that in the era of the *Graphic* (p. 41):

> The height of journalistic enterprise was a photographer's smuggling a camera into the death-house to get a full-page picture of Ruth Snyder struggling against

the bonds of the electric chair as current surged through her, when Bernarr Macfadden's idea of a good front page was a picture of a convict electrocuted at Sing Sing under the stark head "Roasted Alive," when editor Emile Gauvereau's only half-hearted worry about the $12,000,000 in libel suits hanging over him was that the business office might deduct it from his salary, when the editor of one New York paper told his reporters to "bear in mind that from now on it is a waste of time to write a story that cannot stand up under a sensational head."

But yellow journalism did not hold a monopoly on the newspaper business. Journalists of the stripe of Horace Greeley felt they owed an obligation to "the public good." *The New York Times* set a public-duty agenda for itself when it proclaimed it would run only the news "fit to print," and staffers such as Henry Raymond determined that the *Times* should take an active role in promoting the public welfare.

Restated in the vocabulary used by Siebert, Peterson, and Schramm in their landmark *Four Theories of the Press* (discussed in Chapter 2), the Greeleys and Raymonds had moved press responsibility from the stage of total libertarianism into the era of social responsibility.

Note that social responsibility as it is generally applied to journalism entails not only some sort of commitment but a *control* as well. Those controls can be internal (codes of ethics, management dicta, good conscience) or external (government sanctions, libel laws, consumer pressure, press councils, and so forth). Controls and methods of review, while instruments of enforcing responsibility, are also a separate issue, and will be treated as such, and in some depth, in Chapters 11 and 12.

So, again, let's refocus the discussion at this point to the theoretical implications of deriving and imposing responsibility, and address the specifics of enforcement mechanisms in later pages.

The social responsibility theory in its basic form seems a quite reasonable reaction to the threat of excesses by the news media, and by extension can live in peaceful coexistence with the traditional libertarian theories that underlie American society. The "social contract" philosophy often cited as a tenet of social responsibility is also an important principle of libertarianism.

(However, for the sake of accuracy, it should be mentioned that not *all* proponents of social contract theory would be considered libertarians. Hobbes, for example, was quite the opposite; he viewed the social contract as the surrender of liberty to an omnipotent ruler. Locke, though, argued that a ruler is limited by certain obligations to preserve the rights of the people; it would be difficult to find Locke too much at odds with traditional American republican libertarianism since so much of his writing influenced the Founders, and indeed found its way into the Declaration of Independence. The third major proponent of the social contract theory was Rousseau, undeniably a libertarian, who argued that a social contract could coexist with libertarianism because the social contract required the support of the general will of the people.)

In any event, the idea of a social contract is not lost on modern scholars who attempt to link the concept with press responsibility. Professor Hodges (p. 3) recites this almost word for word:

> In the United States, the press comes to have responsibilities chiefly through an implied covenant with society. That covenant is not formally contracted and written, of course, but that fact does not render it any less real. Society seems to promise the press freedom to function if the press will serve society's needs for information.

With any contract or covenant, of course, there exists an "or else" clause: The "or else" is some punishment for violation of the commitment to act "responsibly" within the terms of the social contract. While we won't address specifics of the "or else clause" at this point, it is important to note that it is inevitable that few covenants become universally adhered to rules unless there is a carrot or stick implied in the contract.

It is the stick that worries some members of the press corps and many media observers. While few would dismiss outright the legitimacy of government controls (especially in broadcasting, which is licensed in the public interest), or the legitimacy of libel laws as a citizen's tool for redress of grievances, or the legitimacy of various special-interest groups who seek to impose controls on the press through organized pressure or legislative process, the stick in any fashion also brings to mind the specter of prosecutions for seditious libel, fear of economic ruin because of libel prosecution, and the days of Nixon-Agnew—when those who did not like the message were urged to blame the messenger.

Louis D. Boccardi (1987, p. 11), president and general manager of the Associated Press, takes a wary view of any implicit sanction against the press.

> Press responsibility? Yes, we have a great one. But there can be no doubt about how central a free press is to our system of government. It is no accident or coincidence, that when coups break out around the world, the tanks go to the presidential palace but also to the newspaper and the TV station at virtually the same moment.
>
> It is our responsibility somehow to reconcile the freedom we have from government interference with the legitimate concern of government for secrecy and security. But government must be an honest participant, and we all know that the use and abuse of the national security stamp is legendary.

That is Boccardi's view of the stick implied in the social responsibility theory, and it is a moderate one. Some critics of the theory, though, are not so charitable. Professor John Merrill (cited in Rivers and Schramm, 1969) of Louisiana State University, a distinguished analyst of journalism as well as of philosophy (he is coauthor of the insightful *Philosophy and Journalism*), is quite blunt:

This so-called "theory" of social responsibility has a good ring to it and, like "love" and "motherhood," has an undeniable attraction for many.... Implicit in this trend toward social responsibility is the argument that some group (obviously a governmental one, ultimately) can and must define or decide *what* is socially responsible. Also, the implication is clear that publishers and journalists acting freely cannot determine what is socially responsible nearly as well as can some "outside" or "impartial" group. If this power elite decides the press is not responsible, not even the First Amendment will keep the publishers from losing this freedom to government.

But does the implied stick in "social responsibility" necessarily mean government control? Merrill restates his argument that ultimately, it does.

... since if left undefined by various public or journalistic groups the term is quite relative and nebulous; and it is quite obvious that in the traditional context of American libertarianism no "solution" that would be widely agreed upon or enforced could ever be reached by non-government groups or individuals.

And so we have classic arguments relating to a classic problem: the advocate of the social responsibility theory arguing that under libertarian theory, the press simply cannot control its excesses; and the advocate of the libertarian theory asserting that this nicely packaged "social responsibility" doctrine would translate into government control of the press.

But we have been concentrating on the stick and forgetting about the carrot. What would *lead* the news media toward greater social responsibility, without the implication of government sanction? It has been argued by some that such responsibility, in its ultimate incarnation, rests not with the news bureaucracy, nor with the public, but with the individuals in both camps.

In addition to offering a mild defense against undue intrusion into the process of news coverage, the AP's Boccardi (p. 13) made an offhand reference to what might be a significant problem:

And the society needs to reflect on the fact that despite the connection of the media to almost everything the society does, there is almost no education *about* the media at any level.

A bit overstated perhaps (since there are many media courses offered in colleges, but a good case could be made that in their present form those courses are meant to educate practitioners and not consumers), but a problem nonetheless; Boccardi's complaint is echoed by many journalists. A relevant example is Bill Moyers's story, cited in the previous chapter, of how the press is accused of duplicity because different reporters estimate crowd sizes differently—even though crowd estimation is a notoriously inexact "science." But presumably the critics who cannot forgive the press "for not being able to count" have never tried it for themselves, and have never been held accountable for their estimates.

Headlines are another example of how public misunderstanding of the mechanics of news coverage lead to misdirected complaints. Newspaper reporters are constantly regaled with complaints "about the headline you wrote." But newspaper reporters do not write headlines. Copy editors, editors in charge of checking stories for grammar, spelling, and logical consistency, create headlines—under almost unbelievably tight technical restrictions. (They are given an *exact* amount of space which they must precisely fill with headline characters.)

Now, this is not a blanket apology for sloppy headline composition— merely an expression of personal puzzlement over why certain members of the reading public, people who may have read a newspaper every day of their adult lives, are not aware of, and do not make allowances for, this fact of journalistic life. Is it the fault of the schools, which presumably do not teach students how newspapers are put together? The newspapers, which do not let readers in on the processes of gathering and presenting the news? Or the lack of "inquiring minds" among the public?

All three factors might contribute. And it seems a reasonable contention that the overall lack of understanding of the news process—regardless of whose fault it is—certainly motivates many of the charges of "irresponsibility" leveled against the press. Perhaps a personal example might illustrate this contention.

Radio news involves a large amount of rewriting and reshuffling of copy. The goal, of course, is to avoid giving the listener the impression that the broadcaster is rereading the same news over and over. On slow news days, that is essentially what is happening, but judicious rewriting, coupled with insertion of stories not read during the previous hour and removal of stories just read, can "freshen" the next newscast.

On one particular afternoon our news staff was stretched very thin and I had no option but to prerecord the local newscasts which were to air at 1:30, 2:30, and 3:30 while I was on assignment away from the station, covering some prearranged feature interviews.

Unless a fire, bank robbery, or some unforeseen event occurred during this typically slow period (in which case I would be notified and could break away from the feature stories), the prerecorded newscasts would be run. They contained roughly the same stories, presented a bit differently each time.

But I had made a drastic miscalculation concerning the interests of our local audience. A public official—the commissioner of social services, a major player in the impoverished urban area about which I reported—had been involved in a minor traffic accident in which he and another driver suffered *very* minor injuries. No one was really hurt; no one was ticketed. Unfortunately, though, the commissioner had the bad judgment either to hit or be hit (no one could determine who hit whom) on Main Street, before the watchful eyes, apparently, of every person in the city.

I thought—and *still think*—it was a trivial matter. It barely made the day's newscasts, but since it was a slow news day, the story was included, if for no other reason than to inject some variety into the newscasts. I included the story (reading it as probably the eighth or ninth story out of a total of ten news items) in the 1:30 recorded version of the news. I then reshuffled and rewrote some material and recorded the 2:30 newscast, in which I did *not* include the traffic accident story. The story was reinserted into the 3:30 news.

Again, this was a fender bender in which a local official sprained his thumb: a newsworthy story only because of the celebrity of the official, and *barely newsworthy* at that. On a day with heavier news, it never would have made the air. But as things unfolded, the story did run at 1:30, did not run at 2:30, and did run at 3:30.

When I returned to the station, I found more than the usual stack of "while-you-were-out" slips; in fact, the pile of messages was gigantic. If you cannot visualize the standard "while-you-were-out" slip, remember that it has a line for the time received and several lines where the phone answerer can pass along the message. They were in a neat pile, arranged in order of time taken with the time-taken line neatly filled in each case, so I had before me an interesting chronology of listener reaction to that day's news. Or, more specifically, to the commissioner-cracks-up-his-car story.

All the messages taken from 1:30 to 2:30 accused me of having a vendetta against the commissioner by reporting on his minor accident and trying to embarrass him.

All the messages taken from 2:30 to 3:30 accused me of covering up for the commissioner by suppressing news about his accident.

All the messages taken from 3:30 until I returned once again returned to the vendetta theme, claiming that I "had it in" for the commissioner, etc., etc., etc.

The complaints in and of themselves were not surprising, but the imagined agendas were. Now, in reality, the thought process about using the story had been, if it were to be summed up in a sentence, "This is a minor story but of some local interest because the guy is so well known, and it probably merits a mention once or twice in this afternoon's news; I'll use it near the end of the 1:30 and 3:30 newscasts."

But the imagined agendas reflected some fairly wild and surprisingly intricately imagined assumptions. I returned calls to those who had left their numbers and was treated to a strange tableau of fantasies, most of which included our entire news and management staff huddled around a table plotting the best way to "get" or "cover up for" the commissioner. I made some attempt to explain that the judgment was made by one person under great time pressure and the story was, or so I had thought at the time, of little consequence anyway. I doubt, though, whether any of the callers believed me.

Now the news media absolutely, without question, have their failings and many of those failings are documented unhesitatingly in this work. But when the AP's Boccardi speaks of the lack of education about the news media, and Columbia's Fred Friendly declares that the public needs a "demystification" of the news process, they assuredly make those statements out of the same sense of frustration I felt the day that I was *literally* damned when I did and damned when I didn't.

In a way, the reactions of the irate listeners that day bolsters the case put forward by members of two schools of thought in the argument over where the press's responsibility lies. One particular branch of the social responsibility school puts the onus on an *educated public*. Wilbur Schramm (1966, p. 349) does not rule out external controls of various types, but he does maintain that the social responsibility theory would make the public the "prime mover" in the communications dynamic. "It is my firm belief," Schramm writes, "that the public can come pretty close to having whatever kind of mass communication system it wants. Of course, that requires that the public say what it wants."

In addition, Schramm argues (p. 352) that if the public is going to complain (thus becoming the "stick" in the social responsibility theory), they have an obligation to become an alert, discriminating audience.

> This may require a somewhat different habit of mind from the one we most commonly see on the part of many individuals who by virtue of position or education might be expected to be the leaders of and spokesmen for the public in their demands upon the media. This common attitude—"oh, I never watch television except when there's something like a political convention on—it's just trash"—is fundamentally an irresponsible attitude. It neglects the fact that television doesn't *have* to be all trash, if indeed, it is. Television is potentially one of our greatest windows on the world. It is one of the best ways in which we could expand our horizons, bring a sense of reality to faraway events, make a more informed judgment on public figures, share the lectures and demonstrations at our greatest universities, see the kind of opera, ballet, drama, museums, and concert artists formerly available only to a few fortunate people, most of them in great cities. If television isn't being used that way, what a great social waste it is! What a loss we are suffering! And whose fault is it? Basically, it is the fault of the people who don't watch and don't do anything about improving it.

By implication, it would seem reasonable to extend Schramm's argument to say: If people do not like the "ethics" of news reporting, they should complain; but they should also have some basic grasp of the news process in order to make a more valid complaint and a complaint more likely to be acted upon constructively.

That is a mutual responsibility: The public is responsible to learn and the media are responsible for allowing access and explaining the way news is gathered and presented. In its ideal state, the audience-based social responsibility theory could coax the media to act responsibly without imposition of the controls so feared by the libertarians.

Speaking of libertarians, the varied responses to the story about the social services commissioner do seem to bolster one particular libertarian fear: the trepidation expressed by Merrill when he noted that since people have varied perspectives, it is impossible to gain unanimity on what is responsible and what is not.

The "in the head" concept expressed by semanticists such as Hayakawa is an important element of the news business and not limited to academic abstractionists. Walter Lippmann, for example, used almost exactly the same phraseology in his pioneering book *Public Opinion*, in which he titled one chapter "The World Outside and the Pictures in Our Heads." Lippmann posited that each person creates a "pseudo environment" in the mind, a sort of filter between the real world and the perceived world. While we do not deliberately seek to alter reality, we cannot help but do so because we filter events through the "pictures in our heads."

How difficult it is to draw lines of responsibility when everyone responsible is filtering those responsibilities through the pictures in their heads! Given this enormous handicap, it does seem plausible to assume that responsibility must lie, to a large extent, with the individual, with the collection of individuals known as an audience, and with the individual practitioners of the news media.

Individuals and audiences do have power, and they can affect what they read, see, and hear. But as Schramm would argue, and I would argue by extension, a member of an audience has a *responsibility* to let his or her feelings be known and a concomitant responsibility to shape those feelings into informed opinions.

This would seem the best alternative to what Merrill cites as the danger of extensive government imposition on the press once it becomes plain that those amorphous requirements of "social responsibility" cannot be enforced or even coherently articulated.

Second, this scenario would imply that members of the press have a responsibility to demystify their workings and report vigorously on themselves and on other news media. This is a topic unto itself, and will be considered in a following chapter.

Third, the scenario we have described—which might be termed, for the lack of a better phrase, the *"informed-public-accessible-press" theory of responsibility*—would entail a sharp individual commitment on the part of each reporter.

This means not hiding behind procedures or bureaucracy. As Deni Elliott (p. 42) puts it:

> ... journalists are more than representatives of the media and more than representatives of specific news organizations. First, they are each autonomous moral agents, and thus responsible for their own actions. Illustrations abound to show that a person cannot hide from personal responsibility by attributing his or her action to a supervisor's directive. Individuals are morally blameworthy for their wrong actions even if they were following another's directions in performing the acts. "My editor told me to do it" is not justification for one's actions; nor is, "that's what journalists do."

She goes on to assert:

> Individual autonomy is necessary for the moral health of any profession or group. A plurality of values systems among practitioners is acceptable and even preferred over uniform beliefs. Conventional norms that define group behavior change only through friction. *If all members of a professional group shared exactly the same values, there would be no hope for improvement or growth, no questioning of normative attitudes or actions.*

The last statement (with emphasis added) addresses the final argument for an "informed-public-accessible-press" theory of responsibility. Ethical values do change over time, and as we have seen (and will continue to examine), that change is often the result of individuals saying, "This is wrong." What may have been accepted group practice at one time is not necessarily acceptable as standards evolve.

The accessible and responsible press is an institution in which individuals can say, "This is wrong" and thereby effect change. Such statements have changed the news media's attitudes toward issues of fairness and professional practices, and will be documented in the following two chapters.

Chapter 5
Fairness

"Forget fair."

—John L. Perry, *editor of the Rome, Georgia,* News-Tribune, *advising fellow journalists that an attempt at fairness produces nothing more than "a gray morass of innocuous inanity"*

*I*t is reasonable to assume that no journalist wishes to be accused of being "unfair," but at the same time "fairness" is a difficult concept to define or practice. Worse, mechanical attempts at fairness often backfire. Two such examples will be analyzed in this chapter.

An essential difficulty with "being fair" revolves around the reality that many factors contribute to our perception of fairness, word choice, the selection of elements which comprise a story, the perspective of the journalist and the occasional loss of perspective when a journalist bends over backward to hide his or her perspective, and the mechanics of news gathering and news routines.

These are the background issues; adding them up produces a more clear (or, in the interest of fairness, let's say "less muddy") definition of the problem.

As a starting point, what motivated Rome *News-Tribune* editor John L. Perry to disparage the concept of fairness in the quote used to open the chapter?

As related by *Time* magazine news critic Thomas Griffith (1986, p. 61), the problem began when two men forced a night clerk at a Rome, Georgia, convenience store to hand over the store's cash receipts; the men then raped the clerk. The *News-Tribune* reported the store's name and location, but not the victim's name.

A representative of the convenience store chain claimed the coverage was "unfair"—leading Perry to wonder how he could produce a "fair" story given the circumstances. Griffith writes:

[The store representative complained] that it was unfair to identify the store because that would tend also to identify the victim, ("There is an element of validity in that," Perry concedes), but was more upset that the story had mentioned the chain's name. The only way the story could have been written to satisfy this complainant, Perry says, was "A woman was raped late last night someplace here." People involved in the news do not really want fairness, he insists, they want "favor, exemption, protection from public notice. . . . They want only the "good news published—that their daughter won the scholarship, that their office exceeded its United Way goal."

Perry believed that a newspaper's duty is to be "accurate, timely, incisive and pertinent. Forget fair."

In his analysis, Griffith contends that newspapers are increasingly concerned about their credibility and also about "parading" their fairness. "Let so-and-so be accused of defrauding a widow," Griffith contends, "and The New York Times will meticulously note that he 'did not return phone calls.' [Author's note: Later, we'll examine the wording of the Times policy which motivated Griffith's remark.] A guilty person can no longer just hide out waiting for a story to blow over; he also stands convicted of not answering his phone."

Griffith is not alone in his reproach for the common technique of producing "fairness" by "balancing" the news with mitigating quotes. Edward R. Murrow once opined that adherence to this type of balance mentality would compel reporters to give Judas equal space for his side of the story.

Many news organizations have policies which require that reporters ask for a response to unofficial charges; even when not written in a code of ethics virtually every journalism textbook ever written advises this practice. (The term "unofficial charges" refers to a contention made which is not leveled as part of the legal system; obviously, journalists are not compelled to ask for reaction from someone officially arrested and charged.)

But does the person who "did not return repeated phone calls" suffer from an implication of additional guilt? Intuitively, it would appear so—even if the repeated phone calls were left on an answering machine while the "guilty" party was on an intercontinental jetliner at the time. What about the person who was "not available for comment"? There are good reasons why someone might not be available for comment, and many of them have nothing to do with his or her willingness to face up to a reporter's questioning.

Such reversals of good intentions may also occur when a reporter seeks not to scandalize or offend when handling a sensational case. That was exactly the unenviable situation faced by Newark *Star-Ledger* reporter Diane Curcio and her editors when covering a trial involving alleged sexual abuse at a day-care center. Curcio (interview, 1988) noted that her editors were concerned with the level of explicit detail in news accounts of a ten-month-long trial of a Maplewood, New Jersey, teacher convicted of assaulting 20 of her students. As a result, some stories were edited so that abuse was described in generic terms. The uncopyrighted story "Detective Quizzed in Day-Care Sex Scandal" (Box 5.1) is an example of a story where editors eliminated graphic descriptions and explicit terminology.

The severity of editing varied—often as not, the editing style varied according to the particular editor on duty. On some days, stories written by Curcio retained their explicit detail. Note how "Mom Tells Nursery Sex Trial Her Son Played Nude 'Game' at Pal's Party," an uncopyrighted story reproduced in Box 5.2 (pp. 59–60), describes the testimony in very precise terms.

Curcio pointed out two dilemmas in the fairness issue pertaining to these stories. First, she noted that everyone was, indeed, trying to be fair: The editors who removed explicit detail, she maintained, were making a good-faith effort to excise what they, personally, considered inflammatory and offensive language. But Curcio felt committed to the notion that she should give "the reader the fullest account of the day's proceeding—not for sensationalism, but to educate the public on abuse and the charges. . . . " (Correspondence from Curcio to author, 1988.)

As sometimes happens with efforts to create fairness, the excision of explicit detail backfired—drawing complaints from observers and participants on both sides of the issue. Some who read the bowdlerized version speculated as to why so much coverage was given to an incident when—judging from the expurgated accounts of the testimony—the prosecution had such a weak case. On the other hand, the people involved in the *defense* of the accused did not like the heavily edited versions of the stories, either.

Why? Because the defense's contention was that the acts alleged to have taken place were simply too bizarre, numerous, and blatant to have occurred without everyone in the small school instantly noticing.

The incident reflects a fundamental difficulty in attempting to ensure "fairness" in news coverage: When attempting to fulfill an obligation to fairness, people of goodwill and judgment can differ in their interpretations. Philosopher John R. Searle (1980, p. 243), who has written extensively about the nature of obligations, made this observation:

> . . . most moral conflicts in real life are cases where there are genuinely valid reasons for doing one thing and at the same time reasons for not doing that thing but doing something inconsistent with it.

Reporter Curcio felt *obligated* to give a complete and accurate accounting of events in a sensational trial. Some of her editors felt *obligated* to present that information in a format which would not inflame or offend. Both had genuinely valid reasons; but it appears, at least to this analyst, that the mechanical alteration of events (bowdlerizing the testimony) damaged the effort to be fair.

Box 5.1 DETECTIVE QUIZZED IN DAY-CARE SEX ABUSE TRIAL

Defense tries to weaken credibility of photos and children's testimony

By Diane Curcio

Defense attorney Harvey Meltzer cross-examined a Maplewood police detective for three hours yesterday in Newark, focusing on pictures taken at the Wee Care Day Nursery and statements by children about alleged sexual abuse there.

Sorting through 25 photographs taken of the Maplewood nursery in May 1985, Meltzer questioned Detective Sgt. John J. Noonan about how he got into the building, the condition of the rooms and who was there.

Noonan explained that Diane Costa, a teacher in the defunct nursery, showed him and another investigator the nap rooms, where many children have alleged they were sexually abused.

Costa arranged the children's mats as they would have been during the school year, Noonan said, pointing out how he labeled the mats in the photographs. Meltzer asked if Costa knew which way the children were positioned—drawing objections from prosecutors.

Essex County Assistant Prosecutor Glenn D. Goldberg argued that the defense questioning was irrelevant "because there's no evidence" that any child could see what was happening on another child's mat.

Meltzer represents Margaret Kelly Michaels, 25, a one-time drama student, accused of sexually assaulting 20 boys and girls when she was at Wee Care.

Essex County Assistant Prosecutor Sara Sencer McArdle joined the arguments against Meltzer's cross-examination yesterday, contending there was no evidence that the children were victimized on mats.

Nineteen children have testified in the four-month-old case, detailing various sex acts, sometimes involving knives, forks and spoons, which allegedly took place during naptime and in the school bathrooms.

After more than 40 minutes of testimony on the mat photographs, Superior Court Judge William F. Harth said, "We're spending time out of all proportion... What's your next line of questioning?"

Meltzer then began quizzing Noonan on the statements made by three youngsters. Noonan either interviewed the children himself or was present when other investigators spoke with them.

Meltzer said later outside the courtroom that he focused on the children to show "inconsistencies and embellishments" between what the preschoolers told Noonan in June 1985 and their courtroom testimony.

For example, while one girl testified that she talked to Noonan about one type of sexual abuse, according to Meltzer, Noonan's reports showed her reporting another type.

(continues)

> Noonan said that after taking statements from some of the children and their parents, he and a partner drove the preschoolers to the day care center, where they showed police where the alleged assaults took place.
>
> Meltzer asked if Noonan gave the youngsters toy badges that day and the detective said he did not recall. He testified previously that some Wee Care children had toured the police station in the wake of the investigation and badges then were distributed.
>
> When the children visited Wee Care, accompanied by Noonan and other investigators, the youngsters showed police where they sat in the choir room. The choir room, which is also referred to as the music room or piano room by the youngsters, is where Michaels allegedly disrobed and played "Jingle Bells" on the piano, according to testimony. Children have also said they played a nude pileup game there.
>
> Noonan took photographs of the children as they sat in the choir room pews. These and the other photographs of the facility were given to the jury late yesterday.
>
> The trial is scheduled to reconvene at 9 a.m.
>
> *Source:* Courtesy Diane Curcio, the *Star-Ledger.*

Of course, to this point the discussion has circumvented the root question: What, exactly, is fairness? If we define fairness as a sort of eternal compromise—treading the middle ground so as not to offend or give any hint of sensationalism—the Curcio incident would seem to cast doubt on that definition. Perhaps fairness could better be defined as presenting the most accurate possible portrayal of events within their proper context.

Context, as discussed in the previous chapter, plays an important role in perception, a point not lost on those who claim that word choice plays a larger role than we realize in the fairness of news coverage. At the most basic level of context and word choice are the blatantly biased words with confused or pejorative intentional meanings—words which various news organizations are banishing from their official vocabulary. "Spry," for example, is a word frowned upon by many news organizations because its primary meaning—an adjective applying to an older person who is still active—carries the intensional baggage that older people are expected to be *inactive*, and therefore the "spry" person is the exception.

Word usage is sometimes a factor in, as some researchers put it, "making sense" of changing social situations. For example, University of Michigan communications professors Richard Campbell and Jimmie Reeves, writing in the journal *Critical Studies in Mass Communications* (1989, p. 21), noted that American journalists "discovered" the homeless in the early 1980s, when it

Box 5.2   MOM TELLS NURSERY SEX TRIAL HER SON PLAYED NUDE 'GAME' AT PAL'S PARTY

By Diane Curcio

A mother testified in Superior Court in Newark yesterday that before allegations were raised of sexual abuse at Wee Care Day Nursery in Maplewood she saw her son take off his pants and play a "pile-up game" at a friend's birthday party.

Former students from the defunct Maplewood nursery have testified their teacher Margaret Kelly Michaels engaged them in the nude game during which children would lay on top of one another. Using dolls in the judge's chambers, the children, who were ages three and four when the offenses allegedly happened, sometimes showed how "pile-up" was played.

The mother testifying yesterday in Newark said that at the birthday party her son "had his pants down and a little blonde child with a chunky rear end and he was laying on top of her." She said other mothers saw it too and "I was so embarrassed. . . All of the kids were around there playing like nothing happened, like it was normal behavior."

This birthday party happened on May 4, 1985, according to a stipulation read to the jury. That was three days before another Wee Care preschooler had a routine doctor's visit and mentioned to a nurse taking his temperature rectally that his teacher did the same thing. His remarks touched off the investigation that resulted in three indictments being handed up against the 24-year-old Michaels, accusing her of sexually assaulting and threatening 20 children. The children said they were molested with knives, forks and spoons during naptime and in bathrooms.

The mother yesterday said she knew nothing of the other boy's remark when the incident happened at the birthday party.

Her six-year-old son also testified yesterday, via closed circuit television in Superior Court. The boy said he would draw a picture to tell judge William F. Harth something about his former teacher. But when Essex County Assistant Prosecutor Glenn D. Goldberg asked the child to identify what part of the female anatomy he had drawn under the stick figure's neck, the boy balked.

First, he said he didn't know what it was, then he said it was a "toy." Ultimately, the child whispered into Harth's ear that he had drawn "breasts." The boy had said it was a picture of Michaels.

Twice during his testimony the boy said he was "getting sleepy." He said boys and girls played the "pile-up game." When asked if anyone ever touched him at Wee Care, the boy got up in his chair and pointed to his genitals.

"They touched people in their private parts," he said. Goldberg asked: "Who did that?" and the boy said, "Kelly."

The child is named as a victim in eight counts of the indictment, alleging assorted acts of sexual assault. Defense attorney Harvey Meltzer cross-examined him about each alleged incident and the boy denied they occurred.

When the mother took the stand, however, she said her son had disclosed the incidents to her. The boy told social workers and investigators initially that

(continues)

he had not been abused. During the summer of 1985 he slowly revealed his involvement to his mother, she said. He brought up the subject while they were watching a children's program on television one Saturday morning, the mother testified.

Throughout the 1984-85 school year, the mother said she noticed behavioral changes in her son, who was classified as a gifted child before his enrollment in Wee Care. The mother said she and her husband made "sacrifices" to pay the $175 monthly tuition for her son because they hoped his three days a week at the school would nurture his talents. The parents were in family counseling to resolve their differences when the boy was enrolled in the Maplewood nursery.

While at Wee Care, she said he became a "clean freak," who wanted to change his clothes often, he became a bedwetter and his normally passive inclinations turned aggressive. She said he often came home from school wearing only one sock and he apparently could not have taken a nap because he would fall asleep in the car on the way home.

The mother said her three-year-old son masturbated "excessively" and sometimes used Vaseline and mayonnaise.

After his disclosures about the alleged abuse, the mother said the boy tried doing bizarre things to his body. Once when the mother was coming out of a shower, she testified her son tried to insert a nail file in her vagina. She said the boy was also fascinated by women with big breasts.

Cross-examination of the mother is expected to continue at 9 a.m.

Source: Courtesy Diane Curcio, the *Star-Ledger*.

---

became a "mainstream" issue. As a result, there was a *semantic shift* in the media's perception of the problem. Throughout the 1970s, the authors report, *The New York Times Index* provided no "homeless persons" category, instead listing "scattered articles" under "vagrancy" or "housing." But by 1985, the index listed 235 entries under "homeless persons." Why the change? The authors contend:

> The modification in part represented changes in both the socioeconomic structure and in the numbers and types of homeless persons. Vagrancy conjures up bygone images of tramps and hobos, of drifters who *choose* to wander and live on the margins of society. Being *without home*, however, speaks much more to a severe rupture in the fabric of middle America: to the lack of individual choice.... Being without home transports a person, often violently and unwillingly, from mainstream to margin.

To put it another way, fairness sometimes relates not only to word choice but to what that word means at a particular time. The example above illustrates how the "in-the-head" image evoked by the words "vagrant" and "homeless" altered in less than a decade. A word such as "mistress," according to Wallace Matson, who explored the concept of word meanings in his book *Sentience* (1970, p. 22), "may change its meaning, that is, acquire or lose meaning components in the course of time."

And a case could be made that many implications of unfairness regarding word choice are functions of just this effect. "Spry" was undoubtedly a term coined in an era when active older people were so exceptional as to merit a word intensionally indicating the exception; "homeless" came to signify a different concept from "vagrant" over a relatively brief period in which perceptions and public understandings of an issue changed. In both cases, the *social context* surrounding the words has changed.

In addition to *word choice*, fairness is influenced by *perspective, element selection*, and *the mechanics of the news-gathering process*.

This is not an arbitrary classification; the handbook given to reporters at *The New York Times* (1976, p. 75) mentions or refers to all four of the above factors in its entry on "Fairness and Objectivity." I have flagged the references with comments inserted within brackets:

> Fairness and impartiality should be the hallmark of all news articles and news analyses that appear in *The Times* [a definition of perspective]. Obviously, accuracy is a chief element of fairness and impartiality. But accuracy is easily subverted. For instance, a number of facts, each accurate, can be juxtaposed and presented in a tendentious, unfair manner [element selection]. Even simple, seemingly innocent words can be employed with the same resulting partiality. And even background information can be manipulated (most easily by its mere use or omission) to the detriment of fairness [element choice and news-gathering process].
>
> But avoiding pitfalls like these is not enough. It is of paramount importance that people or organizations accused, criticized or otherwise cast in a bad light have an opportunity to speak in their own defense. Thus, it is imperative that the reporter make every effort to reach the accused or criticized person or persons, or organization, and supply the opportunity to reply. If it is not possible to do so, the article should say that the effort was made and explain why it did not succeed [mechanics of the news-gathering process].

Some of the actions mandated have been discussed earlier in the chapter, and others—such as the eternal conflict between the needs of a particular news medium and the way those needs can distort the message—will be given full treatment in following chapters. But in the effort to define more precisely our perspectives, we will take the tack adopted in the previous discussion of *word choice* and take a very brief look at the above-cited factors of *perspective, element selection*, and the *mechanics of the news-gathering process*.

Perspective reflects viewpoint, and the accurate representation of reality. But the problem is that the cliché that there are two sides to a story simply does not hold true. *The New York Times*'s Russell Baker noted that a reporter can get viewpoints but still not have a fair perspective. "It's almost impossible to get it right," Baker told *Time* magazine writer David Gates (1989, p. 65). "The deadlines are too quick, and you don't have time to go into the background. It's 'Rashomon': you interview four different people, you get four different answers." The "Rashomon effect" is a term coined after a 1951 Japanese film. *Rashomon* (full title: *Rashomon: In the Woods*) concerned the different views of four people involved with a moment of violence. The Rashomon effect is an informal term taken to mean a case where the viewpoints of the participants color their interpretations of events to such an extent that sifting out a "fair" representation is all but impossible. (There is probably no figurative "opposite" of the Rashomon effect, but the ideal of "objectivity" would imply that gathering enough viewpoints would allow the journalist to sort out the "truth.")

Perspective also relates back to the bugaboo of objectivity, which is an elusive quality at best. Media that claim to have a fair and objective perspective may allege that they are free from political bias from the left or the right. But assuming that a news medium could be free from left-leaning or right-leaning political biases, does that automatically make it fair and objective? Perhaps not. Some critics, such as Jeff Cohen, writing in the openly left-oriented press criticism journal *Extra!* (1989), argue that *The New York Times* and other papers promulgate a "centrist ideology," which is in itself an unfair perspective. An example of what Cohen calls "centrist propaganda" is the "inordinate number of (often unnamed) government sources.... Some reporters act more like stenographers for those in power than journalists" (p. 14). Without passing judgment on Cohen's comments, those statements do provide what might be called a perspective on perspective: It is very difficult to find a plateau from which all things and all consequences can be viewed and presented fairly. Even attempting to go "right down the center" can effect an alteration in perspective, as Cohen alleges, and as the arguably centrist editing of Diane Curcio's stories demonstrates to a degree.

Element selection—simply determining what goes into a news story—is a more obvious contributor to overall fairness. Intuitively, one can easily imagine an arbitrary selection of facts arranged to suit any purpose, so that method of "stacking the deck" is reasonably self-evident. So let's take a moment to examine the assertion that the problem can go deeper than arbitrary selection of facts to skew coverage; in actuality, simple arrangement of visual items—things not even given the status of "facts" per se—can be used to stack the deck, too.

A classic example is the framing of a shot in television news coverage. Most journalists who have even a passing familiarity with a video editing control unit understand how shot selection can literally create an "unfair picture." One primary example is the use of the "cutaway" or "reverse" shot, where a reporter's questions are asked again after the interview is completed. To clarify: Most television interviews done on location are taped with one camera and the news report is edited later, back at the studio. In order to picture the reporter, the question must be re-asked.

But what if the reporter adopts an accusatory tone when re-asking the questions, even though the original information was offered willingly? The result might be a feature flattering to the reporter, picturing him or her as a tough investigator.[1]

Reversals and cutaways are problematic. Some organizations do not use them, and many news practitioners feel they inherently produce an unfair and inaccurate portrayal of events. Sanford Socolow, for many years the producer of "The CBS Evening News with Walter Cronkite," favors the use of jump cuts (just chopping the unwanted portion of the interview out and letting the image jump from one part of the screen to the other) instead of reversals. He feels that jump cuts are "more honest" because the viewer "knows that something has been left out of the interview" (quoted by White, 1984, p. 193).

Do we want the interviewee to look nervous? A close-up of hands wringing in the interviewee's lap would do the trick nicely—even though people commonly hold their hands in a position that resembles wringing; at any given time, an observer can usually identify ten "guilty-looking" hand positions in a room full of thirty people.

Do we want the interviewee to appear uncomfortable? Mike Wallace pioneered the technique in the 1950s, and while not admitting to deliberately using an "unfair" depiction of reality, he certainly does indicate his awareness of how selecting visual elements can alter perspective. In his autobiography, *Close Encounters* (1984), Wallace writes (pp. 14–15) of his pioneering no-holds-barred interview program "Night Beat":

> Not for us the traditional and cheerful living room set, with the standard soft lights, the comfortable sofa and fake flowers. Instead, our studio was stark, pitch black except for the white klieg light glaring over my shoulder into the guest's eyes—and psyche. Nor was that all. Just as interviewers never cut too close to the bone in those days, neither did the cameras. They had always been kept at a decorous distance, a medium close-up, to assure the guest that he or she would be seen in the most flattering way. On *Night Beat* we used searching, tight close-ups to record the tentative glances, the nervous tics, the beads of perspiration—warts and all. Not to put too fine a point on it, but in the context of American television in the mid-fifties, this was revolutionary.

And not to put too fine a point on this either, but it is worth noting that tics and perspiration do not always indicate those qualities with which we intensionally associate them. Perhaps the guest tics (or sweats) *all the time*.

---

[1] This issue is discussed at greater length in Hausman, *The Decision Making Process in Journalism*, pp. 72–73.

These actions do not in and of themselves reveal anything about the character of the guest.

Mechanics of the news-gathering process are part of the fairness issue, too, and are strongly related to item selection. Indeed, the Wallace tight-camera technique is unquestionably a staple of certain news-gathering organizations. (Such intrusions of the medium into fair coverage will be elaborated on in the chapter titled "The Medium Versus the Message.") The "mechanical balance" mandated by many news organizations' rule books is standard practice.

Simply put, the way news is gathered and the individual circumstances surrounding individual reporters have a strong impact on whether the eventual story is an accurate portrayal of fact and context.

This can be illustrated, in part, by the findings of a focus group convened by Dr. Lawrence Budner, associate professor of communications at Rhode Island College, and this author, under a grant from the Rhode Island Committee for the Humanities. The group's mission was to study the "fairness" of media coverage of a long and bitter strike; we twice convened a focus group consisting of a reporter who had covered the strike for television, a newswriter for a major regional weekly publication, a journalist who had not covered the Brown and Sharpe strike but had reported on labor issues in other communities (myself), a specialist in labor affairs, and a professor of philosophy.

The background was this: On October 19, 1981, more than 1,600 machinists went on strike against the Brown and Sharpe manufacturing company in North Kingston, Rhode Island. Though the picket lines were withdrawn in 1985, the strike is still technically in effect today. Most of the strikers have returned to work at Brown and Sharpe or elsewhere.

The strike was painful and public, since it was, as many job actions are, partially played out in the media. Charges and countercharges were prominently featured; an incident where strikers were cleared from a street with an irritant gas was given extensive publicity in print and broadcast media.

While it can hardly be claimed that the conclusions are definitive, the members of the focus group (who read an extensive clip file on strike coverage) made the following observations:

1. Strike coverage puts the journalist in the middle of heated issues. The reporters on our panel noted that emotions run very hot in such situations, and they made a concerted effort to project an air of *impartiality* in their stories. One journalist was quite candid in his admission that he feared being viewed as favoring one side or another when covering labor issues, and had an even greater fear of accidentally misstating or representing events in a way that might inflame an already incendiary situation. As such, he was reluctant to advance the story with new information unless that information was

already "proven true" and "neutral" in tone—a factor related to the next point.
2. Strikes are very complex issues, and as such are difficult to cover. The Brown and Sharpe strike, for example, involved court actions, conflicting claims regarding economic issues, intricate labor laws, and a variety of claims from different constituencies. This factor can have two primary manifestations.

First, the depth of coverage is limited because of the complexity of the issue. As one member of the panel noted, there are hardly ever two sides to a story; usually, there are dozens, and it is impossible to accurately portray those Rashomon-like perspectives in 90 seconds or 20 column inches.

Second, reporters who do not have particular expertise in the issues involved may not cover the story in any great depth. The television journalist on the panel noted that stories in TV are typically shunted about from reporter to reporter, depending on that day's work assignments and other variables. Newspaper journalists, even at the largest papers, do not necessarily "specialize" in one type of story, and are often assigned stories with which they have only a passing familiarity.

This is mirrored at the national level, too, and in fact pertains directly to the coverage of labor issues. While once prominent in news organizations, reporters covering the national labor scene have become, according to *The Nation* writer Jo-Ann Mort, an "endangered species" (1987, p. 588). Mort, who had worked as a union communications official, reported that the labor beat is now often split among business departments, life style departments, and in smaller markets, general assignment reporters attached to the city desk.

Do these two factors—hesitancy to inflame a situation coupled with lack of detailed insight into the issue—tend to affect the way decisions, including what we have defined as "ethical" decisions, are made?

A case could be made that they do. For example, an analysis of 41 local newspaper stories about the Brown and Sharpe strike showed that the cause of the strike was mentioned only 13 times. The cause, it should be noted, was a highly complex series of charges and countercharges about the role of seniority at the plant.

To oversimplify, union officials charged that changes in seniority rules would allow management to strip an individual's seniority rights simply by reassigning him or her; that individual, who may have had many years of employment and a concomitantly high salary, could then be laid off in favor of lower-paid workers. Management contended that flexibility in job assignment was essential to maintaining competitiveness with foreign industry.

Investigating such complex issues would be a daunting task indeed, and from this and other empirical observations of media in the area where the strike occurred, that task was not undertaken with any real consistency or diligence. While it was clear that the strike was not per se an economic strike—one where higher wages were demanded—that fact was not clearly pointed out in most stories and it was reported in depth on few occasions. The apparent cause was simply the mechanics of news coverage.

Fairness is a multifaceted issue, and just as fairness relates to previously introduced concepts, it also relates to many of the chapters that follow. We will examine how fairness relates to such issues as professional conduct and privacy, and explore whether fairness is something that can be mandated and enforced.

A point meriting a mention in closing, though, is the relationship of fairness to the so-called informed public-accessible-press theory proposed in the previous chapter. There are attempts to legislate fairness, the latest being the proposed reincarnation of the Fairness Doctrine, a federal regulation that required broadcasters to grant a right of reply to personal attacks or one-sided presentations of controversial issues. The doctrine was repealed by the Federal Communications Commission, on the grounds that it presented an unconstitutional restriction of free speech and press, but Congress has flirted with the notion of reinstating it.

While the doctrine applied only to broadcast media, which are licensed by the government, spokespeople for the print media worry that such mandated "fairness" will be applied to them. John Seigenthaler, former president of the American Society of Newspaper Editors, echoed just that thought in a 1989 speech to the first National Freedom of Information Assembly. As reported in *Editor & Publisher* (1989, p. 14), Seigenthaler chided the print media for complacency and warned that, "Congress is angry. It has had a love affair with the Fairness Doctrine. It wants the doctrine back. . . . There are some members of Congress . . . who actually believe there should be a Fairness Doctrine for the print media."

Seigenthaler's contention, a reasonable one, relates back to the Rashomon effect as it pertains to fairness. Seen through different eyes, many things are *unfair*. "We publish statements every day," he said, "that are unfair in the eyes of government . . . and readers."

But he closed on a point with which many who favor demystification of the press in the eyes of the public, and more responsiveness on the part of the press, would heartily agree. He suggested that newspapers join broadcasters to convince readers, listeners, viewers, and the pubic at large that "we are ethical, responsible, fair, reasonable and open. We need to find ways to explain . . . our positions on journalistic ethics, confidential sources—on why we do what we do the way do it."

Chapter 6
Professional Conduct

Do you pledge that you and your fellow journalists will continue to demand that all politicians get no pay raise, reveal their incomes and stop taking honoraria—while steadfastly, sanctimoniously refusing to do any of those things yourselves?

—Senator John Glenn, swearing in the new president of the National Press Club

A recent survey by San Diego State's K. Tim Wulfemeyer (1989, p. 12) asked news directors what they considered "acceptable" and "unacceptable" behavior. Results showed that in the "acceptable" category were such activities as working at a second job, belonging to a community organization, entering journalistic contests, and going undercover to gather news. In the list of "unacceptable" behaviors were such actions as taking "most freebies," doing commercials, paying for news, and airing the names of accident victims before families have been notified. Some "gray areas" included conducting ambush interviews and using hidden cameras.

This chapter will focus basically on practices that specifically reflect what is implied in the term "professional conduct"—relationships with others and the professional obligations that are part and parcel of those relationships. (Other concerns, including those cited by Wulfemeyer, are addressed elsewhere.)

First, though, we should identify a hidden assumption here, one which needs to be examined before we can determine if a journalist "acted professionally" and whether codes, rules, or sanctions should be in place to ensure "professional conduct."

Is journalism really a *profession*? This is not a trivial question; the implications of the term are disputed, and such differences have a fundamental impact on how journalistic ethics are evaluated.

There are, of course, many different definitions of "profession," but simply citing a dictionary would not prove a prima facie case. However, it is commonly accepted among those who argue both sides of the dispute that a "profession" is a distinct subclass of "occupation." Given that, we can explore some of the finer points, such as the contention by Louis Hodges (1986), director of Washington and Lee University's applied ethics program. He writes that "In a strict sense, 'profession' refers to a certain small class of occupations with special characteristics that set them apart from mere trades or business. Those professional occupations are afforded special privileges and status" (p. 32).

Hodges goes on further to define professions as "self-regulating occupational groups. They establish their own standards of ethics, of right and wrong, and find ways of enforcing on their own members all those proper standards."

Working backward from the last statement, we can make Hodges's definition fit virtually any occupational group commonly accepted as a profession. Physicians, a professional group, have a professional agency with enforcement powers, the American Medical Association. The same can be said for attorneys, certified public accountants, dentists, and so forth. But do journalists establish their own standards of ethics and enforce them? Well, yes and no; the issue will be examined at some length in Chapters 11–13.

At this point, though, the relevant issue is not only whether journalism *is* a profession (and to what degree) but also whether journalism *should* be considered a profession, subject to the "standards" guideline raised by Hodges. For his own part, Hodges argues that journalism *is* evolving into a profession and *should* do so:

> One has to conclude . . . that journalism clearly does not possess all the attributes ordinarily associated with the classical professions. But it does possess enough attributes of the professions to be in the running.
>
>   . . . If the individual journalist and the profession as a whole can find ways to nurture these character traits [traits placing the needs of the audience first, as members of other professions presumably put the needs of their clients first] one sure result will be that the audience will be better served. . . . Thus, in every case the quality of service will improve. All decisions about news stories will be made from the moral point of the audience's interests, not in the interest of the journalist and the news organization.

Journalism as a profession would, according to this reasoned argument, seem to be a universally palatable concept, would it not?

Wrong. While there are many arguments against "professionalizing" journalism, three commonly heard contentions are:

1. That we live in a pluralistic society and journalism is a reflection of our diversity. Imposing standardized codes, the hallmark of a profession, would detract from that diversity.

2. A profession, in our society, is often thought of as a job for which one needs a specific credential, such as a degree or admittance to a society. Critics of professionalism often contend that if we increasingly entertain the idea of "professionalizing" journalism, the imposition of a formal requirement for a professional journalist may follow—an idea which does not sit well with strict adherents to the First Amendment.
3. When a field becomes a profession, it changes in character. It may become elitist, less open to new ideas, and more demanding of conformity among younger members seeking to enter the "priesthood."

Following are examples of such opinion. Professor Merrill (1986, p. 57) fires this salvo:

> ... as far back as 1974 I devoted an entire chapter in *The Imperative of Freedom* to the dangers of professionalizing journalism. Few took my words very seriously then, and few take them seriously now. And there have been others, here and there, who have opposed the trend toward professionalizing journalism. But the trend has continued unabated. . . .

Merrill has a number of arguments against the professionalization of journalism; chief among them is his fear of repression of individual expression. He also proposes a solution:

> ... professionalism is not the only option. American journalism has been getting along pretty well without being a profession. So, another option is to keep what we have: an "open" craft where anyone can be a journalist and where ethical standards are basically determined by the journalists themselves and by the editors, publishers and other media managers on a pluralistic basis. What I am saying is this: What is wrong with our present system of pluralistic ethics which is compatible with, and is working along side of our system of pluralistic journalism exemplified by the diversity of our media and their messages?

Merrill also alleges that much of the desire to "professionalize" (which, by the statements so far presented, we have pretty well narrowed down to membership in an organization with its own rule-enforcement system and prescriptive standards of conduct) stems from the fact that there is some sort of deep-rooted desire among press people to belong to a hierarchy. Indeed, Merrill cites the attitude expressed by Lewis Lapham when Lapham was editor of *Harper's*. Lapham, in an article titled "The Temptation of a Sacred Cow," expressed trepidation over what he perceived as increasing talk about "legitimate" journalists, a term implying a willingness to accept some sort of licensing, certification, or credential that marks one as a "professional" rather than an "amateur" journalist. Rather than turning journalism into an elite, Lapham argued, professionalizing journalism would, in effect, shrink the talent pool, discourage creative work, and promote second-rate work by institutional ladder climbers.

What Merrill and Lapham characterize as a desire for *the prestige* of belonging to a "profession" could also be expressed in sociological terms as an *occupational ideology*. Elliott A. Krause, in his book *The Sociology of Occupations* (1971, p. 89), writes:

> Occupational ideologies are used by specific occupational groups to gain the support and action of target groups, such as the occupation's direct clientele (if there is one), other occupational groups with which the group deals, the government, and the general public.

Krause cites two problems inherent with the professionalization of an occupation. First:

> ... the code and the future goals of the group [which has recently professionalized] may be used as a club to hit the younger generation, who will be expected to live up to the standards. In this sense, in occupations interested in professionalizing there will often be found the most extreme instances of an occupational ideology being used against the occupation itself, in the interest of constructing a greater unity in the future.

Second, Krause argues that a "professional" organization often seeks to exaggerate its expertise for the effect it will have on the public. What he calls an ideology of "total expertise" is useful, for those who seek it, in establishing a type of elitism within the occupation and a priestly facade for the consumption of the general public.

The question of whether journalism is a profession deals with many *implied* consequences: censorship by some as yet nonexistent governing body, exclusion of entry into the field and the resulting constriction on press freedom, the idea of some sort of "credential" which would limit the ranks, and so on. Those arguments, of course, rely on the premise that those who view journalism as a profession will want (or at least allow) events to evolve that way.

On the other hand, "professional" can take the looser meaning of simply being a responsible member of an occupation, a meaning with which no one conceivably would quarrel. But the implied consequences of professionalism could, conceivably, materialize if journalism should follow the "professional" lead of doctors, lawyers, psychologists, and any other field which seeks to enhance its status and exclude those deemed unqualified. (This is certainly not a derogatory characterization in all instances; one certainly would not want his or her neurosurgeon to be a member of an open occupation which one could join just by purchasing the right tools.)

There are no readily apparent answers to the professionalism issue (although I will attempt one in the Conclusion of this work), but it is an underlying issue of great import. At the very least, we can now speak of "professional conduct" and know that the term is not definitive, and that different journalists will have different views of what their occupational obligations are and to whom they are owed.

Let's briefly examine a major category of conflict involving controversy over who owes what to whom: The ever-present occupational/professional problem of how journalists interact with the people they cover.

Many people attempt to influence journalists to produce coverage more favorable to a particular person, organization, or cause. This, in itself, is not a breach of ethics on their part. After all, everyone has some right of access to the press and there is nothing intrinsically wrong with a public relations executive attempting to interest a reporter in covering the PR person's organization. (This process can also provide the reporter with a good story, so the relationship is frequently symbiotic.)

But somewhere in the continuum, professional relationships can become too close. The point at which this happens is not always clearly demarcated. For example, few reporters would feel compromised by having an interviewee buy them a cup of coffee. But what about an expensive meal? Could a reporter feel completely comfortable about his or her objectivity after the subject of the story had spent $50 for the dinner tab? Perhaps more to the point, could listeners, viewers, or readers have complete confidence in the journalist's objectivity if that fact came to light?

As cited in the Wulfemeyer study (the survey of news directors described at the beginning of this chapter), "freebies" are among the most universally condemned of behaviors. Let's accept, just for the sake of argument, a part of Professor Hodges's argument about professionalism—that a professional journalist's primary obligation is to the public. This argument intuitively seems reasonable. Also, owing a responsibility to the consumer of news is compatible with libertarian and social-responsibility press theories. If that argument is accepted, then, freebies are clearly a violation of the transaction.

If the public is "buying" an objective viewpoint, it is obviously cheated if the purveyor of the viewpoint is influenced by bribes or other loyalties. The public is also not well served by a transaction involving a viewpoint which *may* be slanted by bribes or other loyalties; even in the face of the strongest protestations of innocence on the part of the reporter, the public has no way of *verifying* that the transaction is indeed clean and unencumbered.

A relationship that does not involve an exchange of money or other item of worth can still be compromising. For example, reporters come into contact with important people, people such as politicians, people who sometimes fall into the habit of "asking the reporter for advice." This can be quite flattering to a journalist, but it can be compromising as well. First, the journalist is implicitly guaranteeing favorable coverage of the administration in question if the suggestions are followed. After all, how can a reporter criticize what were originally his or her ideas? Second, a journalist can find himself or herself co-opted into the camp of the politician when the reporter becomes a de facto adviser. Third, the reporter may give favorable treatment (or give the appearance of *owing* favorable treatment) to the politician who has bestowed such confidence on him or her.

Even benign-appearing social relationships are cause for concern among some members of the journalistic community. Should a reporter play regular rounds of golf with someone whom the reporter regularly covers? What about attending parties with politicians?

Some journalists frequently socialize with subjects. Others, such as the *Baltimore Sun*'s Lyle Denniston, attend no social functions where they are likely to encounter news subjects. Denniston maintains (1988) that it is incumbent upon him, as a professional, to keep a proper distance from people about whom he may write, thus to provide no appearance of impropriety.

Personal and professional relationships can become particularly vexing when the personal and professional aspects are totally melded, as in the case where a reporter "befriends" a subject, or enters into a business dealing with a subject. That is what happened in the case that inspired an attack on journalism that struck some surprisingly sensitive nerves in the journalistic community.

Author Joe McGinniss entered into a business relationship with Jeffrey MacDonald, who had been convicted of killing his wife and children. McGinniss agreed to collaborate with MacDonald on a book, which would be published under the title of *Fatal Vision*.

The book turned out to be a devastating indictment of MacDonald, not *at all* what MacDonald had expected, so MacDonald sued McGinniss for $15 million. The crux of the dispute: Apparently, MacDonald thought he was hiring a writer—and to MacDonald's way of thinking, a "writer" was more secretarial help than an independent investigator. But McGinniss, writing in *The New York Times* (1989, p. A23), protested that he was a *journalist*, and therefore obligated to write the truth.

In an attack that caused a surprisingly vigorous reaction in the journalistic community, writer Janet Malcolm assailed McGinniss in a two-part *New Yorker* article. In her first article (1989, p. 38), she contended that, "Every journalist who is not too stupid or full of himself to notice what is going on knows that what he does is morally indefensible. He is a kind of confidence man, preying on people's vanity, ignorance, or loneliness, gaining their trust and betraying them without remorse."

No clear consensus on her charge emerged, although many journalists—while vigorously denying their roles as "confidence men"—felt that the fact that McGinniss had entered into a contract with McDonald had weakened his right to call himself an objective "journalist."

Some, such as author Nora Ephron, saw value in Malcolm's critique. She noted (1989, p. 22) that "the world is full of people who honestly don't know that journalists are not their friends." But others, such as biographer Kitty Kelley (1989, p. 22), felt that the issue of reporter-subject trust was less than clear-cut. "If you measure betrayal by a subject's disappointment you are engaging in a useless activity."

But the plot thickens, and in doing so moves us into some new areas. It seems that Malcolm, despite her blanket condemnation of journalistic "confidence games," was sued by a Berkeley, California, psychoanalyst named Jeffrey M. Masson, who was fired from the position of projects director of the Sigmund Freud Archives. Malcolm—in what was originally a two-part article in *The New Yorker* and later a book published by Knopf—painted an exceptionally unflattering picture of Masson. Masson claimed that Malcolm had fabricated quotes which made him look unscholarly, vain, and dishonest (Warren, 1989, p. 10).

And the court trying the case agreed that Malcolm *did* fabricate many of the quotes (p. 18). The majority of the U.S. District Court held, however, that fabricating quotes is acceptable as long as the quotes did not change the substantive content of a public figure. (Masson was deemed a public figure, and therefore under U.S. libel law he was afforded a lesser degree of protection against defamation.)

So the principle of "professional conduct" as it applies to relationships between reporters and those on whom they report took a curious turn: A writer for a prestigious magazine condemned the entire profession, using a one-paragraph indictment which became so widely known that it became the subject of a major article in *Editor & Publisher*, an article in which responsible journalists hotly debated the issue, engaging in a mass breast-beating about this latest crisis of journalistic conscience.

But then the accuser is accused of fabricating quotes, the court agrees, but holds that such a practice is acceptable—prompting *Chicago Tribune* media writer James Warren to speculate whether the court had given the press the right to lie.

This peculiar circumstance is a result of the ways in which principles come into conflict, the subject of the next section of this work. In the case of faking quotes, there is a conflict between the requirements of the medium and the reality of the situation. In some cases, this conflict is relatively benign: Journalists often "clean up" quotes to fix grammatical errors, lend clarity, or eliminate the appearance of ridiculing someone which could be fostered by reprinting his or her dialect verbatim.

Other conflicts put the principles of accuracy and objectivity, social responsibility, fairness, and professional conduct to the test on a daily basis. When push comes to shove—as it often does in journalism—where is the balance between the need to make a profit and the responsibility of the press to the public? How far do we take the principle of consequentialist reasoning when weighing the ends versus the means?

In what is probably the most nettlesome conflict—and the subject of the next chapter—where do we draw the line between the individual's right to privacy and the public's right to know?

PART
Three
PRINCIPLES IN CONFLICT

Chapter 7

The Right to Privacy Versus the Public's Right to Know

We already have in this town so-called respectable publications that print stuff that is untrue, that can be demonstrated to be untrue, and their defense is, "We accurately report real rumor."

—George Will

The delicate balance between the public's presumed right to know versus an individual's right to privacy has historically had a rather elastic fulcrum. Recent events, though, have led some members of the general public and the press corps to believe that the balance has gone entirely out of kilter.

The politics of privacy—and our growing discomfort with the power of the press to shred privacy via the reporting of apparent rumor—became glaringly apparent during the battle over the late John Tower's nomination as Secretary of Defense. As a result, some journalists have begun publicly questioning their own methods and motives in various publications and, as described a bit later, in a rather startling exchange on a popular news program.

A critic who writes under the name of William Boot (1989, p. 18) noted in the *Columbia Journalism Review* that Tower's bid foundered on an FBI report which contained anonymous, uncorroborated assertions of the designee's drinking and "womanizing." What caused some critical introspection in the ranks of the news media was the practice of privacy shredding via uncritical reporting of lurid rumor. As Boot pointed out:

> ... reporters helped carry out the death sentence with lethal injections of venomous claims—reported with such a collective frenzy that it appeared that Tower had won as few friends in the news media as he had in the Senate. There

was the assertion, reported on page one of the February 4 *Washington Post*, that Tower could have jeopardized the national security by having " 'a protracted relationship' with a Russian ballerina. . . . The bureau [FBI] has not yet confirmed any details." The phrase "not yet" implied that it was about to do so. It never did.

As the Tower nomination was writhing in its final agony, television viewers were treated to an odd spectacle: Paragons of self-assuredness such as George Will and Sam Donaldson as much as admitted that they were just as confused about the privacy puzzle as everyone else. Yes, with the onslaught of fact and factoid surrounding such events as the demise of Gary Hart's presidential bid, the toppling of Jim Wright, and the Tower affair, even the most astute members of the press corps have become uncomfortable with the lack of any clearly definable norms concerning the press's intrusion into private lives—even the private lives of very public people.

As examples, consider these excerpts from the discussion of the Tower nomination, which concluded the Brinkley program (March 12, 1989).

George Will posited this contention:

> If we are going to have a wave of virtue in this town and insist that our legislators . . . and it soon will be legislators as well as cabinet members . . . should be role models, then we're going to have a journalism that will dress voyeurism in the fancy cloak of the public's right to know . . . I think we're going to have carnivorous journalism.

Mr. Will went on to state that one manifestation of this type of journalism can be seen in the fact that:

> We already have in this town so-called respectable publications that print stuff that is untrue, that can be demonstrated to be untrue, and their defense is "We accurately report real rumor."

Sam Donaldson offered an observation:

> I thought at one time we didn't report rumors. That was the job of the reporter and the press to check out stories, and if they didn't pan out, you don't print them.

Cokie Roberts joined in the fray:

> That's not entirely [true]. We don't print rumors as rumors. All through the end of the last campaign there were rumors coming into all of our offices about the candidates, particularly the Republican candidates, that none of us printed.

Mr. Donaldson countered:

> Oh, it got into print. It got into print.

CHAPTER 7   THE RIGHT TO PRIVACY VERSUS THE PUBLIC'S RIGHT TO KNOW

Tom Wicker of *The New York Times* affirmed the notion that indeed the rules have changed, and in the days of Kennedy and Johnson certain things were *not* reported that *would* be reported today. He concluded:

> What is going to happen to journalism as such in the long run I don't know.... Whether we'll go back eventually to a kind of blind approach to these things or whether we'll keep reporting these things I don't know, but the very ethic of journalism insists that you have to report.

Finally, Mr. Will summed up it all up with an interesting semantic observation:

> Tom, when you say the rules are changing... *rules that are constantly changing from case to case are not rules.*

One response to the changing rules has been the fact that the subject of privacy is now addressed in formal codes of ethics and informal codes, what we sometimes call "memo-and-meeting" codes. But those codes are typically so broad that they do not provide any measure of realistic guidance on a case-by-case basis. So in effect, the people who write the rules, the people who interpret the rules, and the people who break the rules all share a common problem—they don't know where they stand. As a result, we have what amounts to a high-stakes game with few, if any, rules.

Perhaps the only remaining way to untangle the complex problem of privacy versus the public's right to know is to examine some perspectives of the issue from the point of view of the journalistic profession as well as from other disciplines, such as history, jurisprudence, anthropology, sociology, and philosophy.

This chapter focuses on three cross-disciplinary areas:

1. *The legacy of privacy*. It appears that the lack of a clear-cut heritage of historical and philosophical thought on the subject of privacy is one reason why we're so flabbergasted by the issue today.
2. *The reasons behind the conflict* between the individual's right to privacy versus the public's right to know. We will examine the root causes of this persistent problem.
3. *The current ethical boundaries* and issues relating to privacy, and where we are headed from here.

The most well-known phrase about privacy is, of course, the "right to be let alone," which is usually attributed to Louis Brandeis, former Associate Justice of the U.S. Supreme Court. The phrase actually originated with a judge named Cooley, was refined by Brandeis, and later used by Justice William O. Douglas, who contended that "the right to be let alone is the beginning of all freedom."

But no matter: The intent of the remark was quite clear, but its origin is surprising in two respects. First, the landmark article in which the "right to be let alone" concept made its debut wasn't inspired entirely by scholarly curiosity. The article, titled "The Right to Privacy," by Samuel D. Warren and Louis Brandeis (1890), was inspired by, as you may have guessed, snooping reporters. The coauthor, Mr. Warren, was outraged at the coverage of a party held at his home.

Mr. Warren, and his former law partner Mr. Brandeis, maintained: "The press is overstepping in every direction the obvious bounds of propriety and dignity. Gossip is no longer the resource of the idle and of the vicious, but has become a trade, which is pursued with industry as well as effrontery" (Warren & Brandeis, 1890, p. 193). Hardly an outdated thought, is it?

But there is another interesting aspect of this seminal article: The piece was written only a hundred years ago, and it was arguably the first time in the long history of humanity that privacy was fully addressed as a legal issue. Legal scholars (Prosser, 1960) and philosophers (Schoeman, 1984) have noted that the Warren-Brandeis article was the first truly "sustained and explicit" (Schoeman, 1984, p. 10) legal discussion of the privacy issue in law. The Warren-Brandeis article itself pointed out our paucity of precedent in the privacy area.

Note that our most fundamental legal document, the U.S. Constitution, never *directly* addresses privacy: While Article One indirectly deals with the privacy of one's own thoughts, and Article Four glancingly guarantees the right to be "secure in our persons," and Article Five allows us some limitations on the secrets we're not bound to disclose, privacy as such is given short shrift.

If privacy lacks a long legal pedigree, what about its philosophical heritage? For all intents and purposes that heritage hardly exists. Professor Lisa Newton (1989, pp. 244, 245), of the applied ethics program at Fairfield University, noted that "the concept of 'privacy' has no history in the literature of philosophy. . . . For its philosophical foundations, we look to the literature of human dignity and the literature of private property; odd as the term may seem, one's property in one's own dignity may be the best cognate of privacy."

John Locke touched on the concept when he stated that "every man has a 'property' in his own 'person.' This," Locke maintained, is something "nobody has any right to but himself."

Locke's analysis, while brief, essentially sums up the idea that privacy, for lack of a better definition, is how secure we feel about our control—our "ownership"—of that personal space. Anthropologists and social scientists tell us that the need for personal space is a very deep-seated and instinctive drive, and one which is not limited to humans. The cries of animals are a method of defining territory. If you have any doubt about the innateness of a need for personal space among animals, notice how carefully birds space themselves out on a telephone wire.

So while the birds and the beasts have the problem pretty well under control, we are only beginning to grapple with the critical question: How much "ownership" do I have of my personal space, and how much control can I exercise over what others know about me and say about me? For those of us in the business of dispensing information, the problem is exactly opposite: How far can I go in obtaining private information and within what boundaries can I disseminate it?

This is hardly an easy question, considering the fact that as we just mentioned, those decisions are made in a virtual vacuum of historical precedent. If you have any doubts about how quickly the rules fluctuate, consider one fundamental change that's taken place within the last fifty years: Franklin Delano Roosevelt was rarely photographed in his wheelchair. This rule was entirely an invention of the press. Roosevelt himself did not particularly care to hide his infirmity—he freely allowed photographs to be taken of him in his swim trunks, showing his naked, withered legs. But the conviction of the press that FDR should not be shown in a wheelchair was so strong that on one occasion a photographer who tried to catch such a shot had his camera taken away and smashed—by other press photographers (Davis, interview, 1989).

Times certainly have changed. A mere forty years later we found ourselves treated to animated TV diagrams of Ronald Reagan's bowels and urinary tract.

It seems clear that basic perceptions of privacy have changed. Yes, yellow journalism of the Warren/Brandeis era did produce some scandalous material, but for various reasons, some of which will be addressed shortly, the modern media have unprecedented power to invade privacy. It is also worth noting that at the turn of the century, people like Mr. Warren often felt violated simply by finding their names in print.

Today, however, we have reached the point where, in one particularly extreme example, a newspaper reporter writing a story on a child who choked to death on a Christmas decoration was ordered by his editor to call back the parents of the child to find out the color of the ornament (Goodwin, 1983, p. 232).

As philosophical inquiry fails us, we also come up dry when plumbing other traditions, including religion. "Thou shalt not covet thy neighbor's wife" is a reasonably clear dictum of the Judeo-Christian ethic. But if Congressman X is doing that coveting, do we print it? Our religious/philosophical heritage is not of much help.

Neither is our political heritage. We are a democracy and we value what we call, without truly defining the issue, *the public's right to know*. That "right" entered the popular lexicon after World War II, popularized by Kent Cooper, the former general manager of the Associated Press. Cooper's view, as paraphrased by Conrad Fink (p. 11), maintained that "while the First Amendment gives the press the *right* to freely print the news, the people's right to know gives the press the *duty* to print it. Thus developed the idea of a press serving as surrogate of the people and demanding access to news, as well as freedom to print it, on behalf of the people."

"Right to know" arguments carry considerable weight when dealing with public affairs and tax dollars, but as the issue becomes further removed from public affairs (perhaps a poor choice of words, given the context of the discussion), the basically unresolved "right to know" argument becomes a bit more shaky. In her book *Secrets* (1982, p. 254), Sissela Bok, who teaches ethics at the Harvard Medical School, maintains that such a right is clearly far from self-evident.

> Taken by itself, the notion that the public has a "right to know" is quixotic from an epistemological as from a moral point of view, and the idea of the public's "right to know the truth" even more so. It would be hard to find a more fitting analogue to Jeremy Bentham's characterization of talk about natural and imprescriptible rights as "rhetorical nonsense—nonsense upon stilts." How can one lay claims to a right to *know the truth* when even partial knowledge is out of reach concerning most human affairs, and when bias and rationalization and denial skew and limit knowledge still further?
>
> ... So patently inadequate is the rationale of the public's right to know as a justification for reporters probe and expose, that although some still intone it ritualistically at the slightest provocation, most now refer to it with a tired irony.

In addition to epistemological and moral uncertainties, the idea that the public has a right to know cannot claim a clear-cut legal pedigree. While the American legal system generally gives great latitude for intrusive press coverage under the aegis of a public "right to know," the assumption of that right is not consistent or monolithic. For example, in a case cited by Hiebert, Ungurait, and Bohn (1985, p. 625), the *Missoulian*, a daily newspaper in Missoula, Montana, lost a court case in which the newspaper argued that it had the right to make public the interview process for the presidency of the University of Montana. The *Missoulian* held that closing portions of the interviews to the press and public violated the state's open meeting law.

A lower court disagreed, finding that the right to privacy of the applicants for the position outweighed the public's right to know. The ruling was eventually upheld by the Montana Supreme Court, which contended that a certain amount of privacy in the interviewing process was necessary because frank and private discussion was an essential part of sound management and hiring practice.

To come full circle, scholars have argued that even if the public's "right to know" were a clear-cut legal issue, which it is not, the letter of the law does not necessarily spell out ethical or moral correctness. Christians, Rotzoll, and Fackler (1983, pp. 110–111) argue:

> ... legal efforts assume many debatable questions about the relationship between self and society. ... Shortcuts and easy answers arise from [failing to recognize an area of a person's life which is strictly private and not part of a collective

CHAPTER 7   THE RIGHT TO PRIVACY VERSUS THE PUBLIC'S RIGHT TO KNOW

society].... Glib appeals to "the public's right to know" are a common way to cheapen the richness of the private/public relationship.

Therefore, sensitive journalists who struggle personally with these issues in terms of real people lay on themselves more demands than the technically legal. They realize that ethically sound conclusions can emerge only when various privacy situations are faced in all their complexities.

Yet, the concept of a right to know is not forsaken. Various arguments have attempted to link the First Amendment with the right to know, with varied levels of success. It is difficult to "measure" the linkage since that "right" is only implied and therefore argued by extension. At the same time we cannot eliminate from our collective memory that this country was founded by many people who came to the Eastern Seaboard to escape their pasts—and then moved west to escape the things they had done in the east.

It is clear that we have fallen into sharp disagreement over privacy issues, and reporters are not the only ones complaining about the game with no rules.

Jurists feel this conflict. They bemoan the crazy quilt of privacy and libel laws in this country. Laws are different in all fifty states and now we see the modern phenomenon of plaintiffs jurisdiction shopping across the country to find the most promising venue.

Privacy and related libel laws can also be extraordinarily complex. Former Philadelphia Court Judge Lois G. Forer (1987) noted that in a murder case she can "charge a jury on all elements of the crime, the burden of proof, even mental aspects, within 20 minutes and they will understand it. But in a libel case it takes more than an hour, and the rules are confusing."

Worse, she also contends that this confusion over what you can and cannot publish is indeed having a chilling effect on the media, forcing reporters to back off from covering stories because they simply don't know how the rules apply.

We have pretty much lumped libel and privacy laws into one discussion, but one of the more typical privacy actions, a "false light" complaint, has strong parallels with libel; both actions seek legal redress against a medium which the plaintiff feels has published untrue, misleading, and in many cases defamatory information about him or her.

Another type of privacy action, usually called "misappropriation," usually deals with advertising; it involves the use of names or likenesses in advertising without consent (Dill, 1986, p. 135). "Intrusion" claims involve trespass or taping without consent. They are not particularly common, and sometimes fairly clear-cut (although there is often considerable controversy over what exactly is a "public" place and who has the right to be there).

So-called embarrassment complaints are probably the most nettlesome circumstance confronted in the legalities of privacy, because they hinge on a number of subjective factors: What is "embarrassment," what harm did it cause, did the subject invite the attention?

Here is a mental exercise that illustrates the dilemma of the vagaries of privacy law. Put yourself in the place of an editor or publisher. Do you know the rules about privacy, rules that could put you into bankruptcy? For example, would you feel comfortable publishing an interview with a young man who freely talks about being an unwed teenage father? If so, we may see you in court.

The U.S. Supreme Court recently let stand a ruling that awarded an unwed teenage father $26,500 in damages for invasion of privacy because he was quoted in a story on teen pregnancy in the *Greenville News*, a paper in South Carolina. The court ruled that the newspaper was liable because it knowingly or recklessly published information "not of public importance" (*News Media and the Law*, 1987, p. 25). This ruling came even though the young man—16 at the time of the interview—had willingly spoken to the reporter.

In addition to the press and jurists, government officials are worried about privacy issues. They want clearer demarcations between public information and private information. That, of course, is nothing new. The issue of using and misusing claims of national security and executive privilege to conceal is so pervasive that we can't scratch the surface of that problem. For one thing, the problem exists on all levels of government, right down to the local police station. Every reporter who has worked a police beat knows that law enforcement agencies feel the need to keep information from the public when it suits their purposes—and in some cases justifiably so, because certain facts about a crime must be kept secret. Police need to hide a fact not known to the general public so that they can sort out the deranged people who make a hobby of confessing to crimes they read about in the newspapers. Police also need some key piece of secret information to discredit jailhouse informants who sometimes fabricate stories about confessions of cell mates, and who testify against their cell mates in return for reductions of sentences.

However, we as a nation have a very strong distaste for linking the words "secret" and "police." Reporters like to have police matters out in the open. Police often make reporters feel that they're endangering the public safety every time they ask a question.

Again, those issues concerning the government's desire for a clear line between public and private information are nothing new—but there is an entirely new wrinkle to the situation. In keeping with the concept that rules are bending in bizarre directions, the FBI now wants to protect the privacy of criminals. In the spring of 1989 the U.S. Supreme Court ruled that news organizations don't have the right to access FBI "rap sheets." The FBI fought to keep those records out of the hands of the press and argued that even though these files are compiled from public documents—arrest records and court records from all over the country—the computerized centralization of these records is a threat to privacy.

And while reporters, lawyers, and government play tug-of-war with the rules, some segments of the general public are simply getting fed up with the whole business. A Gallup poll indicated that 73 percent of the American public feels that the press invades people's privacy. (That poll was conducted three years ago; it is hard to imagine that the image of the news media has significantly improved since that time.)

More recently, there has been increasing emphasis on questioning the motives of the messenger. Various members of the press are increasingly using the word "populism" to describe the growing perception that a backlash is growing, meaning that members of the media elite will themselves have to be on their best behavior.

That populism has, on occasion, come full circle and been expressed by members of the working press. Nat Hentoff (1979, p. 23), a writer for *The Village Voice* who has also taught investigative reporting, contends that the press is coming to be regarded as "one of the most fearsome enemies of privacy." He maintains that the press is no more likely to "become humane on its own than bill collectors," and even goes so far as to speculate that it might be "grandly therapeutic" if "one paper in a city would subject reporters and editors of another paper to exactly this kind of privacy shredding." That is, Hentoff says, "headlining the extramarital affairs and ancient arrest records of some of these journalists. The experience could greatly concentrate the victims' minds on privacy when they went on assignment."

Why have these principles in conflict surfaced so dramatically in the past few years? While there are many possible reasons, four are worth considering briefly at this point.

First, we have increasingly sophisticated news-gathering technology. We can gather news quickly and transmit that news across the country or across the globe literally at the speed of light.

A second and closely related point is the fact that the new technologies, including satellite technologies, allow local news organizations to cover national stories. Now that local news organizations have gone national we have what is virtually an enormous national press corps. Of course some would express that sentiment as, "the new technology has increased the size of the pack."

Satellite transmissions and global communications also vastly extend the ability of one party to collect information damaging to another party. This was graphically illustrated by China's interception of satellite signals that carried interviews with dissidents; that intercepted news material, originally intended as a private feed to a U.S. news agency for use in the continental Americas, was turned into a source of domestic intelligence. More recently, the same concerns—that instant global communication translate to readily accessed intelligence data—were expressed concerning news organizations' coverage of the Persian Gulf War.

A third reason why we are having such trouble with rules and the lack of same deals with the changing constituency of the press corps. As mentioned, membership in the ranks of national news media is no longer equivalent to membership in a small, exclusive club. Reporters in Miami or

Figure 7.1 Technology has its price, and raises some ethical questions: In the wake of the Tienanmen Square massacre, Chinese citizens became reluctant to speak with the news media. The reason? Satellite transmissions from an American news organization were intercepted by the Chinese government and used to identify dissidents.

Charlotte crack the big stories just like their counterparts in the networks, wire services, or *The New York Times*.

Some feel the situation goes even deeper. Cokie Roberts (1989) of ABC News, for example, feels that the increasing presence of women in the press corps has changed the rules; men who got off the bus together and drank together, so the theory goes, were more likely to keep secrets. When women "ruined" that bastion of male bonding, the privacy rules changed.

Finally, let's not forget that we have something of a sensory overload in our media-rich society. The segment of the audience that favors luridity has an ever-increasing menu from which to choose. It seems logical that the more we try to shock the public, the harder it becomes; apparently, shock value is subject to inflation, and like money in the Weimar Republic, we now need wheelbarrows full of it to astound the overloaded readers of tabloids, or the viewers of trash TV, or the listeners to raunch radio.

If a portion of our media is devoted to digging for dirt about celebrities or ordinary people consumed by extraordinary events, and a portion of the audience is increasingly devoted to consuming it, erosion of privacy seems a natural by-product.

Given the fluid nature of the rules (and lack of rules) governing privacy, it seems worthwhile to pose questions which relate to the previous discussion. We will examine the current status of the media's views on privacy and some of the questions that will emerge in the near future.

The most obvious question is this: Exactly who is a public person? By extension, does an ordinary person lose his or her right to privacy when extraordinary circumstances thrust that person into the public eye? As a case study, let us examine the incident of a teenager who commits suicide.

In April of 1986 a popular high school athlete hanged himself in a school building. (This is the example stated hypothetically in Chapter 2.) Do you report the case fully, identifying the young man? The *St. Paul Pioneer Press and Dispatch* reported the suicide, but withheld the name. Editor John R. Finnegan contended that it "was a private act. I could not see any major public value to be served."

But the *Minneapolis Star and Tribune* did report the case fully. Managing Editor Tim J. McGuire noted it was the second time a "very visible" student athlete in a local high school had killed himself within recent months, and he stated that the paper decided to publish complete details "because of the extremely public nature of what he had done and where he had done it" (case reported by Stepp, 1986, p. 48).

A related question: How does a journalist strike a balance between the benefits of the story to the consequences which befall the individuals involved? The suicide story is a good example. Many reporters, including this author, have been asked on occasion, by the families involved, not to make public the cause of death of teenage suicide victims. I declined in one case, and I'm sure I aggravated the suffering already felt by the families. But my reasoning was that at the time the event occurred (about fifteen years ago) what was a widespread practice of withholding the cause of death in teenage suicides contributed to the mistaken idea that teenage suicide is not a prevalent problem—an idea given spurious validity because we did not hear about teenage suicide because we never *reported* it. How did this silence affect situations where a teenager talked about suicide but no one took that talk seriously?

Note that this particular concept of deterrence is not universally accepted. News media have, for years, run graphic photos of automobile accidents under the pretext that such photos would somehow let motorists know what awaits them should they become careless behind the wheel. But people continue to have auto accidents, and there is no evidence that conclusively demonstrates the deterrent effect of newspaper photos.

Still, the concept is intuitively intriguing. What may be one of the most gruesome photos ever run on page one of a metropolitan daily newspaper provoked a storm of outrage from some. The photo, shown in Figure 7.2, was carried by the March 9, 1989, Providence *Evening Bulletin*; it showed firemen carrying a badly burned baby, whose charred arms were twisted into an un-

Figure 7.2   This photograph, clearly depicting the body of a baby who died in a fire near Providence, Rhode Island, sparked a storm of controversy when it was printed on page one of the Providence *Evening Bulletin*.

mistakable posture of death. Another photo on page one also depicted the anguished mother being restrained by fire fighters.

However, there were voices that contended that only realistic photos of a tragedy could drive home the point that fires are a threat to everyone. Among those voices was that of the paper's executive editor, James V. Wyman. Wyman contended that the editorial staff agonized over the dilemma of whether to run the graphic photo, but he decided to run with it because "the message it signaled to the public was an overridingly important, powerful and worthy one" (Wyman, 1989, p. B-11).

CHAPTER 7 THE RIGHT TO PRIVACY VERSUS THE PUBLIC'S RIGHT TO KNOW

That message, he argues, is brief:

"Witness the reality of a fast-moving fire.

"Witness the reality of the risks to residents, police and firemen involved.

"Witness the reality of a fact sometimes forgotten or ignored—the grim fact that fire kills."

Wyman acknowledges that in running the photo, the editorial staff was deeply aware of the risk that readers would be offended by the apparent invasion of privacy of the family and, indeed, the small victim. In fact, one letter of protest was signed by the victim's parents and 25 relatives and friends. But Wyman also holds that many of the callers who contacted the photographer who took the shot said that the impact of the photo "had sent them scurrying to check their home smoke alarms." Note the strong strain of *consequentialism* in Wyman's statements; indeed, it is virtually a textbook example of consequentialist reasoning.

The idea of balancing consequences and benefits was brought home with equal force in Washington State, when King County Superior Court Judge Gary Little killed himself after the *Seattle Post-Intelligencer* ran an article charging him with molesting young men in past years. It would appear to any reasonable person that there was some basis to this story—but there were lapses of evidence. (To be fair, almost any story has lapses of evidence.) Also, it is important to point out that while the statements of purported victims gave every indication of reliability, those statements were not made under oath, or subjected to cross-examination; indeed, no aspect of the case was ever tried in a court of law.

That led some critics to contend that the paper hounded the judge to his death. A debate on the related privacy issue raged after the suicide, and that debate demonstrated that these decisions are never quite as simple as one of my freshman journalism students said: "It's true, they printed it, tough."

For example, some serious and sincere people lodged these objections:

—Little had publicly announced plans not to seek reelection to the bench, and was about to move to California when the story broke. In light of this, did the *P-I* unnecessarily report the story?

—The story was planned to cover four full pages. Was it sensationalized? Was it really worth this amount of coverage? Did the paper overdo it because they had a sensational scoop?

—Did the *P-I* rush the story, and possibly compromise its coverage, because they were afraid a rival paper, the *Seattle Times*, was going to beat them into print? Some critics made this charge, and indeed, each paper did know that the other was pursuing the story. According to an article in the 1988–89 *Journalism Ethics Report* published by the Society of Professional Journalists, the *P-I* editorial staff did feel the need to tighten the writing and refine the documentation, but went ahead with the story. Reporter Duff Wilson was quoted as saying, "it could have gone on forever, but we had the basic stuff" (Rowe, 1989, p. 8).

Another privacy question is closely related: How relevant is a public person's private life to his or her public duties? The 1988 presidential campaign was the zenith, or nadir, depending on your perspective, of the character issue in American politics. Gary Hart withdrew after stories linked him with an extramarital affair. Joe Biden's campaign was scuttled after it was revealed he appropriated a speech from a British candidate—and a losing candidate at that—and plagiarized a law-school paper.

Former CBS News President Fred Friendly acknowledged that we're in a game with fluctuating rules when he asked, in the introduction to a panel on the politics of privacy, "Just what privacy should a candidate expect? Media critics have charged that journalists should not be peeping through keyholes, and what someone did 20 years ago is not front-page news. Yet, responsible news organizations have countered that the public has the right to know anything relevant about the character of public officials. . . . The question is, has the press gone too far?" (Friendly, 1987).

Another question brought up in the campaign: How far do we go in printing or broadcasting unproven charges? Do we, as George Will maintained, cloak ourselves in the First Amendment and say "we accurately report real rumor"? There is no question that the American news media engaged in the reporting of "real rumor" when publicizing Michael Dukakis' alleged treatment for depression, or George Bush's alleged extramarital affair, or John Tower's alleged pet ballerina.

The power of accusation can bring about a monstrous invasion of privacy. Harvard Law Professor Alan Dershowitz noted that it is not unusual for prosecutors to hold press conferences at which they appear to equate an indictment with a conviction. "This creates momentum for the case," Dershowitz (interview, 1989) maintains, "helps turn witnesses in their favor, helps win the case, and often is deliberate."

And while there are good arguments to be made against revealing the names of victims of sex crimes, legal scholars, including Dershowitz, have warned that there is a heavy bias in withholding the names of the accuser in sex crimes when the news media prominently feature the name of the person charged (n.b.: *charged*, not convicted) in the case.

Can that bias encourage false claims? A 45–year–old Florida school superintendent recently took his life after widely publicized lewdness charges brought by a 15–year–old girl—a girl who later admitted she made the story up.

That is a difficult issue, and as with many problems it is compounded by the complexities of modern life. In fact, the concept of "media coverage" is changing to the extent that any one of us—no matter how private a person we might be—is subject to sudden, intense scrutiny, even if that scrutiny is something as mundane as a credit report or a report on an employment application.

We live in an information age; but how are we going to govern the way that information is sorted and processed, mixed and matched? Here is a case where all the rules lose much of their meaning, because with the advent of computerized databases and desktop publishing, we don't even have a clear definition of what constitutes a "news medium."

In some states, for example, there are services that publish lists of tenants who have filed complaints against landlords. That list is sold to landlords, who check to see if prospective renters are on that list, meaning, ostensibly, that those people looking for apartments are potential troublemakers. Of course, that list might carry only a report of the fact that an action was filed—no mention of whether it was justified, no mention of the disposition. Is this a medium's invasion of person's privacy, a new wrinkle in the game with no rules? There is good reason to suggest that it is.[1]

Is your name on a database? Probably. Your private life has become a public commodity, and there is a lively commerce in facts about your health, your income, your credit. If you have ever had a life insurance physical, a firm called the Medical Information Bureau—which could logically be termed a specialized type of news media—sells that information to insurance companies. It may contain errors of fact or interpretation. But you will have a difficult time proving that, because you cannot see the report. All you are entitled to see is a general summary provided by your doctor.

An Atlanta firm takes the selling price of homes, a matter of public record, computer matches them with phone numbers, and sells that published list to retailers.

Credit bureaus are by and large accurate in their use of information, but with millions of records on file, we run the risk of becoming the victims of "accurately reported real rumor" as well as simple carelessness. The editor of *Changing Times* magazine, for example, once examined his credit report and found his occupation listed as "changing tires" (Hazard, 1985, p. 93).

Franz Kafka could not invent some of the modern scenarios involving the changing media and their intrusion into private lives. For example, a student of mine was once denied a credit card. He is a very capable and assertive man, and he made a personal trip to the credit bureau, where he was told, by a clerk who somehow managed to keep a straight face through all this, that he had a poor credit rating because he defaulted on a boat loan in 1978.

In 1978 he was nine years old.

When he proved that he had not bought a speedboat at nine years of age, he was told to reapply for his credit card. And he was, of course, rejected again—because of that boat loan.

---

1 The problem of correlating data was recognized in the early 1970s, and the Privacy Act of 1974 placed restrictions on the use of information. It requires consent of individuals before an agency collects and uses information for a different purpose than was originally intended. But there are loopholes, including a loose stipulation that allows "routine use" of the information. Also, in some cases the only notice required is publication of the use of information in the Federal Register.

The point is that the privacy puzzle, the game with no rules, is not an abstract academic problem. It affects private lives and public lives. In some cases it destroys lives. It determines the outcome of credit applications and national elections. And above all, the privacy puzzle points out the fact that all of us—reporters, professors, philosophers, lawyers, consumers of news—have to start putting the pieces together.

Many observers feel that we need to invest some serious thought into the nature of ethics and morals, and our expectations of public and private people. Perhaps our current obsession with morality reflects a perfectly reasonable concern with the values of our leaders and the motives of our messengers. On the other hand, Oscar Wilde might have had us pegged. Morality, he maintained, "is simply the attitude we adopt towards people whom we personally dislike."

Chapter 8
Ends Versus Means

The risk of being overheard by an eavesdropper or betrayed by an informer or deceived as to the identity of one with whom one deals is probably inherent in the condition of human society. It is the kind of risk we necessarily assume whenever we speak.

—U.S. Supreme Court Justice William Brennan

Don Hewitt, the creator and executive producer of "60 Minutes," worked his way up through the ranks of rough-and-tumble journalism. He began his career as a copyboy at the New York *Herald Tribune*, served in World War II, and when he returned to the United States he took on fairly minor positions in wire service and newspaper work, and eventually wound up at the Acme Newspictures agency.

Finally, the big break came. A friend of Hewitt's told him that CBS was looking for someone with picture experience to work in the emerging medium of television.

Hewitt's response (1985, p. 17) was not entirely enthusiastic, given that he was not exactly an expert in the emerging medium: "*Whata*-vision?" he replied.

But his career in whata-vision would span more than forty years, and would involve stints as producer and/or director of "Douglas Edwards with the News," "The CBS Evening News with Walter Cronkite," the first televised presidential debate (Kennedy-Nixon, 1960), and, of course, "60 Minutes."

The news business has always been a competitive one, and no one climbs to the heights Hewitt has reached without an instinct for doing battle.

Some items from the Hewitt biography:

- When working for the Cronkite news program, Hewitt covered the crash of a plane into the East River. Because of a job action, only one tugboat was working the river, and was put to use bringing in bodies. By the time Hewitt arrived on the boat, emergency crews had arrived, and reporters from other networks, wire services, and newspapers were on the deck of the boat, interviewing the captain. The questions were routine, centering on the "burning bodies" and "groaning survivors." Hewitt, though, posed a seemingly irrelevant query: "Who owns the tug?" The other newspeople thought him an idiot—who cares who owns it?—until they found out that Hewitt had called the boat company and *chartered* the tug.

And the first thing he did was to order all the other newspeople ashore. "Get these guys off my boat," he ordered the captain (p. 151).

- About an hour later an NBC crew which had been put ashore by Hewitt found a rowboat, and equipped it with a small transmitter with which they hoped to transmit pictures back to the "Today" show. Hewitt ordered the tugboat captain to maneuver the tug between the rowboat and NBC's receiving antenna so as to block transmission. During the maneuver, the tug accidentally rammed the rowboat, causing no damage but raising some hackles. Complaints were filed against Hewitt; NBC alleged that he tried to sink their boat in the East River.

Hewitt's characterization of the complainants (p. 152): "Cry babies."

- During the 1959 visit of Nikita Khrushchev to a farm in Iowa, Hewitt, arriving to coordinate CBS's coverage, first took care of some small items of business, hijacking NBC's remote truck and hiding it in a cornfield. He then set about the serious task of spying on NBC. Hewitt hired the ex-police chief as a driver, guaranteeing CBS crews access to just about any place they wanted to go. But to prepare for those times when the ex-chief was not around, Hewitt had himself appointed an "honorary sheriff." The next day, sporting his new badge and Stetson, Hewitt wandered over to the NBC remote truck. (They had found it by then.)

"Morning boys," said Hewitt (p. 156). "What's goin' on?"

And the NBC crew told the "sheriff" *exactly* what was going on, including the placement of their "secret" cameras.

NBC again complained, this time about Hewitt impersonating a police officer. "I'm not impersonating anything," Hewitt replied. "I'm an honorary sheriff and I've got the hat and badge to prove it."

This is the stuff of which folklore is made. But it is also the stuff that sets an agenda for the strong ends-justify-the-means (consequentialist) strain of thinking that permeates journalism.

A sociologist might be tempted to call this "mythologization." In the case of many organizations, writes sociologist Peter Tommerup of UCLA (1988, pp. 319–320), mythologization involves stories which become symbolic and play an important role in controlling the organization. Tommerup also maintains that narratives in organizational studies have been found to be largely composed of oral histories which have a major impact on the values of an organization:

> ... Long time employees, who serve as bearers of this heritage [organizational history, which is largely oral history], are seldom more excited than when they are reminiscing about the people and events which they believe are responsible for their firm's past. Organizational history is also principally a "human" history. It is communicated through stories. Stories both *reflect and create* people's social realities [emphasis added].

This is an elongated way of asserting that the folklore of the news business plays an important role in the way newspeople approach their jobs. As Tom Goldstein (1985, p. 10), who testified as an expert witness on journalistic practices in a 1979 trial involving a suit against the *New York Daily News*, puts it:

> In my testimony, I said that journalistic practices are not written down; rather, they are handed down from one generation of reporters to the next by a combination of osmosis and fiat.

Goldstein, a former reporter for the Associated Press, the *Wall Street Journal* and *The New York Times*, left no doubt as to where he felt that osmosis and fiat led in his book *The News at Any Cost: How Journalists Compromise Their Ethics to Shape the News*. But a case can be made that one evolutionary aspect of the way in which those practices are "handed down" is that trickery, fakery, and misrepresentation in the goal of getting the news at any cost are no longer viewed as "business as usual," if indeed they ever were.

This is not a blanket assertion that there is less ends-justify-the-means news practice today than in years past (although that is probably true but unprovable), but rather an assertion that the journalistic community is at least paying closer attention to the dilemma.

Sometimes, old-timers look back a few years and shake their heads. Ed Rooney, a former Pulitzer Prize winning reporter for the *Chicago Daily News*, admits that during the mid-60s he once swiped a photo from a crime scene—a real coup for his paper—but the boss did not even say thanks. "All part of the job, I guess," Rooney mused (1989, p. 9). But he noted, in a story headlined "Once Upon a Time, Reporters Would Use Trickery to Get Story," that today he regrets stealing the photo. He now asserts that "no story is worth a theft or an illegal action."

Rooney's view can hardly be extrapolated to reflect a universal change of collective conscience in journalism. However, hijacking a rival's remote van and spying on one's competitors in the capacity of "honorary sheriff" would certainly raise some eyebrows today, and possibly get someone fired. Journalists can and do get disciplined for even smaller ethical infractions than this (a topic addressed in Chapter 12).

But still, the idea of having rival crew people proudly tell you (the honorary sheriff) about their hidden camera placements: Is it *really* unethical behavior? Or smart, heads-up journalism? As a purely personal response—a response no doubt affected by my exposure to the collective folklore about the news-gathering business—my intellect informs me that, "What Hewitt did was indefensible."

My heart says, "Damn, the guy is a genius."

And such is the ambivalence often encountered when analyzing the issue of misrepresentation, the classic ends-versus-means scenario faced when journalists go "undercover," either assuming another identity or failing to make their identity (or motives) clear. First, the fundamental question: Why, from a practical standpoint, would a reporter pretend to be someone he or she is not?

Journalists typically encounter the same problem often faced by police officers: People often will not openly communicate information which they feel could embarrass or incriminate them *to someone in a position to damage them with that evidence.* Police often solve this problem by sending an officer undercover, a situation not without its own ethical problems.

But *journalistic* undercover operations put the players into true ethical terra incognita. A journalist, after all, is not a public official operating within a prescribed legal framework. The very absence of such legal restrictions makes the reporter's use of misrepresentation an ethical rather than a legal issue, although under certain circumstances legalities could be involved. For example, it would be illegal for a reporter to don the uniform of a police officer and use the guise to pry information out of a reluctant source. The authority of a badge and hat is a privilege relegated only to real police officers and in certain instances to honorary sheriffs. Wearing a police uniform also creates danger for uninvolved people. Suppose a crime occurs and someone in danger relies on the presence of the ersatz officer? Other impersonations would be roundly condemned as illegal and immoral, such as impersonating a physician. But in the case of law enforcement, there are other ways to pose as a police officer without directly lying. It is relatively easy for a reporter who is familiar with police "lingo" to phone a police station and ask for "case file information on the perp in the Smith Jeweler smash and grab." Such an approach can produce the information even if the reporter does not identify him- or herself as a police officer. I have done this myself, using as justification the fact that I did not, strictly speaking, identify myself as a police officer. I have also walked into and milled about crime scenes where I was probably not supposed to be, although one is never really sure in such situations because the rules regarding access are generally made up on the fly. In any event, I did not pretend I was a police officer per se. I simply relied on the fact that at a crime scene, where plainclothes police officers from many different agencies are swarming about, a man with closely cropped hair, a mustache, and a cheap suit is practically invisible.

Unethical? Perhaps. But my *personal* justification rested on the fact that by and large police can restrict access to a crime scene arbitrarily. There is no uniform set of rules, and journalists can be banned from a crime scene—even on public property—depending on the whim of the ranking officer on the scene. That decision would often, it seemed, rest on whether the ranking officer liked reporters in general or wanted publicity.

So rather than taking the chance of being turned down, I simply did not ask, employing a consequentialist line of reasoning: "I am not hurting anything or anyone, I know enough about these situations not to hinder the investigation or damage evidence, and I believe I am entitled to cover this story."

However, it is worth noting that journalists are not always fastidious about keeping their consequentialist and non-consequentialist reasoning consistent. Some news departments "made it a matter of policy"—at least informally, because sometimes it is not written down—not to turn over tapes or photos to police agencies unless those tapes had been aired. The ostensible reason is that turning over tapes or photos to law enforcement officials would co-opt journalists into an evidence-gathering arm of law enforcement, and turning over material every time it was requested was something akin to letting the police rummage through their files at will.

The truth is, though, that some newspeople do not care particularly strongly about the issue, but save themselves from the bother and the time investment involved in an endless string of case-by-case decisions by hiding behind policy. I have invoked "policy" even when it was essentially my personal choice whether to hand over tapes or not. Policy is something ostensibly and conveniently handed down anonymously from on high—much policy exists without anyone knowing *who* made the policy—and so I could not be held accountable. The "policy" excuse was readily accepted by the few police officers whom I turned down and, interestingly, it did not offend them. In fact, at least one officer made it a point to tell me that "rules are rules," and he understood.

So when dealing from a weak position, not wanting to offend people who were my sources—and could, incidentally, decide to ignore the press placard on my visor and start issuing me parking tickets—I justified my actions with non-consequentialist reasoning. But when dealing from a strong position—believing I had an absolute right to be present at a crime scene and knowing that nothing too drastic would happen if I were discovered—I relied on consequentialist, ends-justify-means thinking. (This seems to be a good example of Dr. Gustafson's thesis about the use of consequentialist and non-consequentialist reasoning, which was presented in Chapter 2.)

In any event, there is obviously a continuum along which these ethical values lie, ranging from extreme to extreme, since somewhere between the extremes there is a point where the rightness or wrongness is debatable. There is a broad range of gray area in which misrepresentation is sometimes accepted, sometimes not.

Suppose, for instance, a group of reporters wanted to expose corruption and bribery on the part of city officials, and decided to open up a tavern and take photos of officials and inspectors who solicited bribes? Documenting such thievery would produce a sensational series of stories—which it did. In 1978, the *Chicago Sun-Times* set up a bar, appropriately named the "Mirage," and parlayed the investigation into a stunning multipart story. However, the maneuver did not gain complete acceptance as an ethical method of reporting.

For example, the series did not win a Pulitzer Prize; two members of the Pulitzer advisory board (one of whom was *Washington Post* Executive Editor Benjamin Bradlee, from whom we'll hear more about a later case) objected to the misrepresentation. Bradlee questioned, in effect, how newspapers could promote honesty and integrity when they, themselves, are dishonest in gathering facts for a story.

The Pulitzer's snubbing of the Mirage story came as something of a surprise, since the Pulitzer had gone, on at least four previous occasions, to reporters who assumed a guise. A reporter from the *Buffalo Evening News* who in 1961 posed as a caseworker to expose welfare mismanagement received the coveted award. A journalist from the *Chicago Tribune* who masqueraded as an ambulance driver in 1971 to bring to light the discrepancies in medical care given to rich and poor won a Pulitzer. In 1971, a reporter from the *New York Daily News* pretended to be a medicaid recipient and won the award, as did Bob Greene and a *Newsday* team involved in a story about the drug trade, during the development of which Greene posed as a lawyer (Goldstein, p. 132).

Such stories were fabulous exploits—models for tough, investigative journalism. Note, too, that these stories are relatively recent contributions to the folklore history of impersonation in journalism. As Goldstein noted, "Even though impersonation has lost the blessing of the Pulitzer board, posing still seems to be entrenched among journalists as it has been for at least a century."

Any student of journalism has been schooled in the exploits of Nellie Bly, who exposed the conditions of the infamous Blackwells Island Insane Asylum by gaining admittance after feigning mental illness. Dorothy Kilgallen posed as "a girl from Peoria" in a piece where she attempted to see what it was like for a girl from the Midwest to try to break in as an actress in Hollywood. (Her conclusion: Stay home.) Many journalists, including Ben Bagdikian, have posed as convicts in order to write about conditions within the prison walls.

So, given the assumption that the majority of the journalistic community will accept *some* amount of misrepresentation, where is the line to be drawn? It seems that the determination has to do with the *amount* of artifice used by the reporter to thrust himself or herself into the situation, and the *necessity* of the artifice. Very few critics, for example, would contend that the ever-popular story involving a reporter taking an auto to a car repair shop is a serious misrepresentation. After all, reporters drive cars as do nonreporters, and there is no reason why *any* private citizen could not, if he or she so chose, bring a car to a repair shop to test the competence and honesty of the mechanic. So when the amount of artifice is low, acceptance is high. Too much artifice—pretending to be a police officer or doctor—brings almost universal condemnation.

Sometimes, misrepresentation is given greater tolerance by news executives, and the general public when it is clear that it is *the only way to get a story*. One reporter, for example, got a very good story by posing as a construction worker and documenting the pilferage he observed at the site. He contends that this was the only method to obtain the information; had he shown up in his business suit, notebook in hand, no details would have been forthcoming. But would there be justification for reporters to go undercover to gather readily obtainable information? It seems unlikely that anyone would support such a case.

But debates are not made from easy cases, and not all cases are clear-cut. A number of factors must be weighed. Sissela Bok (1982, pp. 236, 234) addressed the weighing of ends versus means in *Secrets*:

> If a group of editors and reporters have concluded that they see no alternative means and no alternative agencies of investigation to whom the probing of a particular problem can safely be left, they must still weigh the moral arguments for and against deceptive infiltration or other surreptitious methods. Knowing that such means are morally questionable, they must then ask whether their goal warrants the use of such methods. . . .

While acknowledging some validity for impersonation, she also adds an observation which sides with Bradlee's argument against the practice:

> Another consideration that newspaper or television editors should take seriously before going ahead even with clandestine investigations they consider important has to do with the effect on their own credibility and that of the media in general. They know that public confidence in media reliability is already low, and they recognize the existing pressure for rushed stories, forever incomplete, all too often exaggerated or misinterpreted. If the public learns about an elaborate undercover operation such as that of the Mirage bar, many may ask why they should have confidence in the published stories based on information acquired through such an elaborate hoax.

The journalistic community considered both sides of the misrepresentation controversy during a recent case where the factors cited above—*need* for artifice to gather the facts, the *amount* of artifice undertaken, and the *effect on credibility*—were weighed in the journalistic trade press.

In 1987, WNBC-TV (New York) anchor Pat Harper donned old clothes and had fake bruises painted on her face to pose as a bag lady. While many journalists and news critics applauded her, many did not. Some contended that she exploited the homeless in pursuit of ratings.

A sampling of the reaction (one of the best was conducted by the *Washington Journalism Review*) revealed such ambivalence and exposed the fact that news organizations typically handle such situations on a case-by-case basis. While many news organizations officially (in their written policies) frown on misrepresentation, some will condone it when it is the only way to get the story; that is the most typical reasoning process cited.

This ambivalence is probably best summed up by CBS's master trickster Don Hewitt, who said (Palmer, 1987, pp. 20, 21), referring to the Harper case, "Misrepresentation is probably not a good idea, but in specific cases it's a sensational idea." But the longtime opponent of misrepresentation, *Washington Post* executive editor Benjamin Bradlee (Palmer, 1987, p. 21), condemned Harper and NBC. "You can't break the law and you can't tell a lie," he contends, "and you can't pass yourself off as someone you aren't."

Irrespective of Bradlee's contention, the practice of deception continues. While news executives are hardly ever entirely comfortable with the idea, they, and the profession itself, keep the misrepresentation in the toolbox, ready if it is needed, and available in varying dimensions.

For example, a practice similar to misrepresentation by impersonation is misrepresentation by *intent*—in other words, deceiving by misleading the subject of a story regarding what the story is about or where it is leading. "60 Minutes," for example, drew sharp rebukes from a major teaching hospital when it ran a piece on "ghost surgery," the practice of having physicians-in-training perform some or all of an actual operation rather than the experienced physician whom the patient assumes will be doing the procedure. University officials claimed that "60 Minutes" had deceived them by gaining access to the hospital by implying that they were doing a general piece about surgery.

Intent played a central role in a libel suit against the Lexington, Kentucky, *Herald-Leader* over a series of Pulitzer Prize winning articles concerning college basketball recruiting practices. The yearlong investigation involved interviews with dozens of coaches and players, but the libel suit (which was dismissed by the court because no malice was proved) turned on the issue that reporter Michael York had misled a 19-year-old high school basketball player into believing that York was doing a *positive* story about him. York admitted he gave the player "the wrong impression" early in the interview; York conceded he misled, but that the misleading was not intentional.

Writing about the incident for *Editor & Publisher*, University of Kentucky journalism professor Maria Braden (1989, p. 68) observed how the traditional practices of journalism draw reporters along the ethical continuum—sometimes to the point at which she considers "drawing someone out" to be an unethical deception:

I am concerned about where the line is drawn between persuading and misleading, and whether many of us, perhaps unintentionally, mislead our sources.

We know what we are doing when we lob those softball questions early in an interview. If a source should get the wrong idea about what we are after, we may tell ourselves it is necessary to get the story. But is that kind of subtle deception permissible?

Consider what happens at the other end. The source feels tricked and cheated when the story appears. It is one more tear in our tattered journalistic integrity.

Professor Braden concedes that reporters typically save their hardball questions for the end of the interview, and maintains that as long as the source knows "he or she is talking to a reporter for possible publication, that is fine." But, she condemned York's actions because he told the young basketball player that the story would be something other than an investigative piece.

That is a fine line to draw, but her basically non-consequentialist argument (we should not utilize material which is gathered by suggesting to the source that we are working on a positive piece when the opposite is true) is a reasoned argument nonetheless. The question of intent was precisely the fulcrum on which the MacDonald-McGinniss case balanced. MacDonald claimed that McGinniss had promised him a positive story but produced a negative one, all the while keeping MacDonald as a source.

Janet Malcolm used this scenario to label McGinniss "a confidence man" and to imply that all journalists mislead sources and betray them at the last moment. But the question of intent would again surface in the courtroom when Malcolm herself was called before the dock to explain her use of alleged fabrication of quotes.

She argued, in effect, that the ends justify the means; that, as reported by the *Boston Globe* (1990, p. B45), "none of the quotations ... in my ... journalistic writings are, of course, identical to their speech counterparts." She simply was engaging in the "relatively minor task of translating tape-recorderese into English."

But portions of what she alleged were Masson's comments translated from "tape-recorderese into English" were *nowhere to be found on Malcolm's tapes*. Some of the evidence presented in the Malcolm case consisted of typed versions of handwritten notes—not tapes. And the disparity between the evidence that did exist on tapes and the quotations that appeared in the *New Yorker* and the later Knopf book were striking.

The *Chicago Tribune*'s James Warren, in an article that appeared in the *Tribune* on August 30, 1989, and was later reprinted in a Sigma Delta Chi (an organization now known simply as The Society of Professional Journalists) report (1989, pp. 10, 18), disclosed two instances where comments attributed to Masson never appeared on the tapes. In another, he compared Malcolm's *written* quote, *attributed* to Masson:

> [Freud's] entire theory after he abandoned seduction was the product of moral cowardice ...

to the part of the actual tapes that bore the closest resemblance:

> I think [Freud] was a great and remarkable thinker but he was still a . . . a . . . a . . . man who just lost his courage. He was a brilliant mind who didn't have the courage to stick with things he knew were true.

As noted previously, reporters commonly alter quotes in the interest of clarity, and Malcolm indeed has a point when she speaks of the need to translate "tape-recorderese." For example, a literal transcription of the actual portion of the quote which says, "still a . . . a . . . a . . . man" reflects very typical speech patterns, but few if any reporters would exactly transcribe it; doing so, in fact, would probably be considered a "cheap shot." It could be characterized as an attempt to show the speaker as being inarticulate, halting, and hesitant, when in fact everyone speaks that way at some point in their conversations. (William F. Buckley, in fact, stutters; an exact quotation of certain of his speech patterns would be very unflattering.)

Reporters are often trained not to quote someone who uses dialect. A widely used introductory journalism textbook, for example, warns student journalists that "dialect often appears to ridicule the subject in a condescending fashion" (Anderson & Itule, 1988, p. 79). The Associated Press and *The New York Times* stylebooks make similar warnings, advising that unless the dialect is clearly pertinent to the story it is best avoided. The *Times* manual warns that a reporter should try to avoid rendering dialect unless he or she "has a sharp ear" (p. 61).

All of this brings the discussion of ends versus means back to the question of original intent: not the Constitutional meaning, of course, but the original intent of the reporter who goes undercover, misleads a source, or manipulates quotes.

The majority of opinion seems to rely on reasoning including both motivation and consequence, sort of a midpoint between consequentialist and non-consequentialist philosophies, and perhaps a good example of seeking a "golden mean" between two extremes. In general, journalists condone deception when it is the only way to get the story and the story justifies special measures (ends justifying the means) but condemn deception when it is used indiscriminately or to gain privileges and access that could be dangerous or illegal, such as wearing a police uniform or impersonating a physician (an imperative against certain categories of behavior).

But, as we've seen, those who are tempted to bend or break the rules must realize that practices which may be considered unethical often damage news stories or the public and peer acceptance of those stories because the readers or viewers may focus on the *practices* and not the *story*. In this regard, the short-term payoffs often are simply not worth the price of the misadventure.

Again speaking in general terms, journalists allow for a certain amount of deception in their use of quotes when the ends justify the rather mild means employed to fix them. We *know*, despite anyone's protestations, that print journalism cannot possibly consist of nothing but exact quotes. *Newsweek*'s Jonathan Alter (1990, p. 54) summed up the doctoring of quotes insightfully when commenting on the Malcolm libel suit:

> The peculiar truth is that there are no firm rules on any of this. The *New Yorker* magazine, for instance, claims that its legendary fact-checking department ensures accuracy, yet the subjects of its articles all seem to speak in beautiful sentences and perfect paragraphs.

But Alter also acknowledged the imperative thou-shalt-not-lie violation which, in the minds of many, tarnished Janet Malcolm's reputation as a truth teller—and for one of the few cases many observers remember, resulted in press outrage at a writer *winning* a libel suit:

> ... And in a libel suit, Janet Malcolm was reduced to arguing (successfully) that she invents quotes in order to get at a larger truth.

When newspaper columnists play by Malcolm's rules, Alter noted, "they're called 'pipe artists.'"

Chapter 9
Profit Versus Responsibility

It's a chain where the proprietor is more interested in what the financial statements say than what the newspapers print.

—How Richard Behar, in a Forbes interview, described Donrey Media's 54 daily newspapers[1]

Consider, for a moment, these statistics:

- The ten largest American newspaper chains own fully one-third of the country's dailies.
- More than half the revenue of radio stations is taken in by a total of ten corporations.
- Seventy percent of U.S. television stations are network affiliates.

Those facts and figures (Biagi, 1988, p. 276) are compelling, but only tell part of the story. Also of concern to those who worry about such things is the fact that media outlets have become so breathtakingly expensive that, in many cases, only large corporate entities can afford to own them, accounting in part for the type of concentration indicated above.

Radio stations, for example, were once electronic journalism's highly accessible voice in the community; a radio station could be, and often was, a mom-and-pop operation with integral ties to the community. But by the mid-1980s billions of dollars were being traded in the radio market because radio

---

[1] This statement was originally made in *Forbes*, May 19, 1986, p. 144, and later reprinted by Conrad C. Fink in his book, *Media Ethics: In the Newsroom and Beyond.*

stations became an *investment commodity*. The artificially high price ceilings created when a commodity is frequently bought and sold produced *a sevenfold increase* in the amount of money spent on radio station transactions from the mid-1970s to the mid-1980s (O'Donnell, Hausman, & Benoit, 1989, p. 332). Stations became speculative investments, cash cows that offered a better return than condos or the commodities market. Station WLIF in Baltimore, for example, was purchased by American Media in 1984 for $5.5 million and resold just two years later for *$30.5 million* (O'Donnell, Hausman, & Benoit, 1989, p. 338).

Media outlets, even in fairly small markets, became blue-chip commodities. And it became increasingly obvious that what John Dos Passos called "The Big Money" was assuming increasing control of newspaper, television, and radio. Whether this is a positive or negative phenomenon will be debated in a moment, but there is a more fundamental question pending: Why have the media become big business?

One cause is the basic principle of economies of scale. In the economic climate influenced by classic economy of scale production, any business which produces a greater number of units will have a smaller cost per unit, and hence a greater profit. As economics professor William Lasher (interview, 1990) notes, the classic example of economy-of-scale production driving out smaller competitors is the auto industry. The auto manufacturing business once was divided among many small manufacturers, but is now an oligopoly dominated by the survivors of the economies-of-scale war.

Economy of scale almost always works (if "works" is taken to mean "produce a profit"). However, there are two exceptions:

1. Some industries have an inherent need to be localized. Cement plants are the economist's classic illustration of this principle. Cement is so heavy and thus so expensive to transport that building a giant, centralized cement-manufacturing plant makes no sense.

   To an extent, this *used* to be a factor in delivery of the media "product." A small-town radio station, for example, would once have lost money by "importing" extensive portions of its programming; it was simply cheaper to produce it locally. While networks delivered some of the product (news, and in the early days of radio, entertainment programs) modern radio turned a profit by capturing a niche of the local market via a particular format. You could not import a local format—until a few years ago, that is. The present-day wide availability of satellite transmission and reception systems and the drastic reduction of the cost of such systems have convinced many local station owners that it is much more cost-effective to aim a satellite reception dish skyward than to hire a full staff of people to produce the day's programming. The product imported from the heavens (or, less poetically, usually from Dallas via an orbiting satellite) can masquerade as a locally produced product. The technical arrangement allows the local radio station to automate all necessary local insertions, such as weather forecasts, local announcements, and station identifications (O'Donnell, Benoit, & Hausman, 1990, p. 156).

Networks are nothing new, of course, but this technology of delivery is. Print media can be "networked" to an extent, also—sharing a common format and amortizing costs across chain ownership, a lesson not lost on the Gannett Company.

2. There is a theoretical concept known as "diseconomies of scale," a point at which an organization becomes *too* large, and production suffers, primarily due to a lack of flexibility and problems with internal communication. Dr. Lasher, a specialist in organizational finance, notes that while several recent research studies have attempted to demonstrate that diseconomies of scale are affecting General Motors, the concept remains an abstraction.

However, an informal application of the diseconomies of scale theory could be made to the media in general—at least in terms of the *quality* of the product delivered. In fact, many critics and media analysts make essentially that argument.

Before considering those contentions, though, a definition of terms might be useful. It was mentioned earlier that the typical market structure of a media industry is an oligopoly, meaning ownership by a few. (The word "monopoly" is used by many who will be quoted in this chapter, but they use the word informally, since no one entity controls all media, which would be the strict definition of a "monopoly.") Some analysts of media economics, such as Douglas Gomery of the University of Maryland, take the definition of media oligopolies a step further. In an article in which Gomery attempted to standardize terms of analysis in media economics, he wrote (1989, p. 50):

> Actually, the media business consists of a set of oligopolies, separate industrial structures each dominated by a handful of large corporations. The essence of an oligopoly is that the number of firms is small enough that all can be cognizant of the actions of rivals and react accordingly. Take the case of the three networks: When NBC offers a new comedy at a particular time of a particular day, its rivals, ABC and CBS, counterprogram.

In essence, Gomery concludes, oligopolies are in the unique position of being able to *monitor* each other. Think about that uniqueness: In a monopoly there is no competition and hence no monitoring; in a wide-open entrepreneurial market there are far too many competitors and too many differentiated products for any real intramural monitoring and adjustment to take place. So in effect, oligopolies are in a unique position to control the market, but still jockey for a greater share of it, *while operating within certain parameters*. As Gomery puts it (p. 51):

> More often than not, the individual members of an oligopoly want to extract a greater than average share, and soon cooperation breaks down. They begin to differentiate their products. The three television networks are constantly promoting new shows.

But in the end the products they hype seem strangely alike ... in essence, all three "agree" on the rules of the competition and then seek to differentiate their products to make the most money, always knowing what their rivals are up to. The goal is the most profitable profit *within the rules of the game.* (Emphasis added.)

Oligopolies "playing within the rules" have a greater impact than one might at first realize. Consider the fact that within their respective categories, most news "products" appear essentially the same. With the exception of a few differences in the use of graphics and appearance of the individual anchors, for example, television network newscasts are virtually identical in style and, more importantly, in substance.

As an illustration, one study of 180 days' worth of television network newscasts (Rife, 1986) found little real difference in the way the respective newscasts selected news. Another interesting study showed that the concept of oligopolies playing within the rules extended to local markets, too: A strong similarity of content (called *consonance* by researchers) was found in a study (Atwater, 1986) comparing story selection among local stations in Detroit, Toledo, and Lansing. About half the stories were duplicated by other stations in the same market.

Of course, it would be illogical to read too much into this; after all, to an extent news is news and it is obvious that if Toledo's city hall burns down the story is going to be replicated on all Toledo channels. But the studies do reinforce what we can observe simply by turning on the television: News looks a lot alike on any network or in any local market. While competitors differentiate their products to a degree, they typically do not do so in a radical fashion. The same consonance of style and substance can be observed by comparing your local newspapers, should you be lucky enough to live in one of the 30 or so American cities which still are served by more than one (competing) daily newspaper.

And on that note, we're venturing back into the effects of the diseconomies of scale, but now we are examining the situation from an intellectual level: weighing the contention that when media become too big, the quality of their product deteriorates. Ben Bagdikian, formerly of the *Washington Post* and now a noted media gadfly, and Robert Picard of Emerson College both preach this message. Bagdikian, for example, has made media ownership issues his personal quest, and has written many works on the subject, including *The Media Monopoly* (Boston: Beacon). Picard sounded many of the same notes in his work *The Press and the Decline of Democracy* (Westport, Conn.: Greenwood, 1985). Picard, writing in the *Journal of Media Economics* (1988, pp. 61, 62), summed up the view pointedly:

> Although concentration is problematic in any industry, it presents special problems in the newspaper industry because newspapers operate not only in the marketplace for goods and services, but also in the marketplace for ideas. When concentration exists in a newspaper market, significant monopoly power arises that can disadvantage consumers not only in economic terms but also in the availability of diverse viewpoints and access to media channels.

It should be pointed out, though, that while everyone with even a superficial knowledge of media operations realizes that concentration exists, not everyone shares the gloom-doom framework of critics such as Bagdikian and Picard. Benjamin Compaigne, in his book *Who Owns the Media?* (1979, pp. 24, 25), unearths numerous examples of cases where editors and publishers of newspapers taken over by chains claimed that their product had improved. One editor noted that Gannett had settled union problems, renovated the newsroom, improved salaries, and encouraged vigorous investigative reporting. The Knight-Ridder chain is generally credited with improving the *Philadelphia Inquirer*.

Corporate leaders frequently denounce the perception that bottom-line business tactics will corrupt the news. Laurence Tisch, president and CEO of CBS, dismissed the notion at a national conference titled "The Changing Economics of News" held at Columbia University in 1987. Tisch, quoted by Mary Anne Ramer (1987, p. 24), delivered a heated rebuke to those who characterize him as a bottom-liner uncommitted to news.

> It is pure fiction to believe that the independence of the news depends on its economic autonomy. All of us recognize that there are inherent inefficiencies in covering the news. The issue is not what we spend in an absolute sense, but on what and how well we spend it.

Indeed, both sides have a credible case: One camp says that the responsibility of the news organization is compromised by the big money (both in terms of economic concentration and bottom-line profit influences) while the other camp denies it. In fact, some defenders of media concentration contend that a stronger economic base gives a news organization more freedom and greater insulation from the pressures of advertisers and pressure groups; indeed, there would appear to be some legitimacy in that argument because small and marginally profitable media can come under tremendous pressure to conform to advertisers' wishes. A manager of a small television station struggling in a large market once told me, with complete sincerity, that one key to sustaining his news operation was to give good coverage to sponsors' events, such as openings of new stores.

So is concentration good, bad, or indifferent? Can adherents to both philosophies be right?

No one has an answer to the problem of the marketplace of ideas versus the concentration afforded by the influx of the big money, but it is undeniably true that the economic marketplace and the marketplace of ideas operate under different theories. Bagdikian, in his book *The Effete Conspiracy* (1972, pp. 11, 12), issued a sharp warning about the conflict:

> Chains increase absentee ownership. And they deepen the tendency for monolithic politics in an institution already suffering from severe ideological ossification. The largest chains in circulation include Chicago Tribune, Scripps-Howard, Hearst, Newhouse, Knight, Gannett and Ridder. In leadership and in

editorial views they are something less than a representative spectrum of American thought and values.

They tend not only to present single editorial views on any national issue but also to enlarge their corporate size on political grounds [buying news organizations which already share the corporate point of view].

Does centralized ownership provide a centralized point of view? Ownership watcher Compaigne (p. 26) reports that studies show that in presidential elections 85 percent of the papers in a chain typically endorse the same candidate. And reporter Philip Weiss, in a *New Republic* article reprinted by Biagi (p. 282), puts it more colorfully. In his "Invasion of the Gannettheads," Weiss alleges:

> The problem with Gannett isn't simply a formula or its chairman, but the company's corporate culture. The product is the company—cheerful, superficial, self-promoting, suspicious of ideas, conformist, and implicitly authoritarian. But the Gannett story is more, too. For as many as six million daily readers, most of them in one-newspaper towns, Gannett serves as chief interpreter and informer about society—and does so unsustained by ideals of independence or thoroughness.

A stinging indictment of the effect of big money at work, but not the only one; in fact, representatives of other media offer similar warnings. Consider the shrinkage of the marketplace of ideas in the book-publishing market, and what might be termed the resulting intellectual diseconomies of scale (not an inappropriate term, feasibly, for an industry in which one of the leading players, Random House, now calls books "units").

Book publishing, like many other media, had once been an industry where small audiences could be serviced and individual ideas presented with relative financial impunity. Small publishers often had poor seasons, or published financially stillborn books, but some measure of survival was built into the business because small publishers usually did not financially overextend themselves. But within the last few decades, books have become multimillion-dollar properties, and publishing houses have had no choice *but* to extend themselves to the limit. Concomitantly, houses rely on fewer titles and go with proven, multimillion-dollar commodities (such as the endless string of Stephen King novels) which require big money but produce big money.

Organizational sociologists Lewis A. Coser, Charles Kadushin, and Walter Powell illustrated this factor in their pioneering work *Books: The Culture and Commerce of Publishing*. (I say "pioneering" because it was, as far as I know, the first large-scale effort by social scientists to explain the mysterious workings of the publishing industry to the general public.) Coser, Kadushin, and Powell found that the vicissitudes of the publishing market, coupled with the higher costs of acquiring works, were responsible for a constriction of publishing's marketplace of ideas (pp. 7, 8):

Given the built-in uncertainties of the market for many types of books, the book trade, like the fashion business or the movie industry, often operates on the shotgun principle. As one Hollywood mogul is said to have told an inquisitive reporter, "One of the films on this list of ten will be a big success"; but when the reporter queried, "Which one?" the producer answered, "I have no idea." Publishers attempt to reduce such uncertainty . . . through concentrating on "surefire" blockbusters, through large-scale promotion campaigns, or through control over distribution. . . .

Some fifteen or twenty years ago, publishing was still largely a cottage industry. In the past two decades, however, it has been growing out of that stage at a rapid pace. Many formerly independent houses have been taken over by large corporations, and other houses have "gone public" and are traded on the stock market. As a result, publishing executives now worry a great deal about how Wall Street evaluates their operations. Most major houses have rationalized their procedures by installing contemporary management practices borrowed from other industries—including electronic inventory controls, computerized marketing departments, sharply defined lines of authority and assignments of special tasks, and, above all, close attention to the "bottom line."

It would be outright idiocy to argue that any business could or should ignore the bottom line, but many in the publishing industry and other media are now wondering aloud as to the correct balance between profit and responsibility to readers, viewers, or listeners. The recent dispute over Pantheon, a highly respected but unprofitable division of Random House, is a useful example. Certain Pantheon authors (and other authors who have never written for Pantheon, including Kurt Vonnegut) protested the corporate maneuvers which inspired the giant Newhouse chain, which owns Random House, to install a reputedly "bottom-line"-oriented CEO, who in turn attempted to stanch the financial hemorrhaging of Random House's Pantheon imprint.

Now, this is not a black-hat-versus-white-hat struggle, because Pantheon staffers may be partly at fault, too, for their refusal to compromise; but in general the situation does not speak well for the publishing industry's battle of the bottom line. As one observer noted, Franz Kafka once said that a book was supposed to be the ax that broke away the ice of one's soul—but because of the bottom-line orientation of the publishing industry, many readers are feeling a bit colder these days.

In any event, the big money moves, and assuredly will continue to move, many of the media, and people with degrees in marketing certainly will continue to have an impact on the marketplace of ideas. Allow me the indulgence of a personal example. As a book author—well acquainted with the vagaries of finance, both personal and professional—I have come to recognize a certain intellectual diseconomy of scale and concomitant shrinkage of the marketplace of ideas in the operations of those supermarketlike chain stores which have largely usurped the book business. (At last count, Coser,

Kadushin, and Powell [p. 372] estimated that they controlled about half of all general-interest book sales.)

Coser, Kadushin, and Powell also made, as a rather offhand remark, an observation authors might find a bit chilling (p. 372):

> This revolution [chain stores] in the selling of books—and it is truly a revolution—is bound to have significant consequences on the decision-making and gate-keeping functions of publishers. Book chains, as distinct from individual booksellers, are geared to the buying of books in large quantities. The greater the quantity bought, the higher the discount the chains receive from publishers. Such discounts are often up to 17 percent higher than for individual bookstores. It does not pay for chains to clutter their shelves with books that can only be expected to reach a limited public. Hence, as the present symbiotic relation between trade publishers and book chains is further strengthened, publishers have an additional incentive to neglect books that are not likely to have mass appeal.

Does this represent an intellectual diseconomy of scale, a shrinkage of the marketplace of ideas? It could hardly be interpreted any other way. Personally, *I* can find no other interpretation, other than to add that as an author my success or failure seems to ride less on my reviews than on whether the chains pick up the book. I have been told, by more than one publisher on more than one occasion, that my book would "die" if it were not picked up by one or more of the large bookselling chains. And the publishers were inevitably, infallibly, inexorably right. A buyer for a chain store, who may or may not have a publishing background (I don't know, who is the buyer: someone who started out in the fur department at Macy's, perhaps?), now has a major impact on the ideas which will go before the public.

And so while there are no clearly definable answers, there certainly is an identifiable problem. The tug-of-war between profit and responsibility is felt by every communicator, in all media. Take, as another example, your daily newspaper. While publishers do not like to admit this—but it is almost always the case except for the very best papers—the amount of news available in a paper is determined by the amount of advertising sold. The advertising is laid out first, and the available news placed into the remainder of the paper, which is unceremoniously referred to as the "newshole."

The amount of newshole available generally is determined by how much advertising has been sold in order to create the newshole. While electronic newspeople like to imply that a newspaper can simply add on additional pages to cover additional news, that is simply not how the business works. Extra pages are surprisingly expensive, and will rarely be produced unless there is sufficient advertising available to justify making up the extra page and allowing for more newshole. As Conrad Fink puts it (p. 206), "Only managers truly committed to journalistic quality will provide news pages for a big story even without supporting advertising. Done repeatedly, that eats deeply into profits, unappealing to many shareholders and their surrogate managers in publicly owned companies."

Fink offers what probably is a better economic theory about profit versus responsibility than any presented so far in this chapter. When analyzing television, he points to (p. 109) a "Gresham's Law of Journalism":

> Poor quality, low-cost entertainment shows drive out high-quality, high-cost news programming. First-rate network news shows lose viewers when opposed in the same slot by entertainment such as *Wheel of Fortune*. Superb news specials in the Edward R. Murrow tradition of thoughtful, responsible broadcast journalism vanish before stampedes of cops-and-robbers shows.

Fink advises "newsroom ethicists" to carry the fight out of the newsroom, to higher management, and to learn to "talk management's language" by stressing that in the long run, responsible journalism can assist the newspaper or broadcast outlet in reaching the overall goal of profit—while preserving responsibility.

Bob Benson (1989, p. 14), vice president of Radio News for ABC in New York, put a slightly different spin on the situation in an article written in a trade journal for news directors. He notes that while news directors must deal, at some level, with the profit motive, they must remain wary of the old adage that "the guy in the barns at the racetrack shovels horse manure all day, but he's right when he tells you he's in the racing fraternity."

And that is his way of nudging news executives to ask themselves exactly what business they are in.

Chapter 10

The Medium Versus the Message

Reality is nothing but a collective hunch.

—Lily Tomlin

*P*ossibly the most recognizable words in journalism are not from Edward R. Murrow or Walter Cronkite, although "This is London . . . " and "That's the way it is" will always hold a place in most of our memories.

But *every* journalist recognizes these words:

> Jimmy is eight years old and a third-generation heroin addict, a precocious little boy with sandy hair, velvety brown eyes and needle marks freckling the baby-smooth skin of his thin brown arms.

Those words appeared on September 28, 1980, a black day in the annals of the *Washington Post*. The lead above belonged to a page-one story called "Jimmy's World," a story written by Janet Cooke, an ambitious reporter who won a Pulitzer Prize, but had to give it back.

Because she was a pipe artist.

A pipe artist, in the journalists' lexicon, is someone who makes up quotes and stories. Cooke, when the dam first began to leak, initially claimed that Jimmy was a "composite character," an individual conveniently created by melding the quotes and actions from several characters into one, a dubious practice but not necessarily a mortal sin in some journalistic circles. But under ever closer scrutiny from the Pulitzer board and her own editors, Janet Cooke finally admitted that she just made the whole thing up.

The Cooke affair was one of the most traumatic blows ever to the collective integrity of journalism. Many explanatory theories were concocted, among them the hypothesis that there is simply too much pressure put on reporters when they compete for good stories and good exposure. Perhaps there is some truth in that, but the argument does not change the fact that Janet Cooke will always be remembered as the craft's premier pipe artist.

What further inflamed the situation was open speculation by critics and journalists that there is a little of the pipe artist in most reporters. When Tom Goldstein was testifying as an expert witness in the *New York Daily News* libel trial mentioned a few chapters back, he was asked by a lawyer (p. 11): "Is it perfectly acceptable journalism to report as if you are an eyewitness to an event when in fact you are not an eyewitness?"

His answer: "Absolutely. It happens all the time."

The lawyer then read aloud the lead of the story in question:

"A cold wind was ripping up 125th St., and the man in the full-length leather coat dug his hands deep into his pockets as he stepped from the black BMW.

"'Yo,' one of the teenagers standing in front of the Oasis Sandwich shop just off Park Avenue shouted when he spotted the man crossing the sidewalk. Scattering like pigeons, the teenagers crossed to the other side of the street."

Goldstein reports that the lawyer was incredulous that despite the specific detail, neither reporter involved in the case had been at the scene. Goldstein testified that this kind of reconstruction was "common practice" (p. 11). "Since reporters cannot be everywhere all the time," he said, "it is necessary sometimes to reconstruct scenes after the fact."

Was the scene on the Harlem street re-created in too much detail? In retrospect, Goldstein now admits that with the benefit of hindsight, perhaps the depth of detail in this particular case was overly misleading; but the point is that reconstruction of events was and is accepted practice.

How extensive a practice is it? Before writing this paragraph I grabbed, at random, a sheaf of clippings from my file. The very first story in the pile is titled "The Making of a Doctor," and follows several students through a week of medical school. One particularly cloying reference describes a medical student who looks tired because he spent a long, restless, "burning eye" night cramming for a final.

The reference is stated as fact. But the fact is, I personally did not know then and do not know now if the student was tired from studying all night or from dancing the flamenco. He *told* me about his restless night, the cups of coffee, the burning eyes, and so forth. I believed him. But I didn't spend the night with him.

What I did was relatively harmless, I think. What Janet Cooke did was quite damaging. And according to the judge, what the reporters did in the *Daily News* case in which Goldstein testified was legal (not libelous), but disturbing, anyway.

The problem here, of course, is where we draw the line in this particular continuum. How closely must a reporter stick to reality in *portraying* reality? There is a difference. No reporter *repeats* reality; only stenographers do that, and even a stenographer cannot re-create all of the gestures and nuances that are part of reality. Even the "neutral" TV camera is more than an observer. As Mike Wallace's quote in a previous chapter pointed out, a medium-long shot allows the guest an air of decorum, while a tight close-up shows the "tics and perspiration." That camera—which is capable of producing either shot—is hardly a neutral tool.

This chapter continues, to an extent, the dicusssion of whether ends justify means, but examines an ethical dilemma specific to the mass media: The fact that a medium "creates" its own reality. When this happens, the medium and the message—or, stated another way, the drama and the reality—come into conflict.

The fact that cameras, microphones, and notebooks are not always neutral instruments of observation raises a question about just who qualifies as a pipe artist, and to what degree we practice our artistry. And to pose a broader question, what exactly is reality, anyway?

Figure 10.1 How far should a news organization go in presenting sensational or disturbing material? That dilemma arose in January 1987 when Pennsylvania State Treasurer R. Budd Dwyer committted suicide during a news conference. Some television stations, including a station in Harrisburg, broadcast the actual moment when Dwyer's skull exploded from the impact from his .357 Magnum. Some newspapers also ran graphic photographs. In most cases, the news organizations that ran depictions of the instant of Dwyer's death were roundly criticized.

The reality issue is a question which we cannot hope to answer, at least not here. Generations of scholars—philosophers, scientists, sociologists, literary experts, the list goes on—have posed that question, and have not yet produced a definitive answer.

Within the narrow confines of journalism, though, we can at least scratch the surface of the media-created reality issue, and examine whether that media-created image distorts reality. For example, Judy Vanslyke Turk, writing in *Journalism Monographs* of December 1986 (p. 3), made this observation about research in journalistic agenda setting:

> The media present a pseudo-environment, a self-conceived perception of the world which is not necessarily the same as the world that is "really" there. But this pseudo-environment is not entirely of the media's own making. While individuals working for media organizations make decisions as to what does or doesn't get on the agenda of salient, important "news" which is presented as media content, it can be argued that the sources of information upon which journalists rely ultimately have more to do with media content than the selection processes of journalists themselves. News is not necessarily what happens but what the news source *says* has happened because news doesn't "happen" until there is an exchange of information between newsmen [presumably she includes women, too] and the sources.

In other words, we rely on others to create the admixture of words, ideas, and images we use to represent reality. (As I relied on my medical student's report of his "burning eye night.") Sometimes, the people who furnish those words, ideas, and images do so with their own interests in mind, so another layer of distortion is added. In other words, the information is skewed in the first place—say, by a political candidate staging a rally—and then further distorted by our efforts to transplant the information via a mass medium. The situation is likened to a "reality trap" by media analyst W. Lance Bennett in his book *News: The Politics of Illusion* (p. 128):

> Although the goals of documentary ["documentary" meaning, in this case, reporting which relies on eyewitness accounts or accounts from reliable sources] reporting are hard to fault, the practice of the documentary method creates a trap for journalists confronted with staged political performances. Only in rare cases when the performances are flawed, or when the behind the scenes staging is revealed, can reporters document in good professional fashion what they know otherwise to be the case: The news event in question was staged for professional purposes. Since, as [historian Daniel J.] Boorstin pointed out, pseudo-events contain their own self-supporting and self-fulfilling documentation, the documentary method highlights the very aspects of news that were designed to legitimize them and blur the underlying reality of the situation.

The "underlying reality" is frequently difficult to pin down because of the aforementioned (in Chapters 3 and 5) problems inherent in reproducing a fair representation of reality. Media mechanics, at the most basic level—like

Figure 10.2 Although Julio Castillo was not seriously injured when he fell and impaled himself on a metal fence, the resulting photograph caused serious controversy. The photo, which was distributed by the Associated Press, was used by many newspapers, although some papers found it too graphic and refused to run it. There is no question that this is a once-in-a-lifetime eye-catching shot, but there is a question about the appropriateness of running a graphic depiction of an event that is not only sensational but embarrassing to the subject.

> ... arise out of conflict situation—a village falls into factions, a husband beats a wife, a region rises against the state—and proceed to their denouements through publicly performed conventionalized behavior. As the conflict swells to crisis and the excited fluidity of heightened emotion, where people feel at once more enclosed in a common mood and loosened from their social moorings, ritualized forms of authority—litigation, feud, sacrifice, prayer—are invoked to contain it and render it orderly.

Such telling and retelling of the human experience is as much a staple of the news story as any other form of drama; anyone in doubt can attempt to locate a news story without the essential element of drama—conflict. Be forewarned that such stories are few and far between.

Mike Wallace's tic- and perspiration-seeking camera—can distort reality, whatever that really is.

Consider these examples of how the medium intrudes on the message:

- A television reporter covering an acrimonious city council meeting uses up most of the allotted time for the news package with tape of a shouting match between two councilors. The confrontation makes compelling video, but the rest of the items acted upon get little or no coverage.

  This actually is quite a common scenario, and a typical complaint lodged against television news departments. ("We passed a million dollars' worth of appropriations and all you showed was that loudmouth from the fifth ward!")
- A newspaper writer interviews two spokespersons representing opposing viewpoints on an issue. Spokesperson A is colorful and provides pithy, eminently quotable replies. Spokesperson B is softspoken, not very experienced with the media, and while providing reasonably clear responses produces nothing quotable. The reporter leads and closes with anecdotes and quotes from Spokesperson A; while the amount of *space* is balanced in the story, the impression may not be. Spokesperson A clearly comes out the winner in the battle of the pithy quote. (Journalists do debate the ethics of this type of situation. Many reporters feel they must be on guard against a facile, experienced spokesperson, or a slickly staged event, because news that comes to them in a convenient package may not be particularly fair.)

In sum, "balancing" an issue in order to give a fair representation of reality is not always a simple matter of "reporting the facts." Requirements of the medium—including the difficulty of covering a very complex story in a limited amount of time or space, the problems of using compelling video in place of the more routine activities connected with a news event, and avoiding having coverage manipulated by interested parties who have mastered the art of making the journalist's job easier—do intrude on the message, giving new light to Marshall McLuhan's aphorism that the medium *is* the message.

Humans seem to have an innate need for drama, a fact not lost on ancient Greeks, Elizabethans, and every other group of people who have sought to understand the human condition, or at least make themselves feel better, cathartically, by watching someone else struggle with the human condition. That fact—our need for drama—appears in many aspects of everyday life. Clifford Geertz, professor of social science at the Institute for Advanced Study at Princeton, noted (1980, p. 173) that an emerging school of thought tracks drama at all levels of social organizations. Those dramas, he says:

CHAPTER 10 THE MEDIUM VERSUS THE MESSAGE

Conflict, crisis, and denouement (those elements of drama with which we are so accustomed) contribute to our perception of reality, that "collective hunch" about what is going on. In fact, historian Arthur Schlesinger (senior) maintained that we *have* to interpret this drama as a mirror and as an integral part of reality. In his autobiography, Schlesinger wrote (1963, p. 106):

> [In an article, I] argued the need for studying literature as a direct or indirect expression of social and economic conditions rather than as something which had developed "in a vacuum, without relation to anything but itself"; and the essay further urged that researches extend beyond belles-lettres to the reading matter of the masses, which in a democratic country offers the only true picture of the national level of taste and interest.

To rephrase, when Schlesinger contends that the material "of the masses" is the only "true picture" of the national level of taste and interest, isn't he implying, too, that the medium is the message?

Saying that the medium is the message and that the medium sometimes fights the message is really saying the same thing: Since there is no perfect way of conveying reality, we rely on media, which—because of their mechanics and requirements—distort the message, but that distorted message in turn becomes reality.

In many cases, we're hard-pressed to determine what is "real" and what is not. For example, as cited above by Bennett, a political rally is often an event specifically staged for the media; the media, in effect, *create* the event and then *report* on their own creation. Seasoned public relations professionals know, of course, what will "play" in the media and go to great lengths to create usable material, material which reporters can witness and attribute to reliable public figures.

For example, while working as a television reporter I once covered a political "rally" where no one—literally *no one*—was rallying. But there was music (taped) and balloons, and a politician on a dais, and a small hall full of no one but reporters. When I had the camera operator pan the near-empty hall, a campaign manager accused me of taking a "cheap shot" at the candidate.

Was it a low blow? Maybe. It has never been standard practice, as far as I know, for any television station routinely to report crowd sizes at events of this type, so I was departing from standard practice by taking the pan of the near-empty hall. Also, anyone who covers politics knows that the long and grinding obligatory schedule of campaign appearances precludes huge attendance at each and every function, especially for local and statewide races. But on the other hand, is it a fair representation of reality to show a politician who appears to be speaking to an audience when there *is* no audience? Such is the problem of Boorstin's "pseudo-event."

Another closely related factor in the tug-of-war between the medium and the message is the *bureaucracy* of news reporting. Just as Schlesinger's dramas do not spring from a vacuum, neither do our news reports. News is produced within an organization, and reporters must produce material which "sells" to an audience and, in addition, "sells" to the editor. (The point being that reporters compete for space or airtime, and by pleasing an editor—supplying him or her with stories the editor is likely to regard with favor—the relationship of news to reality is skewed by the reporter's natural desire to please a boss.)

In addition, the news process involves many methods of obtaining information; a particular aspect of this news bureaucracy is what Mark Fishman, in his book *Manufacturing the News*, calls "accounting."

> The entire news production process occurs in several successive "levels," stretching from the earliest formulated account of something on up to the reporter's written news story. For example, the accounting process which underlies any one crime story can be traced through successive levels of accounts. Only the top level consists of the police reporter's work of detecting, interpreting, investigating and formulating the story. Behind the news story, inside the agency through which the reporter first sees the story, are the bureaucratically produced accounts upon which the news will be based.

Many who have worked as reporters recognize the problems associated with bureaucratic reconstructions of news. The police reporter, for example, has little alternative but to accept police accounts of arrests as prima facie truths. After all, reporters typically do not witness arrests and interrogations, and often have virtually no access to a person charged with a crime.

The "accounting" which Fishman cites takes place within the news organization, too. Most news organizations maintain a library of sorts, and archival material from that library often comprises the building blocks of future stories (Hansen, Ward, & McLeod, 1987). The material is retrieved for reference purposes—with the practical result that the first account of a situation may indeed provide the "boilerplate" copy, used again and again in recounting following versions of the story. That type of overreliance was what we found in the analysis of the Brown and Sharpe strike stories, detailed in Chapter 5.

One reason for overreliance on boilerplate copy is the fact that reporters handle a wide variety of assignments; they are not, and cannot be, experts in all areas. The library or other repository of archival material becomes an important part of their method or story (and "reality") construction.

Ironically, the bureaucracy of reporting plays a similar role when journalists become excessively close to a story. When we cover a story day in, day out, we tend to leave out details. We take it for granted that the reader, listener, or viewer knows these facts that have become so familiar to us.

Sometimes, we (as reporters) leave out information *because we don't understand it ourselves*. Most reporters will admit that there are many subjects which baffle them, and they simply do the best they can, reporting incomplete information. For example, the first important news assignment of this author was covering a murder trial. While murder trials are completely understandable in TV dramas, some of the real-life aspects of the proceedings can be virtually incomprehensible to the layperson. The vocabulary is arcane, the scheduling and motioning process is mysterious, and sometimes a spectator cannot even clearly hear what is happening. My report may have been fairly accurate—I know I got the verdict correct, anyway—but beyond that, I am not sure.

Many of the effects of this news bureaucracy go unnoticed by the public. Consumers of news are conditioned to accepting incomplete information, and in some cases for good reason. Every story dealing with Middle East conflicts, for example, cannot recount the entire history of the conflict—although occasional stories taking such an approach would certainly be welcomed by many news consumers.

So, try as we might, the battle of the medium versus the message puts a little of the pipe artist in every reporter. This certainly does not imply that reporters cannot be relatively fair, or reasonably objective, or as accurate as possible; only that these qualities are elusive because reality—whatever that is—cannot be picked up and transplanted without *some* alteration in what we see as "real."

There are many theorists from all disciplines who describe this effect in great detail. The best summary comes from one Pogo Possum, who postulated: "We have met the enemy, and he is us."

PART
Four
TOWARD RESOLUTION

Chapter 11
Codes of Ethics

When people are pure, laws are useless; when people are corrupt, laws are broken.

—Benjamin Disraeli

Charles Seib, the former readers' representative for the *Washington Post*, once wrote (in jest, or at least partial jest) that every time three or more newspaper editors get together they are likely to write a code of ethics, unless somebody stops them (1981, pp. 4, 5).

While members of the news business have traditionally been resistant to rules and constraints of any type, the recent spate of code writing which Seib cited is not an entirely modern phenomenon. In 1923, the American Society of Newspaper Editors adopted an ethics code, and three years later Sigma Delta Chi, the Society of Professional Journalists, did likewise. The codes and the name of one organization (Sigma Delta Chi is known now as the Society of Professional Journalists) have changed, but much of the intent remains the same: They are voluntary sets of rules aimed at proscribing certain types of conduct deemed unethical, thereby increasing the stature of the craft or profession (whichever we choose to call it). Other important national codes exist; among them are the code of ethics of the Radio-Television News Directors Association and the Associated Press Managing Editors Association code of ethics. There are also many individual codes at local newspapers, radio and television stations. While no one has tallied the precise figure, statistically reliable surveys, such as a study sponsored by the American Society of Newspaper Editors and conducted by Philip Meyer (1983), indicated that nearly two-thirds of newspapers have some sort of written codes. A later study of sample consisting of print and broadcast newspeople (Davenport & Izard, 1985, p. 5) produced a roughly similar figure. But of those respondents who did not have formal written codes, many noted that they used a patchwork of "piecemeal verbal and memo-published" (p. 5) codes, often referred to as memo and meeting codes. Incidentally, Davenport and Izard's study indicated that many of the informal verbal codes existed at small organizations where presumably lines of communication are more clear and direct than in a larger news organization (p. 6).

"Memo-and-meeting" ethics approaches appear to be widespread. A survey undertaken by Douglas Anderson, of Arizona State University (1987, pp. 341–345), indicated that three-fourths of newspaper managing editors who responded had issued memos on ethical issues, and two-thirds had held seminars. When formal codes existed, about a quarter of the editors responding said that the codes were posted somewhere in the building, while about half said codes had been circulated to staffers.

Some codes are quite brief, no longer than a few paragraphs. Others, such as the code of practices for CBS News, are book-length, and contain precise guidelines on outside employment ("occasional" feature articles or books are acceptable; any hard news reporting for other organizations is prohibited), coverage of civil disturbances, trials, and even the reporting of poll data. Some codes are apparently better-thought-out than others; the Louisville *Courier-Journal*'s policy on use of anonymous sources, for example, spells out a balanced and commonsense viewpoint that has been used as a model by other news organizations. (In a nutshell, the code says that sometimes the use of an anonymous source is unavoidable but on the whole it is a case in which one must exercise "extreme caution.")

It seems clear that ethics codes, like the study of journalism ethics, are a growth industry, too. But as these surveys indicate, not all organizations adopt codes. In fact, some journalists feel codes are a bad idea—even a dangerous one.

But before examining the pros and cons, it might be profitable to explore just what these codes say. Instead of simply reprinting various codes, I have summarized the basic tenets of the four major journalism codes, and followed that with an analysis of factors common to each.

The Code of Ethics of the Society of Professional Journalists was adopted in 1926, and revised in 1973, 1984, and 1987. The 1987 revision was a hotly contested one—the organization's members' magazine still bristles with comment about it—because that revision removed a self-censure clause from the code. The previous code ended with a pledge stating, in part, that "journalists should actively censure and try to prevent violations of these standards, and they should encourage their observance by all newspeople." The 1987 revision modified the comparable portion of the pledge to read: "The Society shall—by programs of education and other means—encourage individual journalists to adhere to these tenets, and shall encourage journalistic publications and broadcasters to recognize their responsibility to frame codes of ethics in concert with their employees to serve as guidelines in furthering these goals."

Moving from "censure" to "encourage" is a sizable semantic shift, indeed, and is an issue that merits further discussion. It is a central topic of the final chapter of this work, in which I report on a survey I conducted in order to learn how a sample of working journalists feels about the idea of self-censure.

Other sections of the SPJ code are grouped under five headings: "Responsibility," "Freedom of the Press," "Ethics," "Accuracy and Objectivity," and "Fair Play." Entries under the first two headings make reference to "the public's right to know of events of public importance and interest," and the "inalienable right" of press freedom. There are six entries under the ethics heading; many restate the obvious ("plagiarism is dishonest") but others are quite specific. Point #2 of the ethics section, for example, advises that secondary employment, political involvement, holding public office, and service in community organizations should be avoided if "it compromises the integrity of journalists and their employers." The ethics section also cautions reporters to avoid freebies. "Nothing of value," the code flatly states, "shall be accepted."

The accuracy and objectivity heading stresses the journalist's responsibility for telling the truth, obtaining information from reliable sources, and ensuring that "newspaper headlines should be fully warranted by the content of the articles they accompany." Photographs and telecasts should "give an accurate picture of an event and not highlight an incident out of context." Reporting and commentary, the code advises, must always be clearly separated and commentary must be labeled as such.

Under "Fair Play," SPJ members are advised that they will at all times show respect for the "dignity, privacy, rights, and well-being of people encountered in the course of gathering the news." Also, there is a specific mention that newspeople should not communicate "unofficial charges affecting reputation or moral character without giving the accused a chance to reply."

In an entry on fair play, it is noted that journalists should be accountable to the public and the public should be encouraged to voice grievances against the media.

The Code of Broadcast News Ethics of the Radio-Television News Directors Association is briefer than the SPJ code, listing seven fundamental points, the last of which is another admonition to "encourage" observance of the code by all journalists. There are many similarities to the SPJ code in respect to integrity (declining gifts) and respecting the dignity, privacy, and well-being of people with whom broadcast journalists deal. The first point in the credo (there are no headings) implores members to be accurate, keep news and commentary respectably compartmentalized, and not mislead the public into believing that something which is staged and rehearsed is spontaneous. (More on this follows later in the chapter.)

The RTNDA code calls for members to respect the confidentiality of sources. The code also advises members to promptly acknowledge and correct errors.

The American Society of Newspaper Editors (ASNE) Statement of Principles was adopted in 1975, and replaced the 1922 code of ethics which was originally titled "Canons of Journalism." It contains six articles, dealing, respectively, with responsibility, freedom of the press, independence, truth and accuracy, impartiality, and fair play. It reads very much like a shortened version of the SPJ code, and calls for the standard virtues of separation of commentary and reporting, freedom of the press (warning that the "press must be vigilant against all who would exploit the press for selfish purpose"). The Statement of Principles also cautions journalists not to give even the impression of impropriety, and includes a mandate that all persons "publicly accused should be given the earliest opportunity to respond." The Statement also urges that pledges of confidentiality be honored "at all costs."

The Associated Press Managing Editors Association Code of Ethics is roughly the same length as the ASNE statement, and is similar in focus. There are four major headings: "Responsibility," "Accuracy," "Integrity," and "Conflicts of Interests." The code is similar to others examined so far, but has an admonishment found in the ASNE code but not RTNDA or SPJ that news sources should be disclosed unless there is a "clear reason not to do so." (In other words, don't use unidentified sources if you can possibly avoid it.) When it is necessary to protect the confidentiality of a source, the code instructs, "the reason should be explained."

The AP code concludes with this observation, unstated and not implied in the three other codes: "No code of ethics," it reads, "can prejudge every situation. Common sense and good judgment are required in applying ethical principles to newspaper realities." Individual newspapers are encouraged to augment these guidelines with locally produced codes that apply more specifically to their own situations.

After examination of the codes, it becomes obvious that certain principles are commonly stressed among most or all of the documents:

1. *Conflict of interest.* All four of the major codes admonish newspeople not to put themselves in positions which compromise their integrity or *appear* to compromise their integrity. "Gifts" are directly prohibited in three of the codes (SPJ, RTNDA, AP Managing Editors) and indirectly in the ASNE statement, which prohibits accepting "anything of value." The codes also make reference to other compromising activities at various levels of specificity.
2. *Accuracy.* The words "accurate" and "truth" are mentioned in all four major national codes. "Objectivity" and similar concepts appear throughout the codes, also.
3. *Constitutional privilege* is mentioned directly by SPJ ("our Constitutional role to seek the truth") and the ASNE. An extensional

privilege, the "public's right to know," is mentioned by the SPJ code, the AP code, and indirectly ("guarantees to the people through their press a constitutional right") by the ASNE code.
4. *Protecting confidential sources of information* is mentioned explicitly in all four codes. The AP and ASNE codes mention that anonymity of sources should be avoided if possible; SPJ and RTNDA make no such mention.
5. Recognition and correction of errors is explicitly mandated by all four codes.
6. Issues of context are recognized in all codes. The RTNDA code and the SPJ code get into specifics about the use of video (for RTNDA and SPJ) and headlines and photos (SPJ); the codes mandate that such elements be used in a way that does not mislead.
7. Separation of news and commentary is mandated by all four major codes. Interestingly, some codes indicate an *obligation* to provide commentary, or at least some type of advocacy journalism. The AP code goes so far as to claim, "The newspaper should serve as a constructive critic of all segments of society. Editorially, it should advocate needed reform or innovations in the public interest. It should expose wrongdoing or misuse of power, public or private."
8. All codes have various allusions to broad principles of respect for the truth, the reading/viewing/listening public, and all prominently mention the word "responsibility." All codes explicitly or implicitly recognize an individual's right to privacy.

Of particular interest in this analysis, I feel, is point 6, the context issue. The AP code gives the strongest recognition to the role of complete context in presenting a fair picture—and invents a verb in the process—when it advocates that, "The newspaper should background, with the facts, public statements that it knows to be inaccurate or misleading." (In other words, don't print a statement out of context when you know that simply printing the statement will mislead; use background material to paint a full picture.)

RTNDA advises that the viewer must not be misled by video, an interesting sidelight to the current "news simulation" controversy, an issue on which the jury is still out as of this writing. Some critics and practitioners feel that simulation—having actors portray news events within the context of a news-type report—is a harmless practice. Others believe it oversteps the boundaries of news coverage.

What adds further interest to the issue is the fact that the trade journals published by RTNDA and SPJ have recently been rife with debate over not just news simulation, per se, but the new technologies which could take simulation to previously unheard of levels. For example, a recently perfected video device allows the televised image of a person to be placed within a scene which might be thousands of miles away; this technology could, for example, allow a reporter in Iowa to be electronically "placed" on a street in Moscow.

Other devices available to still photographers allow them to remove distracting or unwanted images from the photograph without the manipulation being apparent to the reader.

This discussion may seem to be veering off the track of an examination of codes of ethics, but it is a good example of the way in which any sort of written regulation—code, statute, or law—has difficulty keeping pace with technology. As mentioned in the earlier chapter dealing with this issue, lawmakers are struggling without overwhelming success to build a legal fence between the incredibly intrusive technology of the computer (and other information-gathering technology) and the individual. We're observing roughly the same problem when we examine codes that require us "not to mislead" but do not address the possibilities invoked by current technology.

To provide a little background on this idea, note that anyone over the age of 30 remembers that television programming used to be replete with incessant announcements that "portions of the preceding program were prerecorded." This was a direct reaction to the invention of videotape and the general advancement of technology, which allowed easy insertion of recorded material. Television executives were uneasy about the idea that viewers would get the wrong impression about whether a program was indeed "live," and the reality problem sparked an endless litany of reminders that everything we saw did not necessarily happen at the instant we saw it. In fact, radio executives had suffered through the identical problem decades earlier; the practice of playing recordings instead of live bands was considered, by some, to be deceitful, and was not at first universally accepted.

Today, those concerns seem overreactive. (Quickly, now, can you think of any real confusion caused by the availability of videotape?) Perhaps the current concern over news reenactment may, someday, seem similarly overreactive. But maybe not; while simulation may seem relatively benign in a Connie Chung feature story on Donald Trump, simulation could be used for some high-tech pipe artistry.

This fear is reinforced by the observation that there are indeed members of the viewing public who have considerable difficulty distinguishing fact from reality. Actor Alec Guinness once noted that he received many sincere letters from people who honestly did assume that he was the literal personification of his character in *Star Wars*. On a more serious level, many teachers of mass communications are surprised to find that a good number of their students have based their conceptions of the workings of the news business on the film *Broadcast News*. Now, *Broadcast News* was entirely a work of fiction; it did not even don the cloak of docudrama. But many otherwise intelligent people base their opinions of the news business on a *complete and total simulation of events—a pure work of fiction which makes no claims whatsoever to a basis in truth*. So perhaps "re-creating" the passage of a spy's briefcase might not be so innocuous as, at first blush, it appears. And perhaps the writers of codes are beginning to notice the lag between their principles and the technological reality.

News simulation is just one example of a case where events come into apparent conflict with codes; I say "apparent" because some portions of ethics codes are so loosely written that they defy precise interpretation, and that leaves us with a semantics problem. (Ahem . . . now what exactly do we mean by "deceive"?)

That is one reason why codes meet with opposition: News executives are reluctant to agree to abide by rules which cannot meet every circumstance. Others go further and insist that the codes simply will not work in the first place. When Michael Gartner was editor of the Ames, Iowa *Tribune*, he condemned codes in a remark quoted by Conrad Fink (p. 89):

> Everyone, so it seems, has been adopting codes over the past decade or so, ranging from the simplicity of the Ten Commandments to the complexity of a corporate prospectus. All have one thing in common: They don't work.
> A bad person does not become a good person because his newspaper has an ethics code . . . [if] readers don't like what we're doing, they'll quit buying our papers. The marketplace is the best regulator the press can have.

Implicit in Gartner's statement is the fear that if the public stops regulating, other regulators will step into the gap. As Fink (p. 89) extends Gartner's reasoning:

> Opponents, who include some of the nation's leading editors, argue against sweeping codes for a number of reasons:
> There is a danger that any definitive and widely accepted code, particularly if endorsed by major newspapers or television operations, could become—in the eyes of judges, legislatures, or the public—a general standard of behavior to be enforced on *all* media. That is, opponents view written codes as a self-inhibiting first step toward licensing the media under a universal standard of conduct.

The idea of media accountability via a code is an intriguing idea to certain government officials who don't much like the way they are treated by the media. While on the surface a reasonable contention, it is nevertheless important to consider the deeper implications. Consider this recent development: The mayor of Pawtucket, Rhode Island, called on the Providence *Journal-Bulletin* to adopt the SPJ code of ethics. Mayor Brian Sarault, a vocal critic of that paper's coverage of his administration, said in a news release reprinted in the *Journal-Bulletin* (1990, p. A-4):

> We need to establish some sort of standard by which we can assure fair and unbiased reporting of events. As an elected public official, I take an oath of office and am responsible to the voters and to a state Ethics [commission]. Clearly some sort of clear and uniform ethical standard is needed for media.

The implication is quite clear: The mayor is responsible (meaning he faces some sort of sanction if he is *irresponsible*) and the press should be put in the same position. The *Journal-Bulletin*, for its part, declined to take up the code of the 18,000-member organization. A spokesperson said the newspaper had "its own policies which we think meet or exceed the guidelines of the various journalism societies."

And that is a very clear and public example of Fink's point. The *Journal-Bulletin* was quick to point out that it had its *own* policies, and was not about to let its standard be set externally, and by extension open itself to some undefined responsibility for meeting that standard.

The idea of a "standard" and the inevitable link to a sanction is particularly problematic for news organizations, many of which, like the *Journal-Bulletin*, jealously guard their independence and parade First Amendment guarantees. As discussed in the next chapter, organizational sanctions against press behavior deemed unethical have largely proved to be dismal failures. SPJ, as a brief example here, attempted to adopt a method of code enforcement in 1983, and a task force was charged with the responsibility of setting up a grievance procedure. In 1984, the organization's national board tabled the idea pending a national survey, which produced little evidence for support of the SPJ grievance procedure. Some of the objections included fears that the procedures would invite lawsuits, and that code enforcement against SPJ members discriminates against *them* because the grievance mechanism would not apply to *all* journalists.

Other avenues are available, though, and they will be explored in the following chapter on internal and external controls on the media. This transition away from ethics codes to consideration of other aspects of press control is not meant as a tacit supposition that codes are worthless. Indeed, they have their place and are acknowledged as positive entities by many in the news business.

But there remains a problem deeper than the enforcement issue, and that is the general philosophy surrounding codes of conduct. What the Ames, Iowa, *Tribune* editor said—a bad person does not become a good person because his [or her] newspaper has a code of ethics—echoes the idea that virtue simply cannot be enforced. In journalism, a field where practitioners have, by the very nature of the craft, considerable autonomy, "creating" virtue by fiat becomes even more difficult. How do we enforce an "objective viewpoint"? Or a "fair attitude"? In other words, how do we force people to be virtuous?

Spinoza (1964 edition, p. 247) recognized this basic conflict: "[The person] who avoids crime solely from the fear of punishment, in no sense works from love, and in no sense embraces virtue." And Walter Lippmann (1929, p. 170) recognized the difficulty of attempting to impose static regulations on fluid situations:

> The attempt to construct moral codes on the basis of an inventory is an attempt to understand something which is always in process of change by treating it as a still life and taking snapshots of it. That is what moralists have always attempted to do. They have tried to capture the essence of a changing thing in a collection of fixed concepts. It cannot be done.

Chapter 12
Methods of Review

A person of bad character is not likely to be reformed by lectures.

—Aristotle

Throughout this work, many of the discussions have centered on the concept of "accountability" and the implication that if the news media were somehow accountable to someone or something, the person or thing who "keeps accounts" would be able to exact a punishment.

This chapter examines the concept of accountability, first discussing to whom accountability may be owed, and then probing the methods of review which enforce accountability. We will examine *internal* methods of control, such as intradepartmental discipline and ombudsmen who write only for internal consumption, and *external* methods of control, including press councils and the U.S. legal system.

So, to begin the discussion: To whom does the press owe "accountability"? Klaidman and Beauchamp (1987, pp. 211–221) note that the concept of accountability is basically unclear and invites many interpretations. One possible definition they offer (pp. 211–212) views accountability primarily as a moral issue:

> In ordinary English *accountable* means "answerable" and "liable to be called for an accounting." These terms are essentially synonyms, however, and therefore unilluminating. The concept of accountability as we use it assumes responsibility of the sort captured by the expression "the buck stops here." The person owes an account in the form of a clarification, explanation, or justification. Any valid

account generally entails a relevant and justifiable explanation of one's actions given to someone to whom it is legitimately owed.

Klaidman and Beauchamp note that accountability extends not only to the public as a whole, but to *employers, subjects of stories,* and *sources.*

Accountability to employers is problematic, in that journalistic considerations and business considerations often ride a collision course. Klaidman and Beauchamp contend (p. 217) that the "classic example is an editor failing to publish a legitimate news story that is potentially detrimental to the interests of an important advertiser, because the advertiser has made it known that he will discontinue the advertising if the story appears."

That situation certainly does blur lines of accountability; to whom does a newsperson owe "an accounting," the boss or the public? This can be a real dilemma; as a television and radio reporter I had often been assigned coverage of store openings—events of no real significance except to the sales department of the station. While I offered token resistance to the idea of producing blatantly commercial "news," I *did* produce news reports on the store openings, a factor which on a philosophical level probably indicates I felt a greater accountability to my employers than to the public (who could have been better served by stories other than the grand opening of a new supermarket). On a pragmatic level, the situation simply reflected the fact that I wanted to keep my job.

Despite the typical protestations of media executives, advertiser pressure does affect editorial content at some operations. A recent survey published in the *Journal of Mass Media Ethics* (Hesterman, 1987, pp. 93–101), for example, documented that exactly half of the responding editors of one hundred of the most popular American consumer magazines (in the magazine trade, "consumer" means "general interest") said they felt some pressure from the business office. While most (78.3 percent) said that giving favorable coverage to advertisers as a trade-off for those purchasing advertising space was not allowed, more than half of the editors noted that they would consult the business office before buying a well-documented story on the dangers of a product which also was advertised in the magazine.

This must not be interpreted as a blanket statement that editorial/business trade-offs are a common practice, since at many organizations they clearly are not, but the accountability of reporters to employers does sometimes include this issue. Employer/employee accountability runs vertically through the entire structure of an organization, so that while there is not always a specific role for the editorial arm of an organization in "plugging" sponsors, it is undeniable that news is in some respects a profit center, and the fact that news is expected to draw an audience has an undeniable effect on content.[1]

---

[1] Richard Clurman has done a thorough job in examining the role of corporate profits in news operations in his book *Beyond Malice: The Media's Years of Reckoning* (New Brunswick, NJ: Transaction Books, 1989).

News organizations obviously have accountability to their subjects, too. It is certainly immoral (and legally actionable) to picture someone in a false and damaging light. Also, newspeople by and large feel they owe a duty not to place people innocently involved in a situation *they did not create* in a position of public ridicule or scorn. For example, as a totally unscientific but probably meaningful measure, a panel of news executives surveyed at Emerson College's Second Conference on TV & Ethics (1987) unanimously agreed that they would have no qualms about withholding the name of a person who witnessed a bank robbery where the robber escaped. Using the name of the witness would in no way advance the story, they concurred, but could endanger the witness.

By and large, it has been my observation that responsible journalists do harbor concern for subjects who have not brought exposure to themselves. As Henry Schulte (interview, 1987), professor of journalism at Syracuse University and former United Press Chief Correspondent in Spain, notes, there are times in a reporter's life where he or she must hurt someone on purpose, "but you must never hurt someone by accident."

Accountability to sources also entails protecting their confidentiality if the reporter has indeed made that promise. Actually, it extends somewhat further than that: A reporter must be sure that he or she has the *authority* to grant anonymity; it is not unheard of for an editor to decide that the reporter was out of line in granting anonymity and demand the use of the name.

But in general, it is expected that the reporter will exercise his or her accountability to subjects involved in the story by respecting their anonymity if that is what is promised. Indeed, this is, as John Hulteng (1985, pp. 89–95) notes, virtually a sacred trust, a deeply ingrained tenet in the canons of journalism. In extraordinary circumstances, of course, journalists have been known to violate confidentiality under consequentialist reasoning if a greater good, such as saving a life or preventing a serious crime, would be the result.

Sometimes, journalists are compelled to violate their confidences by the legal system. In one of the more eminent cases, a Los Angeles television station manager named Will Lewis was jailed for refusing to turn over to a court a letter and tape recording sent to him by a group claiming involvement in the Patty Hearst kidnapping. Lewis was initially jailed for refusing to hand over the material, released pending an appeal of his contempt citation, and then ordered back to jail when he lost the appeal. At this point, Lewis surrendered and turned over the evidence.

But other journalists stuck it out. William Farr (in a case cited by Gillmor, Barron, Simon,& Terry, 1990, p. 359), a reporter for the *Los Angeles Herald Examiner*, spent two months in jail after refusing to disclose the identity of an informant.

Such accountability to sources weighs heavily on the minds of many journalists, even in states where there are so-called shield laws. A shield law is a state law (there have been unsuccessful attempts made at passing a national shield law) which protects a reporter from legal compulsion to reveal information. At the time this was written, more than half of the states in the nation have shield laws, and many others have have various combinations of laws that serve the same function.

But a shield law can be circumvented. A judge in California, a shield law state, once sent the managing editor, the city editor, and two reporters from the *Sacramento Bee* to jail for refusing to divulge the source of a sealed transcript which wound up printed in the pages of the *Bee*. Through some complex reasoning, the judge simply decided that the shield law did not apply (Gillmor, Barron, Simon, & Terry, 1990, p. 359).

Confidentiality problems are illustrative of how journalists can become caught in conflicts of accountability. It is very tempting to offer anonymity to a source for a number of reasons directly related to the concept of *accountability to the source*:

1. The source is spared embarrassment and possible retribution. Someone providing information on mismanagement within his or her city department, for example, will surely feel heat if identified.
2. By extension, the source is allowed access to the media. Some people simply will not, and in their eyes, cannot, come forth with information if they are going to be identified. Anonymity allows them to bring such information to the attention of the public.

But if it is assumed that the journalist is responsible to the *public*, use of anonymous sources can compromise that accountability, for a number of reasons.

1. There is no guarantee that an anonymous source is going to tell the truth. Strictly speaking, there is no guarantee that people quoted on the record will tell the truth, either, but at least *they* will in turn be held accountable for *what they say*. A journalist who relies heavily on anonymous sources may violate his or her accountability to the public because of this "accountability gap."
2. Anonymous sources may be manipulating the press for personal gain. The classic example of this is the "trial balloon"—a piece of information "floated" anonymously to see how the public reacts. (For example, a politician leaks details about a new highway project; if reaction is negative, the politician can simply drop the issue and never be held accountable to the public for his or her initial statements.)

The anonymous source problem shows how accountability is a two-edged sword, and also illustrates some of the practical realities of journalistic decision making. Some stories—including the series of Watergate revelations—probably never could have materialized if it were not for use of anonymous sources. But there is no certainty of that. Some journalists maintain that they can get *anything* on the record if enough effort is expended, and that use of anonymous sources is simply a symptom of lazy or deceitful news practices.

There may be some element of truth in that. Even highly controversial and sensitive stories have been constructed entirely from on-the-record comments. For example, the *Pittsburgh Press* presented a powerful and dramatic series about the buying and selling of human kidneys—and did it all on the record. Series coauthor Andrew Schneider, in an interview with the *Washington Journalism Review* (Leslie, 1986, p. 33), said that he decided to do the story without anonymous attribution because he wanted an entirely credible, bulletproof piece. "It's really hard to talk about fictionalizing something or taking it out of context when you've got a couple of hundred doctors, nurses, procurement people, and donor families all talking [on the record] about the issues at hand."

Arguably, discussing such intimate details was not pleasant for the subjects of the story. And perhaps that constituted, in some measure, a lack of accountability to those subjects. But the public was undeniably well served: They were given important material on a relevant subject which was—by the very nature of its construction—virtually guaranteed to be free of any whiff of pipe artistry.

Given the fact that we now have some notion of the dimensions of accountability, it is interesting to note how accountability is exacted. We'll move from the highly internal methods to the most obviously external means of enforcing accountability.

Internal discipline. As a strictly employer-oriented form of accountability (although it may be brought on by a breach of accountability to the public) internal discipline is difficult to describe and measure for the obvious reason that it is typically carried on behind closed doors.

But some data do exist. A study by the American Society of Newspaper Editors, reported in the *Journal of Mass Media Ethics* (1986–1987, pp. 7–16), showed that at least 78 newspaper journalists were dismissed or suspended during the three years previous to publication of the study. In this admittedly unscientific study, it was postulated that the results, at the very least, showed that contrary to "critics' charges that transgressors are never punished, the survey shows that editors are policing the newsrooms" (p. 8).

However, the study also admitted that the public hardly ever reads about it—and more about that will follow later. To return to the findings, it was interesting to note that editors had a difficult time making the determination of whether an action was or was not "unethical." There was a broad gray area involving the propriety of doing free-lance work, serving as a radio or TV commentator (this was a survey of newspaper editors, remember), and doing work for nonprofit groups. There was roughly a 50–50 split on whether it would be ethical for a staffer to make a campaign contribution to a candidate the reporter does not cover.

But there were some strong areas of agreement as to what should be punished. Plagiarism, profiting from insider information, and accepting discounts from companies with which the paper has contact were almost universally condemned (p. 9).

Some main points from the survey's summary illuminate the scope of in-house punishment. Quoting directly from the study (p.9):

- More than one out of every three editors reported at least one ethics violation occurred at his/her paper in the past three years. A total of 240 ethical violations was reported by the 122 respondents who answered the question; 11 papers reported six or more violations.
- About one out of six editors said at least one newsroom employee had been dismissed because of ethics violations in the past three years. Another 11 percent said at least one employee had been suspended in the past three years for an ethics violation.
- Slightly more than a third—37 percent—of the editors said they had a written code of ethics. More than half—54 percent—said they did not. Four percent said they were preparing one and 6 percent did not answer the question.

Other points paraphrased from the study: About 30 percent of the editors who had written codes said that the penalties were described directly in the codes, and the most frequently encountered ethical violations listed included inappropriate social contacts between reporters and newsmakers, and reporters who rewrote competitors' stories without verifying the information.

It was mentioned earlier that this survey indicated that the public generally did not hear about these transgressions. That is often the case; but in other scenarios, papers employ a reader's representative to report on the workings of the news organization. The reader representative, often termed an "ombudsman," also is considered to be an independent source for handling complaints from the public about news coverage. ("Ombudsman" is a term of European origin originally pertaining to an official appointed to investigate complaints against the government; the word, in its present usage, has no gender-neutral form.)

Ombudsman practice is not widespread; estimates vary, but one recent tally by Klaidman and Beauchamp (1987, p. 227) indicated that there are only about three dozen ombudsmen at newspapers across the country. Other figures are generally in line with this, and estimates for the number of ombudsmen at broadcast outlets are much lower.

External methods of review. Sometimes, the ombudsmen work only internally, writing memos; that, for example, is the case with the Louisville *Courier Journal*. Others are quite visible, such as ombudsmen at the *Washington Post*. Many of the *Post*'s ombudsmen, including Richard Harwood, have become noted press critics. Harwood, in fact, recently returned to the ombudsman's position at the *Post*—he was the first, twenty years ago—and proposed a new agenda for the movement.

In his role as reborn ombudsman, as reported in the Society of Professional Journalists' publication *The Quill* (Cunningham, 1988, p. 12), Harwood stated:

> I would like to see us establish a tradition of criticism and analysis that goes beyond explanations of why the letter "r" was omitted from the word "shirt" or why a demonstration against dogs by a dozen cat lovers was improperly covered or covered not at all.
>
> We should begin looking at the news business the way we look at the business of politics and government. What ethical and professional standards do we profess, if any, and how often do we violate them?

Noble ideas—but are they practicable? There is no way reliably to calculate the net effect of the ombudsman practice, or the actual degree of independence they enjoy. But incidents do abound where ombudsmen refused to toe the company line—sometimes taking the editors to task in a very public forum.

Richard Cunningham, a former ombudsman himself, noted (1988, p. 12) that an ombudsman at the *Calgary Herald* publicly called an editor on the carpet for allowing the identification of a teenager who had talked freely about her sexual activities. The case caused intense reader reaction and a student picket line at the paper; the primary objection was that the direct attribution embarrassed the students cited (one in particular gave explicit details) and the paper should have known better than to report such detail—even if the student did not know enough to keep her mouth shut.

"Life Today" editor Mark Tremblay told *Herald* ombudsman Jim Stott that the decision to run the quotes was made after weighing the harm caused to the individual young woman against the potential gain of saving Alberta teens the problems associated with pregnancies and sexually transmitted diseases. He claimed (Cunningham, 1988, p. 12) that the decision was guided by "doing the greatest good for the greatest number." (To point out the consequentialist rationale of that remark is really unnecessary, no?)

Ombudsman Stott disagreed, concluding that the onus of the decision was on the editors, and they drastically underestimated the impact of using the quotes on the students in a small school and the particular students quoted. And he said exactly that in a published analysis.

So at least in this case, an ombudsman had teeth and used them. (It should be noted, though, that the ombudsman practice is more common in Canada than in the United States.) Whether it is a practice that can or will reform journalism is unclear, although the ombudsman is a benefit to the news organization from the standpoint that he or she can handle complaints that *somebody* must field; at least, with the ombudsman system in place, the complaint-handling process is centralized.

This allows the ombudsman to keep consistent track of problems, and that is exactly what *Sacramento Bee* ombudsman Art Nauman has done. A recent article in *Editor & Publisher* (Stein, 1989, pp. 20, 21) analyzed Nauman's statistics, and found that 355 corrections were published in 1988. The analysis of the mistakes showed that a quarter of them involved numbers, statistics, ages, times, and dates. About 17 percent concerned names which were misspelled, omitted, or misidentified, and about 11 percent were problems with telephone numbers and addresses. Ten percent related to photos or other graphics.

Twenty-one percent of the complaints regarded substantial matters of fact, such as incorrect statements, misinterpretations, and misquotes. In a statement directly relevant to the bureaucracy of news reporting (discussed in Chapter 10 and elsewhere in this work) Nauman asserted (Stein, 1989, p. 20) that the *Bee* is not always to blame for the mistakes, since much of the material comes from public relations sources and there is not always time to verify it.

There have been attempts to make the news-correction process much more public than the partly internal, partly external practice of having an ombudsman report in the pages of his or her own media. Press councils have been proposed and established, but have rarely flourished.

It is interesting to note that the press council concept originated in Great Britain, and enjoyed some success. One largely unrecognized reason for this is that the British press council was viewed as a viable alternative to litigation and government interference; litigation, to a small degree, and government interference, to a much greater extent, are more troublesome to British journalists than to American journalists.

Local press councils were given a go in the United States during the 1960s, 1970s and 1980s. Most are now defunct. A national news council was formed in 1973. As recounted by Robert A. Logan, of the University of South Florida (1985, pp. 68–77), its panel consisted of judges, law school deans, journalism professors, editors and publishers of newspapers and magazines, television production executives, former U.S. representatives, business executives, television news executives, plus religious leaders and civil rights leaders. Logan notes (p. 69) that the advisers were selected to reflect a "wide diversity of professionals, political perspectives, and geographical locations."

An admirable idea, but a short-lived one. The council closed its doors in 1984 after tepid support from the news media and other parties. It did produce some interesting work, though, and the opinions rendered were very much in line with the opinions on ethical quandaries discussed elsewhere in this work. When those opinions went against the press, they frequently chided the news media for out-of-context use of broadcast news footage, which gave a distorted view of events; also criticized were conflicts of interest.

The National News Council had no legal authority, although it and its local siblings were often viewed as logical alternatives to litigation.

Litigation in the form of a libel suit is the most common form of government review of press practices. While libel today is a civil action (with very, very rare exceptions: there are little-known criminal libel statutes which still exist), the parties involved are compelled to appear before a government representative—a judge and/or jury—and face government-imposed sanctions.

A primer in libel is in order for readers of this book not directly involved in the study of mass media. Libel—in very general terms—is any *untrue* published statement which causes damage to a person's reputation, standing in the community, or business or personal finances. The word "published" also refers to things spoken over the mass media.

The word *untrue* is the operative term in the above definition. In most cases, the person claiming he or she was libeled must prove that the reporter was wrong. (Another defense, not particularly relevant here, applies to so-called privileged statements, such as those made during debate of governmental bodies or in court while court is in session.) But proving the reporter wrong is *not always* enough to win a libel case.

The reason involves a tenet of U.S. libel law which applies libel law differently to *public* and *private* people. "Public" people who feel they have been libeled must not only prove that the charges against them are untrue but also that the reporter made those charges *knowing* that they were untrue. The plaintiff *who is a public person* must prove that "a defamatory statement was made with actual malice, that is, with knowledge that it was false or with reckless disregard of whether it was false or not."

Those words—"actual malice," "reckless disregard"—have become intrinsic parts of the journalistic lexicon, and are the linchpins of the *New York Times* v. *Sullivan* decision, the 1964 Court ruling which has come to dominate libel law. To summarize briefly, L. B. Sullivan was a Montgomery, Alabama, police commissioner who sued the *Times* because the paper printed, in an advertisement carried by the newspaper, some unflattering remarks about the commissioner's treatment of blacks. The advertisement contained several errors, but errors which were essentially minor.

The U.S. Supreme Court ruled that a public official *exposes* himself or herself to public criticism, and in order to collect damages, must prove libel to a higher degree of fault: to wit, actual malice and reckless disregard on the part of the media as to whether or not the statement was true.

The trend of court cases in the decade following *Times* v. *Sullivan* broadened the scope of those who invite criticism—and therefore must prove libel cases to a higher degree of fault—to include "public figures" as well as "public officials." In the 1970s, the trend of court decisions would shrink, somewhat, that broad definition of public figures. (For example, a woman involved in a melodramatic divorce case was not held to be a public figure even though she had held press conferences about the case.)

Despite the vagaries of determining who is and who is not a public figure, and the succeeding cases which have modified *Times* v. *Sullivan*, the landmark case continues to be the cornerstone of libel law. In effect, *Times* v. *Sullivan* sent the message that the judicial branch of government worried about the "chilling effect" of libel verdicts against the media; in other words, that threats of libel suits from public officials and those ill-defined "public figures" would discourage public discourse and debate about public affairs.

Is there a "chilling effect"? A cursory examination of any of the media trade journals would indicate an epidemic of the "chilling effect." A body of formal research backs this perception, to an extent; a survey conducted during a convention of a professional group called Investigative Reporters and Editors (IRE) found that more than half of the respondents claimed that concern over libel had some effect on decisions involving what they covered and how they covered it (Lubunski & Pavlik, 1986, pp. 43–45).

Given this fear of the "chilling effect," it would seem that members of the news media would wholeheartedly endorse the principle of *Times* v. *Sullivan*. And in most cases, they do. But *Times* v. *Sullivan* is not without its critics, one of whom is veteran reporter Clark R. Mollenhoff. Consider this analysis (1989, p. 27):

> ... what has been a worthwhile shield for some journalistic projects in the best tradition of a responsible press also has been a convenient fortress for some of the worst practices that plague the profession today.

Mollenhoff, who now teaches journalism at Washington and Lee University and who has written a text on investigative journalism, further recalls (p. 28):

> I had been able to operate as an investigative reporter for more than 20 years without the *New York Times v. Sullivan* rule by doing the detailed digging work necessary to document my stories to the satisfaction of the very demanding editors and lawyers for the *Des Moines Register*, the *Minneapolis Tribune*, and *Look Magazine*.

And if you still harbor any doubt as to Mollenhoff's perspective, consider his observation that *Times* v. *Sullivan* changed the investigative reporter's credo from "When in doubt leave it out" to "What you don't know won't hurt you" (p. 28):

> No longer is the highest premium put on the truth of a story in some newsrooms. Instead the key questions may be whether its target is a "public official" or "public figure" under the malice rule of *New York Times v. Sullivan*, and whether

the reporters and editors *believe* (rather than *know*) the charges and facts in the story to be true.

In other words, ignorance is the best defense, and, if one subscribes to the Mollenhoff contention (p. 27):

> It has been said that patriotism is the last refuge of scoundrels. *New York Times v. Sullivan* similarly has provided a significant refuge for a few willful falsifying scoundrels, for a larger number of scoop minded incompetents, and for many reporters and editors who are just plain lazy.

Stated in terms relevant to previous discussions in this book, *New York Times* v. *Sullivan* (if one concurs with Mollenhoff) provides a nonconsequentialist doctrine behind which the lazy and incompetent can hide *when they are caught*. (This, of course, corresponds with Gustafson's thesis that we tend to use non-consequentialist reasoning when arguing from a position of weakness; we are certainly weak when we have to defend ourselves.)

Consequentialist reasoning, continuing the same argument, often is used when arguing from a position of strength. And that is a logical extension of the case that Mollenhoff makes when implying that the ends are used to justify the means when editors and reporters decide to use defamatory information when they *believe* it to be true but don't—because of the position of strength afforded them by *New York Times* v. *Sullivan* protection—particularly worry about having to *document* its truth.

The continuum of review and control ends at the point of government control and censorship. Censorship was only recently revived as a major issue after the outbreak of the Persian Gulf War; until that time, the last critical problems dealing with censorship dated back to World War I. And even though the effort to restrict press activities in the Persian Gulf War raised hackles initially, the outcome of the war—the surprisingly easy success—seemed to have dampened continued criticism. While at the time of this writing a suit brought by several news organizations against the military was pending, alleging unreasonable censorship on the part of the government, much of the initial outrage expressed by the press apparently had subsided.

Some would argue that we have short memories; others would contend that the government did not, after fine-tuning its public relations effort (which was undoubtedly heavy-handed at first), restrict the flow of information inordinately. In any event, despite the pull and tug over the Persian Gulf War, Panama, and Grenada, it would appear that while the issue of censorship has caused concern among American journalists, that concern has not been of enormous consequence.

The probable reason is that censorship simply has not worked very well in the modern United States, nor has it been needed to any great extent. There was field censorship during World War II, of course, but the press and radio were primarily put on their honor (Hohenburg, 1978, p. 149) to keep vital state secrets. Field censorship did not work particularly well in Korea, and in the chaos of Vietnam, censorship as a coherent policy was virtually nonexistent and unenforceable.

It may be overgeneralizing, but in general the news media have rebelled at any mandate to keep secrets that really did not warrant classification; but the media have, in general, kept secrets that posed true threats to national security. When the press and the military formed an uneasy truce in the Persian Gulf War coverage (after the military obviously overplayed its hand, forbidding—and being caught forbidding—completely innocuous interviews), some reporters went so far as to admit that they welcomed the presence of the censor because they feared accidentally reporting tactical information of use to the enemy. Reporters who had advance knowledge of the pincer movement that eventually brought the Persian Gulf War to a close kept the plans secret, not attempting to thwart or circumvent the security restrictions in place at the time.

Almost a half-century ago, a secret that would have had truly devastating effects had it been leaked was openly divulged to the media, and kept secret by the media, and the way it unfolded reflects an interesting view on how perspectives change when they are brought to the level of the individual.

As CBS correspondent Fred Francis (1990, p. 14) recounts the situation from historical records, 58 correspondents were invited to accompany the troops on the first wave of the D-Day action at Normandy. (Remember, it is not overstating the situation to say that the fate of the free world lay in the outcome of this maneuver.) The reporters were asked to wander over to a block of flats and knock on the door of 38 Edgerton Gardens.

Colonel Barney Oldfield met them all, individually, at the door. He asked them for some basic information, such as addresses and home telephone numbers. He discussed their assignments.

And he asked them to write their own obituaries.

Anthony Stout, president of the U.S. Committee for the Battle of Normandy Museum, noted that this ploy made the accountability of "secret-keeping" an "individual imperative."

It became clear, Stout noted, that "reporters could bleed from indiscretions as well as soldiers."

Chapter 13

Critical Self-examination

The press does not have a thin skin; it has no skin.

—Edward R. Murrow[1]

ITEM: When *The New York Times* dropped a column by controversial Pulitzer Prize winning writer Sydney Schanberg in 1985, the paper reported, on page 18, only that he had accepted another assignment. Although the *Times* received hundreds of letters of protest, it never offered any explanation of the move. In addition, the *Times* stonewalled on the issue, refusing to comment on the case to other news organizations interested in finding out more about the situation (Klaidman & Beauchamp, 1987, p. 213). The same year, the *Times* did not cover the fact that the paper had encountered a small outbreak of Legionnaires' Disease (Clurman, 1988, p. 31).

ITEM: Media critic Ben Bagdikian reported in 1987 that just 29 corporations controlled half or more of the media business in the United States. Bagdikian predicted that in the 1990s, media control will shrink to only half a dozen giant corporations. Of course, the giant corporations typically do not air or print this in the media they own; the story was promulgated by a Sonoma State University (California) research effort called "Project Censored," which labeled media concentration the "most under-reported story" of 1987 (*Editor & Publisher*, 1988, p. 11.)

ITEM: The editor of the *Reader's Digest* was removed from his post for what may have been political reasons; we say "may have been" because although there were rumors to the effect that the *Digest* board removed him for printing articles

---

1 Quoted by Goldstein (1985, p. 243).

contrary to the corporate party line, the story was relegated to the bottom of the last page of the business section of *The New York Times*. The story was virtually ignored by the media even though the *Digest* has a circulation of more that 27 million—roughly the size of the combined populations of Israel and East Germany (Clurman, 1988, p. 30).

ITEM: When Gerald Lanson and Mitchell Stephens of New York University were doing a profile about *The New York Times*' A. M. Rosenthal for *The Washington Journalism Review*, they ran into an unexpected problem: Many at the *Times* wouldn't talk. Twenty-four top staffers refused to be interviewed or did not return phone calls. Of 44 who agreed to be interviewed, more than half required that their names not be used (Goldstein, 1985, p. 245).

Richard M. Clurman, chair of the board of Columbia University Seminars on Media and Society, and a former correspondent and editor of *Time* magazine, is an eloquent spokesperson for the contingent of the news media which believes that the press can effectively dish out criticism—but has never learned to take it. Clurman, writing in *The Quill* (1988, p. 30), contended that a major problem with the news media is their "failure to report energetically and critically on themselves and on each other just as they do on the rest of the world." In addition to the first two items listed in this chapter's opening, he also noted that when he covered the press for *Time* (p. 32):

My editors wanted intensive reporting and criticism of others. But it was taken for granted that when I had to write about some development at Time Inc., itself, I would shift into the spare prose of a corporate press release.

Clurman maintains that the twin problems of the news media's failure to report on themselves and the fortress mentality often encountered are worthy of some soul-searching and self-examination. But the call for self-censure has not been universally accepted. The Society of Professional Journalists, for example, recently dropped a censure clause from the organization's code of ethics. The *Chicago Tribune*'s Casey Bukro, the author of the original code which called for journalists to "actively censure and try to prevent violations of [the standards put forth in the ethical code]," maintained that self-censure has largely been a failure because journalists are uncomfortable with calling attention to the sins of fellow professionals (Bukro, 1985–1986, p. 10) and contended that while journalists are quick to hold others to ethical standards, they are afraid of having ethical enforcement principles imposed on them.

Is this a widely held attitude? Do journalists still cling to the notion, expressed by former *Columbia Journalism Review* editor James Boylan (1986, p. 30), that for a member of a news organization to offer such criticism is to "foul one's nest"?

There appears to be little if any existing quantified data to support or oppose this contention, so I decided to begin the process of extracting some by conducting interviews and a pilot study into the issue. The purpose of this pilot study was to construct a questionnaire dealing with the issues of media self-criticism, self-censure, and whether journalists do, indeed, feel reluctant to report on the sins of their colleagues.

Fundamental concepts for the questionnaire were developed during focus groups on media ethics issues. Members consisted of the author (a journalist and journalism professor), another journalism educator, a television reporter, a writer for a weekly news magazine, and a professor of ethics.

Further evaluation of the basic questions was undertaken through in-person administration of an early version of the questionnaire to a television news director, a radio news director, a news magazine editor, and a former daily newspaper publisher and editor.

The pilot questionnaire that was eventually mailed is shown in Figure 13.1.

The sample to whom the questionnaire was mailed was drawn from the listing of radio news directors in the *Broadcast/Cablecast Yearbook*. Radio news directors were chosen for this pilot study because they represented a relatively homogenous group, from which inconsistencies in responses might be more easily recognized.

The methodology of the questionnaire administration, for those who are interested in examining the procedures and statistical methods, is explained in Appendix C.

The tabulations as shown in Figure 13.2 (pp. 150–151) show that many respondents agreed with the criticisms leveled by Clurman and Bukro (that "the press should learn to take it" and "journalists prefer not to call attention to their sins," respectively). In addition, a majority agreed that media self-censure would be an effective deterrent to unethical journalistic practices. Respondents split more or less evenly on whether the public concern over journalism ethics is trendy "media bashing," with a small majority feeling that it is not.

As would probably be expected, responding news directors showed a greater zeal for pursuing a story about a public official (the state representative) caught in an unspecified conflict of interest than in pursuing similar stories about an insurance executive, a reporter for a rival media outlet, and a co-worker in their department. As was pointed out in marginal comments by many respondents, a publicly elected figure would, by the very nature of his or her office, merit more vigorous coverage than more "private" figures. Willingness to pursue a negative story about a rival reporter and a media co-worker, respectively, finished last in the list of scenarios which would be pursued "vigorously."

Most respondents, about 60 percent, disagreed or strongly disagreed with the contention that they had frequently observed other journalists avoiding stories which involve negative coverage of other journalists.

There was a strong correlation, though, between those news directors who felt they *had* frequently observed journalists avoiding negative coverage of other journalists and those who agreed that the press should "learn to take

Questionnaire

Directions: Please check the blank in front of the appropriate response. Then, mail this questionnaire in the attached, self-addressed stamped envelope. Note that the wordings of these questions do not reflect a bias on the part of the surveyors; they are asked in an effort to determine how members of the working press react to one aspect of current media criticism. You are, of course, free to disagree or strongly disagree with the premise stated.

1. Former *Time* magazine correspondent and editor Richard Clurman recently wrote an article headlined: "The press can dish it out; now we should learn to take it." He argued that the news media have failed to report energetically and critically on themselves and on each other. How do you feel about this statement?

   ____ Strongly agree   ____ Agree   ____ Disagree   ____ Strongly disagree

2. There have been various proposals for the press to actively censure wrongdoers in their profession by publicly reporting on the ethics and competence of other journalists. But those proposals have not met with universal success. In fact, the Society of Professional Journalists recently dropped the section of the society's code of ethics which called for journalists to "actively censure" colleagues who violate the code. Some observers, such as the *Chicago Tribune*'s Casey Bukro—author of the original code which called for censure—feel that while journalists embrace ethical principles, they are afraid that those principles will be imposed upon them.

   Bukro writes that "the problem is that journalists, like doctors and lawyers, prefer not to call attention to their sins." How do you feel about Bukro's statement?

   ____ Strongly agree   ____ Agree   ____ Disagree   ____ Strongly disagree

3. Media self-censure would be an effective deterrent to unethical practices in the journalistic community.

   ____ Strongly agree   ____ Agree   ____ Disagree   ____ Strongly disagree

   (continues)

Figure 13.1 The questionnaire used in a pilot study of journalists' willingness to criticize themselves and others publicly.

4. Much of the public concern over journalism ethics is "media bashing"—a trendy concern not really warranted by the facts.

____ Strongly agree ____ Agree ____ Disagree ____ Strongly disagree

The following questions relate to this hypothetical case:

You have evidence that Mr. Smith, a well-known member of the community, has a conflict of interest which, in your judgment, compromises his ability to function in his job.

5. Mr. Smith is a state representative. I would be likely to vigorously pursue the story. (Check the response which indicates how strongly you agree with the assertion that you would vigorously pursue the story.)

____ Strongly agree ____ Agree ____ Disagree ____ Strongly disagree

6. Mr. Smith is a vice president of a major insurance firm. I would be likely to pursue the story vigorously.

____ Strongly agree ____ Agree ____ Disagree ____ Strongly disagree

7. Mr. Smith is a reporter for a rival media outlet. I would be likely to vigorously pursue the story.

____ Strongly agree ____ Agree ____ Disagree ____ Strongly disagree

8. Mr. Smith is a reporter in my department—a co-worker. I would be likely to vigorously pursue the story.

____ Strongly agree ____ Agree ____ Disagree ____ Strongly disagree

9. During my career, I have frequently observed journalists avoiding stories which involve negative coverage of other journalists.

____ Strongly agree ____ Agree ____ Disagree ____ Strongly disagree

Responses to Questionnaire

(First figure indicates raw number of respondents. Second figure indicates percentage of total respondents)

Frequencies for Question 1: "How do you feel about [Clurman's] statement?" (press should learn to take it)

Strongly Agree	Agree	Disagree	Strongly Disagree
16/13.3%	75/62.5%	26/21.7%	3/2.5%

Frequencies for Question 2: "How do you feel about Bukro's statement?" (Journalists prefer not to call attention to their sins)

Strongly Agree	Agree	Disagree	Strongly Disagree
17/14.3%	77/64.7%	20/16.8%	5/4.2%

Frequencies for Question 3: "Media self-censure would be an effective deterrent to unethical practices in the journalistic community."

Strongly Agree	Agree	Disagree	Strongly Disagree
12/10%	68/56.7%	32/26.7%	8/6.7%

Frequencies for Question 4: "Much of the public concern over journalism ethics is 'media bashing' — a trendy concern not really warranted by the facts."

Strongly Agree	Agree	Disagree	Strongly Disagree
5/4.3%	49/41.9%	56/47.9%	7/6.0%

Frequencies for Question 5: ". . . state representative. I would be likely to vigorously pursue the story."

Strongly Agree	Agree	Disagree	Strongly Disagree
51/43.6%	60/51.3%	6/5.1%	0/0.0%

Frequencies for Question 6: ". . . vice president of a major insurance firm. I would be likely to vigorously pursue the story."

Strongly Agree	Agree	Disagree	Strongly Disagree
30/25.6%	62/53.0%	25/21.4%	0/0.0%

(continues)

Figure 13.2 A table of responses to the questionnaire shown in Figure 13.1.

Frequencies for Question 7: "... rival media outlet. I would be likely to vigorously pursue the story."

Strongly Agree	Agree	Disagree	Strongly Disagree
22/18.6%	56.47.9%	36/30.8%	3/2.6%

Frequencies for Question 8: "... reporter in my department — a co-worker. I would be likely to vigorously pursue the story."

Strongly Agree	Agree	Disagree	Strongly Disagree
17/14.8%	39/33.9%	48/41.7%	11/9.6%

Frequencies for Question 9: "... I have frequently observed journalists avoiding stories which involve negative coverage of other journalists."

Strongly Agree	Agree	Disagree	Strongly Disagree
6/5.2%	41/35.3%	53/45.7%	16/13.8%

it" and "doesn't like to call attention to its sins." A modest correlation was also found between those who reported observing journalists avoiding negative coverage and those who felt media censure would be an effective deterrent to unethical behavior.

The various mathematical correlations and their derivations, along with an explanation of correlation for those who are not mathematically inclined, are also included in Appendix C.

The results indicate that, among this small sample, many news directors do feel that the news media could and should be tougher on themselves, and most feel that self-censure—giving coverage to unethical practices among journalists—would be an effective deterrent to journalistic malpractice.

The fact that four out of ten respondents agree or strongly agree that they have "frequently observed journalists avoiding stories which involve negative coverage of other journalists" would seem to indicate that this is a legitimate issue. In addition, it might be inferred that those who have observed the news media treading lightly on stories involving other media are—at least for the purposes of this questionnaire—more critical of the news media as a whole. In sum, the figures from this small sample do support the contentions of critics such as Bukro and Clurman, and provide some quantifiable data on a subject which has previously been discussed only in qualitative terms. The next step will be to see if these factors are supported by larger samples from across the journalistic community.

I do hope that I and other researchers will have the opportunity to follow this thread further, this research to include many of the above-cited factors—and shed greater light on the problem of how much light the news media wish to shed on themselves, and whether the media choose to cover themselves, as one editor put it, "like porcupines making love—tenderly, very tenderly."

Conclusion

Despite what might be interpreted as a negative tone in the last chapter of this work, I do see the news media making ever-increasing efforts at critical self-examination. Like the Berlin wall, the media "stonewall" may someday completely crumble. As an informal tally, I remember seeing or reading recently:

- An ABC News piece demonstrating how modern video equipment has the capability of misleading the viewer—warning that television can become a new tool for propagandists and tacitly warning that the news media are not always capable of filtering out the propaganda.
- A seminar during which WCVB, the local ABC affiliate television station in Boston, devoted an hour of uninterrupted, commercial-free airtime to a no-holds-barred discussion of press coverage of the Stuart murder case.
- A series of articles in major magazines and newspapers dealing with the ethical charges and countercharges among our friends Mr. MacDonald, Mr. McGinniss, and Ms. Malcolm.

Yes, I do believe that the news media are gradually opening their gates and making themselves more accessible to the public. By doing so, many dilemmas about ethics may be resolved.

But before examining that point any further, allow me to make the tone a bit less formal here, and offer an observation about the nature of journalism and ethics. First, let me make it clear that I do not pretend to be a philosopher/ethicist. I am a journalist and writer who got a job in TV news at age 16 and has worked in the media for almost exactly twenty years as of this writing. While I picked up a graduate degree along the way and teach as a communications professor, I still actively work as, and think of myself as, a journalist.

But while I make no claims of being a philosopher, I don't believe that most philosophical thoughts are so abstruse that they cannot be understood by almost anyone. (I regard myself as the lowest common denominator; if I can figure it out and explain it, anyone can understand it—that, in a nutshell, is the way I make my living.) After all, in a very cursory and informal way we have dealt—without naming them as such—with such branches of philosophy as metaphysics, the study of questions concerning "reality." Several chapters touched, quite briefly, on the idea that we have some trouble distinguishing what's real and what isn't. We've backed into some discussion of epistemology, the problem of what we really know and how we know it; and have landed lightly on issues in another branch of philosophy known as logic when evaluating the validity of arguments relating to many of the issues discussed in this work. And, of course, we've waded heavily into the branch of philosophy called ethics.

In a roundabout manner, we've dealt with some of the divisions into which ethics is traditionally broken. Metaethics, which evaluates the meanings of ethical terms, was, in a loose way, the topic when we attempted to clarify what we mean by "fair," "objective," and "accurate."

The bulk of this work dealt with what is commonly termed normative ethics, a term usually taken to mean the examination of established ethical principles and how those principles relate to the problems of the world.

Some philosophers, such as Christina Hoff Sommers (1985, pp. vii, viii), divide normative ethics in halves: social ethics (meaning applied ethics) and private ethics, which refers to the individual's own sense of virtue.

I recently taught a course in applied media ethics, and have taught the subject as part of various courses at a variety of colleges and universities. For one of the few times in my career, what I had to offer was met with market demand, because ethics is a big business on campus these days. There are, according to a study by the Hastings Center, about eleven thousand courses in applied ethics on the books at American colleges and universities.

But to tell the truth, I've always harbored some doubts about the real value attached to the way many applied/social ethics courses are taught, including my own. I never quite had the nerve to express those trepidations, though, so luckily I came across a piece in which Professor Sommers did it for me. On the subject of the resurgence in interest about ethics, she wrote:

> ... not all is cause for self-congratulation.
> In reading the articles for a course in applied ethics, students encounter arguments by philosophers who take strong stands on important social questions like

abortion, euthanasia, capital punishment, and censorship. By contrast, they may find little to read on *private individual virtue and responsibility*. [Emphasis added.] Many college ethics courses are primarily concerned with the conduct and policies of schools, hospitals, courts, corporations, and governments; again, the moral responsibilities of the students may be discussed only occasionally ... the effective purpose of such courses in applied ethics is to teach students how to form responsible opinions on social policies—a purpose that is more civic than personal. "Applying" ethics to modern life involves more than learning how to be for or against social and institutional policies. These are important, but they are not enough.

It has always seemed to me that private ethics, personal virtue, and individual responsibility have more bearing on journalism than do elaborate systems of social or institutional ethical "puzzle-solving."

The belief that we solve some ethical dilemmas by developing a system of an informed public coupled with an accessible media, which—I hope you've noticed by now—is the underlying theme of this book, must rely on the energy and integrity of the individual. We cannot have an informed public if it is made up of individuals who do not know about the existence of the First Amendment, much less its ramifications; we cannot have a responsive media if individual reporters and editors hide behind stone organizational walls. Knowledge, I believe, is the key to developing a personal view of media ethics, both for the informed public and the responsive media. And this means not only knowledge of how the media work—which is vitally important—but of all the cultural factors that come to bear on ethical decisions. Ethical decisions cannot be made in a vacuum. They cannot be made in a vacuum of knowledge. They cannot be made in a vacuum of *personal virtue*. And personal virtue cannot be upheld by someone unwilling to take risks, to stand alone and say, "This is wrong."

Just as I make no claims to being a philosopher, I can't call myself a historian either, or a political scientist, or a scholar of law, or a sociologist; but I have attempted to bring some perspectives from those disciplines into this study of ethics—perspectives which all contribute to my field of journalism and mass communications.

I suppose, though, that I can call myself a historian manqué, since I have published some works on history and I do make an attempt to keep current on things not current. Given that, I'd like to close this work with some lessons from the history of journalism.

When the junior senator from Wisconsin was graphically demonstrating the link between groupthink and mass hysteria, the news media of the United States—who, God forbid, didn't want to be known as *sympathizers*—largely sat on their hands. Two journalists, Edward R. Murrow and Fred Friendly, bucked the corporate timidity at CBS and produced a documentary that exposed Senator McCarthy for what he was—a documentary Murrow and Friendly in part personally financed. They risked their careers and their savings, but the time had come for them, as individuals, to say, simply, "This is wrong."

About a decade later, as Lyndon Johnson began in earnest to pour money and men into a war which he apparently was incapable of either winning or losing, the American press corps again was largely passive. But this couldn't last forever.

Barbara Tuchman (1984, p. 342) characterized the growing opposition, in this case the antiwar activities of Walter Lippmann, by writing that "dissent spread to the establishment." With apologies to the late Ms. Tuchman, I'm not sure that "spread" is the right word; it implies a sanitized, gradual shift, and that was not the case. Lippmann faced the wrath and ridicule of a bullying president and was scorned by many members of the press corps who still held to the party line. While Lippmann's position would become popular later—when it was *safe*—he initially acted alone, and suffered the consequences. So did Harrison Salisbury, who was bitterly repudiated by many of his contemporaries for his unfavorable coverage of Vietnam policy.

But they simply had had enough. They knew the score, they knew the stakes, and they decided to say, "This is wrong."

And that is the way that ethical changes seem to be made. By individuals. Not by groups. Not by professions. That is why I, personally, am wary of the ever-growing intrusion of big business into the media and the threat that we'll see a shrinkage of diversity. Part one of the worst-case scenario, in my personal view, is streamlined, bottom-line, monolithic news media too afraid of rocking the corporate boat to allow one man or woman to say, "This is wrong."

The state of American journalism is, to wield some gigantic understatement, less than perfect. But we haven't done too badly, either. Through a system of pluralistic politics and pluralistic ethics we've been able to maintain, though not without some struggles and setbacks, a free nation and a free press. And while the excesses of free speech and press have been duly noted, in these pages and elsewhere, the consequences of *deficiencies* of free speech and press are much worse. That is why part two of my personal worst-case scenario would involve excessive, backlash-inspired restrictions on the press.

Finally, I believe John Merrill's contention that "the diversity of our media and their messages" could be threatened by a well-intentioned but ill-advised "professionalization" of the news media, because professions, as such, tend to inbreed and restrict membership. It would be unfortunate, indeed, if part three came to pass, and some sort of credentialing were to evolve as a way to separate the "legitimate" from the "illegitimate" journalists. It would be most fortunate if this trend could be averted by increasingly vigorous critical self-criticism, as opposed to credentialing and regulating.

Ayn Rand, who professed certain politics with which I personally don't agree—but, hey, let's hear it for pluralism—made a cogent case for a free and unrestricted press, an "open craft," if you will.

"If there is any way to confess one's own mediocrity," she wrote (1971, p. 46), "it is the willingness to place one's work in the absolute power of a group, particularly a group of one's professional colleagues. Of any form of tyranny, this is the worst; it is directed against a single human attribute: the mind—and against a single enemy: the innovator."

Appendix A

Notes on Further Readings in Philosophy and Ethics

Many of the concepts discussed in this book were derived from the field which, for lack of a better term, we have called "classical philosophy." And while this has not been a work of philosophy per se, it is apparent (at least I hope it is apparent) that many of the dilemmas which occupied the minds of classical philosophers are still the topic of debate today.

In some cases, the modern reincarnations of classical thoughts surface word for word, as in the case cited in Chapter 3, where the newspaper reporter felt he was right in running a story that resulted in a suicide because it "produced the greatest good for the greatest number." In other instances, the arguments form a web of thoughts which affect us today, even if they are not immediately traceable to their original sources. For example, the school of philosophers known as "intuitionists" felt that certain concepts of right and wrong did not need to be proved; they were *self-evident*. You'll remember that a group of very pragmatic people adopted this philosophy in relation to the subject of human rights: They wrote that, "We hold these truths to be self-evident. . . . " That document was dated July 4, 1776, and is still quite relevant in modern political thought.

In any event, it soon becomes obvious to even the casual reader that writings in philosophy—while relevant and very much a part of everyday life—are often not particularly accessible to the nonexpert. What follows is a recommended list of readings which may help the nonphilosopher penetrate the unfamiliar vocabulary and the sometimes arcane methods of presentation utilized in writings about and related to the field of ethics.

First, three important points:

1. Some readers of philosophy are discouraged and distracted by the fact that much of the writing seems to be centered on intramural squabbling about points raised by another philosopher. If you feel this way, you are right; that is the nature of much of the work. Even the great George Santayana took the (then) young Bertrand Russell to task for this predilection, scolding Russell for living in "an atmosphere of academic disputation which makes one technical point after another acquire a prepondering influence in his thoughts." That did not, of course, stop either Mr. Santayana or Mr. Russell from spending the remainders of their careers in some reasonably technical "academic disputation."
2. Other readers who attempt to dip into philosophical thought are dissuaded by the apparent obscurity of the verbiage. If so, take some comfort in the fact that you are not alone. Philosophers can and do criticize each other for incomprehensibility, so you should feel no reluctance to acknowledge that you cannot understand certain passages, either; it may be a legitimate complaint.

    Part of this problem can stem from a poor translation. Some words and ideas suffer badly when transposed from one linguistic system to another. As an example, writers who create works for international consumption often engage in a practice called "cross-translation," meaning that the original document is translated from English to, let us say, Japanese. The Japanese version is then given to another translator and changed back into English to check the accuracy of the denotations and connotations of the words. Sometimes, the two English versions are startlingly different: "Connect terminal number one to the network lines," might become "Mate the conclusion of the first number with the web of stripes."

    You can imagine the difficulties inherent when translating thoughts on the meaning of life from German or Latin into English—not only preserving the meaning of the words but the *flavor* of the original document. Some translators succeed; some do not. So if you are having a great deal of difficulty wading through Kant, for example, try another translation.
3. As a final suggestion, I have included some works *about* philosophy as well as the original works of the philosophers. Many such works (a few are listed below) can be helpful not only in explaining the work itself but in putting it in perspective; that is, explaining some of the thoughts and theories to which the author was reacting, and showing how the economic and social climate of the author's times may have affected his or her thinking.

A word of warning: Some writers who set about to analyze a philosopher's works equate profundity with incomprehensibility. In other words, do not be surprised if the explanation of the work may be much less clear than the original work itself. Take comfort in the fact that when Professor Hypothetical delivers a seemingly incoherent analysis of flawlessly clear writings of Plato, the fault just might lie with Professor Hypothetical and not with Plato. Do read books about philosophy, but also be a wise consumer.

What follows are some suggestions on works which may be of particular interest to the scholar of journalism ethics or ethics in general. With the exception of the first category ("General References . . . "), they are listed by author and contain some brief explanatory notations.

The only acknowledged bias utilized in recommending these works (aside from their relevance) is availability. Each book recommended has been checked against a national data base listing the number of libraries in which they are housed. Works housed in many collections were favored in compiling this listing. However, do remember virtually any book can be obtained through interlibrary loan should the work not be available locally. Also, note that in the list below, when no particular publisher is mentioned, the book is such a standard commodity that it exists in many editions. Unless there is a compelling reason (i.e., a particularly good translation) only the title is given.

GENERAL REFERENCES ABOUT PHILOSOPHY AND ETHICS

Will Durant's *The Story of Philosophy*, now available in an inexpensive and widely available paperback edition from Washington Square Press (you will find it in most major bookstores, in fact), was first written in 1926 and later revised; it is one of the finest works of its kind. While Durant's narrative does tend to become a bit overheated from time to time, he does convey the excitement of exploring great thoughts, and he explains those ideas within a broadly knowledgeable perspective.

A History of Philosophy by Frederick Copleston, S.J., is currently in print (New York: Doubleday Image Press) as a three-book set containing three volumes in each book. Book One contains volumes on Greece and Rome, Augustine to Scrotus, and Ockham to Suarez; Book Two's volumes are Descartes to Leibniz, Hobbes to Hume, and Wolff to Kant; Book Three ends with Sartre. The strength of Copleston is that he draws relationships and comparisons among the various lines of thought he analyzes. *A History of Philosophy* is probably the most understandable of all the references and goes into greater depth than does Durant's book. The only problem with Copleston is that the "volumes" are indexed separately—meaning that there are six separate indexes among which you must choose, a minor limitation if you are searching for information on a broad topic which spans several time periods.

Introductory Readings in Ethics, edited by William K. Frankena and John Grandose (Prentice-Hall, 1974), is a textbook which offers a wide selection of readings, grouped by general category, and includes some cogent prefatory remarks. Widely available books of a similar structure include *Ethics: Theory and Practice*, 3rd edition, by Jaques P. Thiroux (Macmillan, 1986), and *Morals and Ethics*, 2nd edition, by Carl Wellman (Prentice-Hall, 1988). Among the works which relate classical ethics to current affairs is *Ethics for Modern Life* by Raziel Abelson and Marie-Louise Friquegnon (St. Martin's Press, 1982).

There are many widely available works dealing with quite specific aspects of modern ethical problems. A reader interested in the ethics of business will find *Ethics and Profits: The Crisis of Conscience in American Business* by Leonard Silk and David Vogel (Simon and Schuster, 1976) to be lively and informative; the book essentially lets businesspeople speak for themselves—reporting their remarks from a large-scale conference held in the 1970s—and then provides thoughtful analysis. Silk, an economist and writer, and Vogel, an economist, provide a painless dose of classical economic philosophy while exploring modern dilemmas.

Ethics and politics are often considered to be contradictory terms, but a book of that title, edited by Amy Gutmann and Dennis Thompson (Nelson-Hall, 1986), is a fascinating study of such problems as violence, deception, disobedience, and justice. It includes current and historical entries and insightful analysis. (As an example, a section on nuclear deterrence includes not only modern commentary, but also an article written by then-Secretary of War Henry Stimson concerning the decision to detonate the first atomic bombs over Hiroshima and Nagasaki.)

Many authors who are philosophers in their own right have written broadly based introductions to the field. G. E. Moore's *Principia Ethica* (there are many editions, and as is the case in further references to classic works, no publishing reference will be made unless there is a specific reason to cite a particular edition) provides a wide-ranging view of the efforts to define the basic ethical question of what is "good." John Dewey wrote what might be termed a "survey" in his book *A Theory of Ethics*. Dewey's work, clear and sincere, is among the finest expository writings about ethical thought.

What follows now is a listing of recommended readings grouped by author. The list is composed chronologically according to the author's date of birth.

PLATO

Plato (c. 427–347 B.C.) chronicled the thoughts of his teacher, Socrates, and produced the familiar *Dialogues*. The dialogues are not specific discussions of ethics, but rather exercises in exposing vacuous thinking, demonstrating the dangers of applying overly broad thought to specific ideas, and challenging accepted ideas. On a broader level, the *Dialogues* espouse the idea that everything in the universe has a purpose and fits into an overall scheme.

Plato maintained that these ultimate ideas, or "forms," are formed previous to experience and are independent of experience. As an example, in the grand scheme of things we *know* what an absolutely perfect circle is even though we cannot physically draw it.

While there are innumerable versions of the *Dialogues*, a good option is *The Collected Dialogues of Plato*, edited by Edith Hamilton and Huntington Cairns (Princeton University Press, 1961). Ms. Hamilton's succinct introductory remarks are splendid. Those readers interested in gaining an initial understanding of Socrates and Plato might wish to start with the later dialogues, particularly the *Apology*, also known as *Socrates' Defense*. (By *later*, I refer to the dialogues set in the final days of Socrates' life; as far as I am aware, no one has any definitive notion as to the order in which Plato wrote his *Dialogues*.)

ARISTOTLE

Aristotle was a pupil of Plato, but did not idolize and chronicle Plato in the manner that Plato idolized and chronicled Socrates. In fact, some biographers suggest that Aristotle and his teacher, Plato, did not particularly care for each other. Will Durant put it in more genteel terms when he noted that geniuses mix with each other about as well as dynamite and fire.

In any event, Aristotle's philosophy was more strongly based on *observation* than was Plato's. Aristotle did not feel that there was an independent "good," or an abstract "form" of virtue. He believed that basic morality could and should be studied by examining the workings of our everyday lives.

A recommended starting point among the works of Aristotle is the *Nicomachean Ethics*, which examined those aspects of everyday life and recommended the path toward virtue. The *Nicomachean Ethics*, the first, as far as we know, Western system of ethics, is best known for its advocacy of "the golden mean," that point which is halfway between two extremes of behavior.

Aristotle postulated that "good" was closely related to happiness, but admitted that he could not clearly define happiness. He did, however, link happiness with the powerful "activity of soul."

While this is admittedly a simplistic differentiation, it is safe to assume that readers comparing Plato and Aristotle will find Plato more abstract, more interested in overarching, nonobservable ideals; Aristotle will be more concrete, more concerned with measurement and observation. This distinction will remain significant throughout the history of philosophical thought.

EPICURUS

Only a few of Epicurus' writings are extant, but his doctrines are available from secondary sources, such as Lucretius' *On the Nature of Things*. Epicurus (341?-270 B.C.) took up the problem of defining "good" and "happiness" and in the process became one of the first public figures with a legitimate claim to having been misquoted. Epicurus postulated that happiness, and therefore the "ultimate good," is the serenity derived from simple pleasures. His doctrine, the root of the primarily pejorative adjective "epicurean," actually advocated *moderation*. In other words, Epicurus, like Aristotle, warned against too much of a good thing, noting that pursuit of pure pleasure only leads to hollow disappointment.

EPICTETUS

Epictetus was a Greek by birth who imported the thoughts of an Athenian philosopher named Zeno to Rome. (Romans, as you remember, were quick to appropriate Greek property, citizens, ideas; even gods.)

Epictetus, who probably lived c. A.D. 50 to 130, either wrote very little or had all his writings lost; however, Epictetus' lectures on ethics were transcribed and edited by his pupil Arrian. One such volume is *The Discourses of Epictetus*.

Those lectures formed the basis of *stoicism*, which remains a familiar concept to this day. Stoics (the word derives from the Greek *Stoa Poikeile*, "painted porch," the school of Greek philosophy founded by Zeno, who presumably held court on that painted porch) were known for their rigorous self-discipline. The Stoic ethic held that humankind is self-sufficient and must hold itself indifferent to life's vagaries and troubles. It is your attitude toward your toothache, Epictetus contended, that determines your happiness, not the fact that your tooth is aching. (If legend is to be believed, this was not mere braggadocio on the part of Epictetus; he once allowed a teacher to break his leg and then calmly remonstrated his tormenter by saying, in so many words, "I told you that would happen.")

Above all, the Stoic philosophy as put forth by Epictetus is significant in that it holds that the good and ultimately happy person is the person who *values virtue for the sake of virtue*. This concept will surface repeatedly in ethical reasoning.

ST. AUGUSTINE

St. Augustine (354–430) was a follower of Plato, and as such was committed to the idea that the universe has an overall purpose and our actions fit into a predetermined scheme—concepts independent of experience. Augustine, though, believed that this was an entirely biblical framework, a chain of events based in theology.

His most noted works are *Confessions* and *The City of God*. *Confessions* is the more readable of the two works. It goes into great detail about Augustine's personal ethics and how those ethics flowed from his previous transgressions.

The critical point to be remembered when reading Augustine is that he was a converted Christian who had searched for meaning—and failed to find it—in many philosophies before turning to Christianity. He did not become a Christian until the age of 32. His was the zealousness of a convert to a recently established religion which, at the time, tolerated little if any deviation from formal doctrine. (The council of Nicea had defined basic Christian doctrine in 325 and declared that any deviation thereto was heresy.)

ST. THOMAS AQUINAS

Nearly a thousand years after Augustine interpreted Plato in terms of Christian doctrine, Thomas Aquinas (1225–1274) would resurrect the ideas of Aristotle in Christian terms. While Augustine the Platonist championed faith in the unseen ideals of the universe (in this case, the Christian universe), Thomas Aquinas the Aristotelian engaged in a precise and explicit examination of Christian doctrine and used Aristotle's logical rigor in the effort to prove conclusively the existence of God.

Summa Theologica is his most noted work.

Incidentally, Thomas Aquinas' influence in ethics extended beyond the realm of pure Christian ethics. He wrote extensively about the law, and was one of the first ethicists to argue with rigor that the law should aim at "the common good." To him, the common good meant something a bit different from what might be meant by a modern user of that term; the common good referred to what was best for the people of a particular society—not simply for the privileged members of that society or for those who live outside of the society.[1]

NICCOLÒ MACHIAVELLI

The name Machiavelli (1469–1527) became synonymous with the ethical concept that the end justifies the means, a theory which would resurface (though with a different overall perspective) in works by utilitarian philosophers.

---

[1] This becomes a rather technical point, explained well by C. Wellman (1988), *Morals and Ethics*, 2nd ed. Englewood Cliffs, NJ: Prentice-Hall. pp. 183–185.

The Prince is a straightforward examination of a ruler's ethics or lack thereof. And while it is not spiritually inspiring, it certainly reads beautifully.

SIR FRANCIS BACON

Bacon (1561–1626) was a pioneer in the Renaissance philosophies which integrated politics, hard science, and psychology. An astute politician, Bacon was a devotee of Machiavelli (even though Bacon professed adherence to Christian ideals). Bacon also was an admirer of Epicurus.

An interesting body of work to sample is the *Essays*, written between 1597 and 1623. These essays expand the realm of thought (which is, in retrospect, what the Renaissance was about) in ethics to related fields, such as psychology. Will Durant, for instance, bluntly credits Bacon with inventing the field of social psychology.

Bacon, it seems, was among the first philosophers to understand that philosophers need to "diligently inquire into the powers and energy of custom, exercise, habit, education, example, imitation, emulation, company, friendship, praise, reproof, exhortation, reputation, laws, books, studies, etc.; for these are the things that reign in men's morals; by these agents the mind is formed and subdued."

THOMAS HOBBES

A contemporary of Descartes (see next entry), Hobbes (who was British; Descartes was French) shared a fascination with the certainty of mathematics, and attempted to apply seventeeth-century scientific method to the ethical and governmental problems of the era. An avid reader of Copernicus and Galileo, Hobbes (1588–1679) attempted to apply a mechanistic rigor to philosophy. He developed strict measures for ruling people by means of a formula of so many parts desire to so many parts aversion.

Hobbes was a defender of the concept of absolute monarchy, maintaining that only a supreme ruler could dispense those mathematically correct doses of desire and aversion. His works *De Cive* and *Leviathan* reflect his theory that ultimately, morality is based on social authority, an authority which stems directly from the sovereign.

He also planted seeds of utilitarianism with his view that a successful member of society acts from self-interest and not from altruism.

RENÉ DESCARTES

In much the same way that Bacon moved philosophy and ethics toward social psychology, Descartes (1596–1650), a mathematician by training and temperament, pushed philosophy toward "the scientific method"; see *Dis-

course on Method. While not usually considered a major figure in ethics, per se, Descartes was influential in developing concepts which today play a role in ethical analysis, including epistemology (the branch of philosophy which investigates how we know what we know). *Cogito ergo sum*—"I think, therefore I am," now a familiar catchphrase—was Descartes's entry into epistemological inquiry.

But perhaps of more significance to the student of ethics was Descartes's influence on Spinoza (see below).

BENEDICT DE SPINOZA

Born Baruch Spinoza, Benedict de Spinoza (1632–1677) changed his name to the Latin equivalent when he was expelled from his Jewish community because of his radical views.[2]

Spinoza's *Ethics* is considered one of the more important works in the field, despite the fact that it is extraordinarily difficult to read. Some scholars theorize that Spinoza was hampered by the fact that he wrote in Latin, and that Latin, long dead as a living language, had not evolved to the point where it could express Renaissance ideas.

In any event, Spinoza's *Ethics* defies capsulization, except to describe it as an interconnected system of theorems which attempt to bring, by way of Descartes, an overall mathematical order to an obviously ethically disordered world.

A recommended work about the *Ethics* is David Bidney's *The Psychology and Ethics of Spinoza* (New York: Russell, 1962). Bidney spent decades studying Spinoza's *Ethics*, and his book offers some insight.

DAVID HUME

Hume (1711–1776) is perhaps the most noted skeptic in the field of ethics, but although his writing carries the tone of intellectual mistrust of conventional thinking, it is invariably good-natured. (His skepticism was not entirely born of simply a phlegmatic nature; many of the "enlightened" scholars of the era

---

[2] Much is made of Spinoza's excommunication, but we do not often hear of the "extenuating circumstances." Will Durant provided an interesting perspective when he noted that Jews of Spinoza's era were quite literally being exiled from continent to continent and faced incredible hardships irrespective of their destinations. Their reputed wealth caused hostility even when that wealth was mythical; in some cases, penniless Jewish emigrés were disemboweled in search of the jewels they were rumored to have swallowed. Durant points out that it is not surprising that exiled Jews, such as Spinoza's ancestral community (which emigrated to Holland from Spain), were motivated by survival instinct to huddle together and insist on strict orthodoxy.

produced what might, in modern vernacular, be termed "crackpot" ideas, so Hume's skepticism might have been entirely healthy.)

Of particular interest to a reader pursuing the subject of ethics is *An Enquiry Concerning the Principles of Morals*, in which Hume made a heroic effort to attach accurate definitions to all of the psychological attributes being used, he felt, rather loosely. *An Enquiry . . .* was a follow-up to an earlier failed (in terms of public acceptance) effort titled *On Morals*, which also attempted the same systematic definition of value judgments.

A useful guide to Hume, which can be found in many libraries, is John B. Stewart's *The Moral and Political Philosophy of David Hume* (Columbia University Press, 1963). This book examines the entire scope of Hume's work—there is a great deal of it—by category.

Much of Hume's writing is categorized as epistemological because he investigated not only morals per se but *why we feel* actions are right, *how we know* actions are right, and—in the extremes of skepticism—how we *really know* we know anything at all. A useful work which focuses on this subject is Jonathan Harrison's *Hume's Moral Epistemology* (Clarendon Press, 1976). It is thorough and rigorous but rather difficult to follow.

Hume may be widely noted for his enquiries into the psychological origins of our moral judgments, but he was also a diligent investigator of economic theory. *David Hume: Writings on Economics*, edited with an introduction by Eugene Rotwein (1970 edition, University of Wisconsin Press), is an ideal mixture of original text and commentary. Hume is at the helm but Rotwein steers us through the difficult waters, especially the now-obscure references to events and people of the times.

IMMANUEL KANT

Kant (1724–1804) was the champion of *a priori* ethics. He held that ethics are derived from universal principles and are not based on empiricism. Hence the famous categorical imperative, a contention that good can only stem from goodwill; hence, motives, not consequences, are the important factors in making moral judgments. According to the categorical imperative, we must act on that goodwill *always*, acting as though "the maxim of your action were to become through your will a universal law of nature."

Two works of particular interest to the student of ethics are *The Moral Law* and *Lectures on Ethics*.

Kant is obviously worth exploring; he and Aristotle are often considered the tallest historical figures in ethics. Kant's writing is neither overly abstract nor difficult, although it can become tedious. Kant has an undeserved reputation for obscurity, based, perhaps, on poor translations; in any library you will find numerous translations of all Kant, so choose wisely. Anything translated and annotated by T. M. Knox is likely to be quite readable.

G. W. F. HEGEL

Hegel (1770–1831) does not usually receive major treatment in ethics texts, probably because it is difficult to relate his obtuse prose to specific issues. While Kant was not reluctant to discuss such homely problems as marriage, money, and sex, Hegel's verbiage dwelt in the stratosphere.

Hegel's dialectic (a complex method of synthesizing opposing thoughts) was waged on a grand scale, and reflected the idea that an "absolute mind" was attempting to set the world in a perfect order—and would do so, regardless of our actions.

The worldly outcome of Hegel's cosmic, deterministic prose was the connection (an impression not discouraged by rulers of the era) between the determinism of this absolute mind and the totalitarian power of the Prussian state.

Determinism would remain a powerful force, though, so Hegel cannot be taken lightly. Marx was a follower of Hegel, and adapted Hegel's determinism (a sort of historical determinism) to what might be called a Marxian economic determinism. Some have argued that Freud was influenced by Hegel in Freud's development of a theory based, to an extent, on *psychological* determinism.

Given that lengthy prologue/caveat, you may wish to wade through *Philosophy of Right*. The translation with notes by T. M. Knox (Oxford University Press, 1967) is as good a version as any.

JOHN STUART MILL AND JEREMY BENTHAM

A British utilitarian, Mill (1806–1873) championed the "pleasure and pain" formula for determining the greatest good. J. S. Mill's most relevant work is *Utilitarianism*. Mill and the other famous utilitarian, Jeremy Bentham (1748–1832), differed on some minor points, but their thrust was essentially the same. One difference worth noting (which might be illustrated by reading Bentham's *An Introduction to the Principles of Morals*) is that Bentham was less concerned with philosophy and more interested in practical implementation of social policy.

(Note: It might be misleading to dismiss Mill and Bentham as sharing the same thoughts and differing only on matters of application of theory and other "minor points," so here is a simplified and probably simplistic explanation of what those minor points are: It is usually held that Bentham stressed quantity of pleasure rather than quality in determining the utilitarian scheme of things; Mill was a bit more concerned with defining the quality of pleasure. Bentham was an *act utilitarian*, believing that the ethical worth of each act should be judged by the good of its consequences. While the jury is still out on this one, Mill is usually thought of as a *rule utilitarian*, meaning that the judgments of acts should be based on how those acts conform with certain tenets of the utilitarian doctrine.)

FRIEDRICH NIETZSCHE

Nietzsche (1844–1900) offered a harsh critique of morals and put forth a radical view of his own. Essentially, he rejected *everything* and suggested, more or less, that superhumans invent their own morals. The ascendancy of the superman, he argued, would result in a perfect state where individual creativity is balanced with a fair system of justice. Nietzsche made this argument in an odd juxtaposition of the Greek legends relating to Dionysus and Apollo. Read *The Birth of Tragedy* if you are interested.

JOHN DEWEY

A uniquely American thinker, a Vermonter by birth, a midwesterner by transplantation, Dewey (1859–1952) concerned himself with the practical application of thought and ethics to everyday life. He clearly espouses the notion that philosophy and ethics are methods of understanding and managing life—not merely mental calisthenics.

Dewey is eminently readable, and in addition to his own philosophy he makes earlier works much more understandable through thoughtful analysis. For starters, the student of ethics may wish to explore Dewey's *Theory of the Moral Life* and the finely crafted *Ethics* by Dewey and James H. Tufts.

G. E. MOORE

Moore's *Principia Ethica*, as mentioned, is not only a statement of a theory of ethics but a lucid explication of other theories. Moore (1873–1958) is important in the "analytical" movement in ethics, where fundamental assumptions are reexamined. In point of fact, Moore gives some very practical advice to the student of ethics in the preface of the *Principia*: "In ethics," he maintains, "as in all other philosophical studies, the difficulties and disagreements, of which history is full, are mainly due to a very simple cause: namely to attempt to answer questions without first discovering precisely what question it is which you desire to answer."

If you are contemplating putting together a personal reading list on classical ethics, this volume, along with Dewey and Tuft's, might be the books with which to begin.

LUDWIG WITTGENSTEIN

Wittgenstein (1889–1951) was luminescent in the areas of linguistics, epistemology, and logic; by extension, his work has had important ramifications in modern ethics.

Essentially, he held that many disputes evolved from the fact that we simply misuse and misunderstand language—a powerful and reasonable argument in an era of widespread mass communications.

While reading Wittgenstein's intensely thorough examination of "language-games" requires some fortitude, that and other topics in *Philosophical Investigations* are perfectly understandable. Another of Wittgenstein's works, the *Tractatus Logico Philosophicus*, is not so easily accessible, and the reader might benefit from a guidebook. H. O. Mounce's *Wittgenstein's Tractatus: An Introduction* (University of Chicago Press, 1981) is available in many libraries and is helpful for "cracking the code" of the *Tractatus*.

This reading list is obviously not definitive, nor is "ethics" a definitive label. The philosophy of determining right and wrong, of separating good from evil, is inextricably linked with philosophy in general, including linguistics, logic, aesthetics, epistemology, and metaphysics. Also, the field of ethics as a whole is difficult to comprehend out of context, leading to the inescapable (and totally obvious) conclusion that a broad and interdisciplinary education is the most necessary tool for understanding the way we analyze and resolve ethical and moral dilemmas.

Appendix B

Further Readings in Journalism Ethics and Related Subjects: A Critical Annotated Bibliography

The following analyses deal with works cited in this book, and several works not cited but which contributed, in some way, to the effort. This is not a complete listing of all sources (the unabridged listing is located under "References"), nor a complete bibliography of works on journalism ethics, but rather a bibliography of works that were particularly useful in the writing of this work and are of particular interest (in my judgment) to the reporter studying the broad range of issues relating to journalism, history, and ethics. Two categories are listed: works specifically related to journalism ethics, and books which deal with other subjects but have a bearing on relevant questions of ethics, philosophy, history, and culture.

A note on the tone of these analyses: These are largely personal reactions and should be taken as such; the writer makes no pretensions to holding a lofty "critical" perspective from which to judge the work of others. It is my opinion that those who claim to know the secrets of writing good books could more profitably occupy their time doing just that.

Agee, Warren K., ed. (1969). *Mass Media in a Free Society*. Lawrence: The University Press of Kansas. This collection of lectures gathered the thoughts of prominent observers—most of whom were destined to achieve greater prominence in the two decades following publication—on media ethics in particular, and the social responsibilities of the media in general.

Ben Bagdikian, for example, sounded an early theme (he was beginning his reincarnation from Pulitzer Prize winning reporter and editor to "press critic") when attacking the integrity of the American newspaper. He contended that the institution had lagged in its traditional role as the "watchdog of society," and insisted that the press must return to its function of a national conscience.

(It is worth noting that this theme was repeated virtually word for word in an address by Mr. Bagdikian that the author viewed in June of 1989. No direct indication was given as to whether conditions had improved, declined, or remained static in comparison to 1969.)

Other addresses include reflections on the media's role in covering social crises (Carl Rowan), the nascent role of television news (Theodore F. Koop of CBS), a satirical view of the media by Stan Freberg, and a call for social enlightenment on the part of filmmakers, by Bosley Crowther.

While the material, by and large, is reasonably standard fare, the remaining entry, "The Press and Government: Who's Telling the Truth" by Bill Moyers, is a provocative statement by one who knows whereof he speaks. Moyers, characterizing his role as Johnson's press secretary as "having gone over to the enemy," admits his ambivalence toward both the press and the government, and offers a thoughtful analysis of how both camps slant, distort, and otherwise mangle the news. It is a good lesson on the imprecision of "truth," and the ways—intentional and unintentional—in which the filtration process of the media change our perceptions.

Bagdikian, B. (1972). *The Effete Conspiracy: And Other Crimes by the Press*. New York: Harper & Row. When Ben Bagdikian speaks, the press listens—or, at least, is reluctant to dismiss his comments out of hand. The reason, of course, is that Bagdikian established his credentials before turning to a career of nibbling (or needling) that hand that fed him. In addition to a Pulitzer, which he shared, Bagdikian owns Peabody and Sigma Delta Chi awards, and had a distinguished career at the *Washington Post*.

The Effete Conspiracy was one of the first sustained arguments on a theme which would dominate Bagdikian's later criticism: the increasingly monopolistic control of the media. The book section titled "The Conglomerate Discovers Newspapers" is incisive and portentous. If you agree with Bagdikian in his argument that monopoly control of the news media is destructive, you will also note how much more troubling the modern situation has become.

Bagdikian still warns against the threat of media mega-monopoly; indeed, it is difficult to pick up a copy of a journalism trade publication without finding reference to what may be one of the nation's most underreported stories. *The Effete Conspiracy* is dated, but still a valuable work in that it provides historical data on a continuing and escalating problem.

The remainder of *The Effete Conspiracy* deals with "crimes of the press" such as PR and advertising and how the practitioners of those fields affect news. Also, the work deals extensively with the largely forgotten (although they should not be) alliterative attacks on the press by then Vice-President and now ex-felon Spiro Agnew.

One final note: While of undeniable value, *The Effete Conspiracy* is an edited collection of essays and as such really lacks a central theme; it is an excellent collection but not a particularly cohesive book.

Compaigne, B., ed. (1979). *Who Owns the Media?* White Plains, NY: Knowledge Industry Publications. *Who Owns the Media?* is a study of the concentration, degree, and pattern of media ownership. The work is a compelling and admirably balanced tract.

There is a temptation to ascribe a conspiracy theory—or at least a negative connotation—to any hint of "cross ownership" or "media concentration." Compaigne's work is refreshing in that it poses some basic questions *without assuming the answer*. For example, we are presented with a detailed analysis of exactly "how big is too big?" Another assumption is challenged: Is "localism" really beneficial? What is the definition of "concentration"?

Certain basic assumptions taught in most mass communications curricula are challenged, also. For example, Compaigne points out that while there are fewer competing newspapers today, that factor is not necessarily a result of conglomerates eating up the small fry; another explanation might relate to the increase of *all* media (television, radio, etc.) in competing markets and the resulting shortage of media consumers (and advertising dollars).

These are excellent if unanswerable questions, and while the contributors do not provide those answers, they do offer a wealth of anecdotal and statistical information which lets the reader form his or her own opinion.

Casebier, A., & Casebier, J. J., eds. (1978). *Social Responsibilities of the Mass Media*. Washington, DC: University Press of America. This is not a widely distributed book; it is held in few libraries but provides a worthwhile examination of press and media ethics. The work is a transcript of a conference on mass media responsibility held at the University of Southern California.

Of particular note is Chapter Two: "Professional Press Ethics—A Case of Conflicting Concepts," by Anita Silvers. She maintains a view contrary to many media critics: That "journalists seem not at all hesitant to decry perceived disparities between the practices and the ideals of their profession." She further maintains that, "Doctors seem less worried about their failures to heal, and lawyers about failures to provide due process, than do journalists about failures to attain objectivity."

The definition of objectivity is, of course, nebulous, and that occupies most of the remainder of her paper. But the fundamental premise stated above is one of the few times where such a case has been argued in print, and it is worth exploring.

Christians, C., Rotzoll, K., & Fackler, M. (1987). *Media Ethics: Cases and Moral Reasoning*. New York: Longman. This is a well-known and widely used book; indeed, Christians has become a recognized leader in the academic analysis of media ethics.

It is therefore somewhat heretical to find fault with the work. After all, it does cover the standard case histories referred to in all such efforts, and makes a valiant effort (and a good one, considering the difficulty of the task at hand) to introduce concepts of ethical analysis. The authors, for example, introduce the concept of the "Potter Box," a philosophical construct for evaluating definitions, identifying values, understanding related ethical principles, and identifying loyalties.

But in my *personal view* the book has a rather hollow ring. First of all, it speaks with a pomposity which has proved downright offensive to the few working journalists with whom I have discussed the work. Statements such as, "Obviously the newspaper had failed in its public obligations...", or "The paper violated the basic moral principle that we should not cause harm, but should prevent it when doing so does not subject us to a result of comparable harm" might appear profound to a college freshman but seem arbitrarily judgmental to experienced professionals and academics who are aware of the complexities—*and the truly agonizing introspection*—which were involved in these cases.

Equally disturbing is the excessive use of unidentified and undocumented "examples." Are these hypotheticals, real situations with the names withheld, or what? Who, for example, is the writer whom we are told watches TV while he writes, and "needs to read a good book before he can write one"? Given the plethora of all-too-real cases, the continued use of blind references seems a bit too convenient to be convincing.

Crawford, N. A. (1970). *The Ethics of Journalism*. New York: Knopf. While this work was republished by Knopf in 1970, it actually dates from 1924. Still, it is a more relevant document than many of the efforts entered into the modern ethics market.

Crawford was among the first writers to make a sustained argument that the process of publishing news carries a heavier responsibility than being a *printer* of news. To the modern reader, that distinction is obvious; in the 1920s, it was an emerging perspective.

Crawford lays out a carefully documented tableau of the abuses of newspaper reporters and owners, and takes a long and careful look at the uneasy relationship between journalism and advertising. In addition, Crawford offers what might be regarded as a devastating sociological-psychological-political analysis (written comprehensibly) of the way *fear* plays a role in journalism. Reporters fear editors; editors fear publishers; publishers fear the public, who can choke off their profits. In addition, Crawford argues, people within the news organization often fear their *perception* of others; those perceptions may or may not be accurate.

He pulls no punches, noting that a young reporter often feels that attempting to part from the editorial line is futile, and that the young reporter is "perhaps encouraged in his belief by the city editor and the copy-readers—men who have grown old and cynical in the newspaper office and who could not readily find employment outside of it."

The Ethics of Journalism is must reading, if for no other reason than to confirm the aphorism that the more things change, the more they stay the same.

Goodwin, H. (1983). *Groping for Ethics in Journalism.* Ames: Iowa State University Press. Goodwin, a fine reporter, uses a journalist's perspective in this work.

He has assembled what appear to be (from examining the bibliography) several hundred interviews done in a cross-country trek, during which he met with editors and reporters. Each interview and each case history is extensively and exhaustively documented; there are very few hypotheticals. We get the complete menu of names, dates, and places, proving—at least to me—that a good journalist can get even the most controversial cases on the record if he or she works at it.

The author does an outstanding job in garnering perspectives on what he feels to be the fundamental areas of conflict in journalism: business verus professional interests, conflicts of interests, freebies, the relationships between reporters and sources, misrepresentation, sensationalism, privacy, the obligations of journalists as citizens, and the competence and responsibility of the press corps.

Goodwin does not engage in extended philosophical or historical analysis. That is not the thrust of this work, nor should it be. *Groping for Ethics in Journalism* is a straightforward piece of reportage and a superb standard by which to judge the current state of thinking and practice concerning journalism ethics.

Gross, G., ed. (1966). *The Responsibility of the Press.* New York: Fleet. Gross assembled a wide-ranging book with selections addressing much of the basic theory behind mass communications in general and ethics in particular; as a result, the work hardly seems dated in the slightest.

A couple of points: First, there are generally neglected areas explored at some length. The ethics of book criticism, for example, are examined. Attorney Edward Bennett Williams—in what surely must be a unique entry into the literature of media ethics—comments on the perception of the TV lawyer and how that perception squares with reality.

Second, two prime movers in communications and ethical theory offer their views. Wilbur Schramm submits an argument which is still fresh and probably still as unpopular among the general public as it was when introduced in 1966. (That date refers to the publication of this article; Schramm's theory, of course, had surfaced in various incarnations for many years before this publication.) Briefly, Schramm argues that the responsibility for ethical press coverage lies not only between government and the media, but among government, the media, *and the public*. This, as the author remembers it, was anathema to a basically passive public in the 1960s and probably remains so today, but it is—again, in my opinion—a telling point. The section is worth hunting down, because it is probably the most succinct distillation of Schramm's theory relating specifically to who is responsible for the quality of mass communications (which is, word for word, the title of the selection).

Gross' work also contains a chapter by Theodore Peterson which explores what he feels is a break with the traditional libertarian theory of the press and a move toward ethical standards reflecting the social responsibility theory—with a twist.

That twist is—shades of Schramm—that the newspaper-buying public shares in the responsibility as well. This material is, of course, available in longer form in F. S. Siebert, T. Peterson, & W. Schramm (1973), *Four Theories of the Press*. Urbana: University of Illinois Press, and W. Schramm (1957), *Responsibility in mass communications* (the chapter in Gross's work is the final chapter of *Responsibility*), but this collection places Schramm and Peterson's work in a stimulating context.

Hohenberg, J. (1978). *A Crisis for the American Press*. New York: Columbia University Press. Hohenberg ostensibly has written a work detailing ways in which the government suppresses media—more on that in a moment—but his book may be of more interest for its subtext.

That subtext is, in essence, a reasoned defense of the adversary system in American journalism. Hohenberg argues, in effect, that journalism and government cannot sleep in the same bed, and points to the successes of the press corps when it firmly established itself as the fourth estate operating as an adversary to entrenched power structures.

Hohenberg's main text is a comprehensive thesis that national security (including "executive privilege") and legislation limiting press rights are chilling the media's effectiveness. While much of what Hohenberg wrote in 1978 is no longer page-one news (seizures of newsroom notes, jailing reporters for refusal to disclose sources, etc.), these problems are still concerns of the journalistic community. Hohenberg's work, then, is a valuable historical prologue.

Curiously, though, Hohenberg does not appear overly concerned with the bizarre patchwork of libel and privacy laws which, at least from this writer's perspective, do indeed have a preemptive and chilling effect on news coverage. Perhaps the libel climate when this book was written did not seem so alarming as it does today.

Jaska, A. A., & Pritchard, M. S. (1988). *Communication Ethics: Methods of Analysis*. Belmont, CA: Wadsworth. This slim (172–page) volume is a painless and engaging introduction to the study of communications ethics, moving gracefully from quoting *U.S. News & World Report* to analyzing Bentham with nary a glitch.

Without explicitly indicating it (at least, as far as I could perceive), the authors created an interdisciplinary approach, weaving current and ancient philosophical reasoning into the current controversy surrounding media. While not done in the same depth as Merrill and Odell, the book does examine classical philosophy and makes it comprehensible. In addition, we're offered a psychological view of moral development; the names Freud, Kohlberg, and Piaget are rarely found in ethics texts, although a reading of Jaska and Pritchard convinces one that they should be.

Incidentally, this is a *text*, in the sense that it is designed for classroom use and contains questions for discussion, further readings, and references to current newsworthy topics. (The *Challenger* disaster and the ethical/organizational aspects of NASA decision making are treated with aplomb.)

Communication Ethics is an introduction, and not a substantial reference, but it makes no claims to be what it is not. Whatever it is, it is worth reading, as it provides a solid framework for anyone interested in the concepts of good and evil and right and wrong.

Lichter, S. R., Rothman, S., & Lichter, L. S. (1986). *The Media Elite: America's New Powerbrokers*. New York: Adler & Adler. The book bills itself on the dust jacket as "the first systematic study of the people who tell us most of what we know about the world around us." While that claim might be overblown, the book *is* highly systematic, and brings something which, in this author's opinion, journalistic criticism certainly needs: perspective from other disciplines.

The authors are political scientists, and use their research techniques to analyze the media as a power bloc. (Incidentally, readers interested in this type of cross-disciplinary examination might also examine *Books: The Culture and Commerce of Publishing*, by sociologists Coser, Kadushin, and Powell, published by Basic Books in 1982.)

Some of what the authors contend in the *Media Elite* is pretty much old hat: They assert, for example, that reporters are mostly liberal and media owners primarily conservative. That is certainly no surprise, in that the claim has been backed up in numerous studies and is instantly verifiable by anyone who has worked in a news organization other than *The National Review*, the *Washington Times*, or perhaps the Manchester *Union-Leader*.

Other findings are novel but certainly not conclusive (nor, in fairness, do the authors claim that the findings are conclusive). For example, the authors showed pictures representing various scenarios to members of the "media elite," and concluded—this, of course, is a broad generalization of the findings—that journalists tend to read an overabundance of oppression and class struggle into the scenarios, and have a strong predilection to root for the underdog.

A reader intent on searching for hard fact will find some concrete analysis of news coverage of major stories; *The Media Elite* purports to show how personal perspectives bias news coverage. Again, almost any working journalist will admit that objectivity is less than a precise commodity, but Lichter, Rothman, and Lichter do put a fresh face on what journalists and critics alike have suspected all along.

Hulteng, J. L. (1981). *Playing It Straight: A Practical Discussion of the Ethical Principles of the American Society of Newspaper Editors*. Chester, CT: The American Society of Newspaper Editors. The original code of ethics, called the "Canons of Journalism," of the ASNE survived virtually intact from its inception in the 1920s until 1975, when it was supplanted by the "statement of principles." Hulteng's work seeks to make the principles more concrete and directly related to journalism practice.

For the person engaged in the study of media ethics, it is a valuable document. First, it is more or less an "official" statement of position on the part of the ostensible guardians of newspaper ethics. Second, it relates real-life examples (although, unfortunately, often couched in blind hypothetical situations) to interpretation of the codes.

Second, *Playing It Straight* steers clear of arbitrary pontification. The blurred lines are readily acknowledged. For example, some careful analysis is given to the dilemma of the interviewee who offers to buy the reporter a cup of coffee. While this may not be an earthshaking quandary, it is the beginning of the series of small compromises which often lead to larger problems. Do we stick precisely to our ethical code which prohibits acceptance of "anything of value," and in the process appear to be hopelessly rude and doctrinaire? Or do we accept the coffee—and maybe a second cup, and possibly a drink . . . ?

These are the building blocks of real dilemmas, and they are dealt with realistically. While *Playing It Straight* does not offer definitive answers on responsibility, freedom of the press, independence, truth and accuracy, impartiality, and fair play, it does make a good-faith effort to survey the issues *realistically* .

Klaidman, S., & Beauchamp, T. L. (1987). *The Virtuous Journalist*. New York: Oxford University Press. The virtuous journalist is not mentioned by name, although we are given a reasonably clear picture of who he or she is.

The Virtuous Journalist does, though, present a very realistic attitude toward the concept of journalism analysis. The authors do recognize that the "catch-it-on-the-fly" nature of daily journalism makes it futile to examine every second's output of news as though it were representative of the news industry as a whole.

The authors do provide an overall framework—in particular, freedom, morality, rules of duty, virtue, competence, and fairness—as a way to analyze journalistic ethics, and the scheme seems to work. The analyses seem logical and their relationship to the framework unforced.

Of special importance is a chapter devoted to the concept of accountability. A good question is proffered: To *whom*, precisely, is the press accountable? Does it have a duty to invite criticism? Do reporters owe accountability to their sources, the subjects of their reports, to the government? That fundamental question seems to have been dropped from discussion during the decades following the heyday of Peterson and Schramm, but it is a question which will not readily disappear.

Merrill, J. C., & Odell, S. J. (1983). *Philosophy and Journalism*. New York: Longman. Here is what may be a unique book: a work that marries classical philosophy, including but not limited to ethics, to the practice of journalism. In addition, and to the reader's delight, the work is written in clear, comprehensible English.

Odell, a philosophy professor, inserts his vocabulary and thinking process into the world of journalism. He explains inductive and deductive reasoning, conceptual analysis, ethics, and epistemology *and* relates those concepts to journalism. Merrill, a journalism professor, does just the opposite; he relates journalistic practice to axiology, rhetoric (including theories of persuasion), political theory, and metaphysics.

To digress and make a critical observation on form, there are, in this writer's opinion, two factors which make this book a success:

1. The authors have written extensively and seem—and this is an excellent feature—to be rethinking their own bases of knowledge. They often quote and analyze themselves (from previous publications) and each other.
2. The book is written entirely without any attempt at obfuscation. At the same time, the material is not visibly "dumbed down" for the masses. It is incisive and compelling.

Of particular interest is the section by Odell on semantics. The journalistic precept—some would say myth—of objectivity is predicated on the meaning and submeaning of words. Odell's work, in conjunction with Hayakawa (cf), makes sense out of a subject which is generally made incomprehensible to the uninitiated.

Paletz, D. A., & Entman, R. (1981). *Media Power Politics*. New York: Free Press. An insightful but somewhat overheated work which paints the media consumer as a "powerless" (literal transcription) person, force-fed preprocessed information by a media possessed of less than noble intentions.

Once the reader penetrates the hyperbole, the work is insightful, and offers an excellent analysis of the "routinization" of news coverage. As an example, the authors (political scientists) analyze the overblown importance the media place on early presidential primaries and the resulting overflow effect from Iowa and New Hampshire.

But some of the material, at least to my point of view, does not ring true. A great deal of emphasis is placed on an alleged partnership of the police and press to manipulate the news; if that partnership does exist, I never knew about it, and through several years of police reporting never found one officer interested in any partnership. Rather, it was my experience that most police officers dislike and in some cases *detest* the press. A press/police conspiracy seems, then, a bit farfetched.

But this is a personal observation, and perhaps not an accurate one; the book as a whole has considerable merit.

Rivers, W. L., & Mathews, C. (1988). *Ethics for the Media*. Englewood Cliffs, NJ: Prentice-Hall. In the glut of media-ethics books, it is a formidable task indeed to come up with any new approaches to the field. Rivers and Mathews do manage: While much of the examination is standard (which is not meant as a pejorative description), the authors introduce a much-needed chapter on ethical leadership.

The work, in nature and in scope, is somewhat reminiscent of Swain (cf) but broader in content.

Ethics for the Media was treated harshly in a review in *The Journal of Mass Media Ethics*, in which it was attacked for "failure of scholarship," which often translates into academic resentment of anything written in comprehensible English. In addition, it was alleged that the "deepest problem" with the work was that it does not teach a way of thinking about moral issues.

Granted, the work does not prescribe a method of thinking. It makes no such pretention. It is, rather, a useful and factual volume.

Rivers, W. L., Schramm, W., & Christians, C. (1980). *Responsibility in Mass Communications*, 3rd ed. New York: Harper & Row. This latest update of a venerable work offers yet another incarnation of the four theories of the press along with sections on other entries. Of particular interest is a section on popular art; it is rare that a serious critic of the media takes on the critics themselves, those people who, it might be argued, determine what is viable art and what is not.

By the way, *Responsibility* offers a succinct and readable history and synopsis of communications theory. But the primary advantage of having *Responsibility* in your library is the section on the four theories, which offers a concise but still relatively complete summary of the *Four Theories* work. It is also an interesting book for interdisciplinarians.

Rubin, B., ed. (1976). *Questioning media ethics*. New York: Praeger. Rubin has collected some unusual entries for his work on ethics, including an analysis of crisis reportage, an investigation of the generally dismal history of press councils, and various explorations of how the media treat certain groups, including women and (via advertising) children.

All of the material is reasonably standard fare except for a delicious chapter titled "Small-Town Journalism Has Some Big Ethical Headaches," written by Loren Ghiglione. Ghiglione makes the point that the small-town paper is susceptible to certain types of problems commonly not encountered by its major-market counterparts. "Boosterism" is examined; so is advertiser pressure exercised by merchants who do not find the publication employing the proper level of boosterism. Witness:

> To operate a small-town paper in defiance of these expectations is to risk retaliation. Recently, our 6,200-circulation paper published a front page article about building-code violations, precipitating a letter to the editor from one landlord who also happens to be a restaurant owner. The letter concluded with great subtlety: "The article is very unprofessional!! If I ran my restaurant so unprofessionally, I'd be shut down. Who shuts down the local newspaper? Nobody, I guess... unless it's your advertisers!" A week later, when news and editorial page coverage of the building-code violations continued, the restaurateur pulled his ads.

This is not to imply that large-market media do not have advertiser pressure, but the advertiser dismay at lack of boosterism is unique to the small-town market and a case could be made that advertiser pressure could be far more crippling. In his article, Ghiglione explores the idea that pulling back from reporting because of local pressure is a greater act of irresponsibility than abusing First Amendment freedoms.

While there is no question that the national media are the primary movers in news coverage, we cannot forget that small- and medium-size communities are consumers of news, too—and a story by a small-town newspaper can dramatically alter someone's life as readily as a piece in *The New York Times* can affect the life of a New York City resident.

Two notes about Ghiglione and a brief disclosure: Ghiglione has significantly expanded his holdings to include much larger markets since this work was written, and he has become an influential member of national press associations. Also, the author has previously written for several Ghiglione-held publications.

Schramm, W. (1954). *The Process and Effects of Mass Communication.* Urbana: University of Illinois Press. Schramm defines, in simple terms, the basic elements of mass communication, and compiles a work which deals with some questions as relevant today as in 1954.

Walter Lippmann noted in *Public Opinion* that although people live in the same world, they think and feel in different worlds, with a "pseudo-environment" between themselves and the real environment; the title of Lippmann's opening chapter was "The World Outside and the Pictures in Our Heads."

This is mentioned because Lippmann's quote also serves as the introduction to Schramm's *Process and Effects*. Schramm's work investigates the ways in which we make meaning of ideas and symbols to form those "pictures in our heads."

Some pioneering work is contained here, and, mercifully, the book was written before it became fashionable to express ideas and theories about mass communications in indecipherable and pretentious jargon. *Process and Effects* offers clear, readable, and even exciting perspectives on such issues as how rumor spreads, how opinion is influenced, and the ways in which the individual's perception alters the reception of a message.

International communications are also addressed.

Of primary interest to the ethicist is the work's attention to the effects of communications (as one might easily guess from the title). Such effects are complex and can only be readily understood by a thorough reading of the book, but one recurrent theme which surfaces throughout this book (and much of Schramm's work) is that the mass media are not omnipotent shapers of opinion.

Schramm, W., ed. (1963). *The Science of Human Communication*. New York: Basic Books. Schramm pulls together what he terms the strands of human communication: sociology, psychology, political science, and modern scientific rhetoric. Collected articles include examinations of attitude change (which are still being referred to today in the books and journals which deal with advertising and politics), and the way in which communication produces an effect.

What is largely left unspoken (perhaps because it was so obvious in 1963) is some communication theory, and much of the work presented in this book emerged from research into propaganda conducted during World War II.

Despite the age of the work, it relates precisely to modern communication analysis. For example, one then-controversial tenet put forth from the wartime researches (and later investigations) was the idea that people are difficult to "convert" by means of the media; they are more likely to be "mobilized." Fascinating: Every four years media "analysts" dissecting political campaigning and advertising serve up this truism as though it were a dish invented yesterday.

Siebert, F. S., Peterson, T., & Schramm, W. (1973). *Four Theories of the Press*. Urbana: University of Illinois Press. The four theories proposed by the authors, the authoritarian, libertarian, social responsibility, and Soviet Communist paradigms, have become standard features of most mass communication textbooks. But the theories, as such, are not as important as their historical and philosophical origins, which are traced and documented in *Four Theories*.

The authoritarian theory, for example, traces its roots back to Plato. This is certainly not standard mass media text fare, and the initial reaction to this assertion might be one of skepticism. But on reflection, didn't Plato advocate the rule of philosopher kings? And did he not advocate the banishment of those who produced works of art not squaring with his view of the world? Yes, authoritarian censorship was very much a part of Plato's view, as well as views of Machiavelli and some utilitarians, including Hobbes.

The connections made by *Four Theories* extend to Milton, Mill, and Locke's contributions to the libertarian theory; the authors neatly make the connection between libertarianism and natural rights. Likewise, they make some rather strained (by necessity) connections between the social responsibility theory and Milton while documenting the evolution of this primarily modern theory. And, of course, they relate the philosophical views relating to the flow of information as interpreted by Marx and eventually trampled by Stalin.

Four Theories of the Press is not so much a set of theories, per se; rather, the work traces the evolution of important thought as it relates to the press. It gives especially important illumination to the libertarian and social responsibility functions of, in the words of the authors, "the British and American press," although one might argue that there is a significant difference—especially in terms of British government control over the bottomless well of state "secrets"—between the two nations' systems.

Stephens, M. (1988). *A History of News: from the Drum to the Satellite.* New York: Viking. This is an intriguing concept: comparing accounts of the Peloponnesian War to the modern-day coverage of ax murders in New York City... tracing the development of cave drawings to modern-day newspaper layout. While some might argue that the book sets itself an impossible goal—unifying a vast topic in a single volume—the interdisciplinary exploration is well done, carefully documented, and—in its uncovering of unexpected detail—reminiscent of Barbara Tuchman. Much of this material simply hasn't been mined and collected in such a fashion before. For example, Stephens's comparison of "journalistic" sensationalism in the Roman marketplace to that of the modern media does, intuitively, make sense.

The connections are expressed in a lively manner, and as one reviewer noted, this book does point out, as a reviewer notes, that news was not "born yesterday."

Swain, B. M. (1972). *Reporters' Ethics.* Ames: Iowa University Press. Many journalistic decisions are essentially private ones, an aspect of ethics addressed coherently in this work. And while these are very personal stories—involving the individuals' decisions when facing such dilemmas as accepting a freebie, keeping perspective, resolving a sticky relationship with a source, or a conflict of interest—the cases are documented and *on the record.*

This is what makes Swain's work a valuable resource for other researchers into journalism ethics. In some works (some works considered the "classics" in the field, incidentally), the reader is left to wonder whether the incident is apocryphal, a "composite" representation, or simply an invention for the sake of discussion.

Swain's book does not provide an overall framework, or an overarching theory of journalism ethics, and that's probably a good thing, since such an approach would run contrary to the book's intent. This is a work which makes no pretensions of being anything other than a book of reportage on reporting, and it is a valuable, if somewhat dated, resource.

(As an example, standards regarding freebies are typically much more strict today than in 1972. For example, accepting gifts from people directly or peripherally involved in news coverage is almost universally verboten today, but in 1972 the lines were not so clearly drawn.)

Thayer, L., ed. (1980). *Ethics, Morality and the Media*. New York: Hastings House. Edwin Newman, a contributor to this book, once did a story on the sixtieth anniversary of the teddy bear, and said that one of the attractive things about the teddy bear is that it has not been excessively humanized. Later, an indignant viewer called and accused Newman of saying that the teddy bear was not civilized.

Such are the problems of those who transmit information to the public—a rather fickle public which can take offense at what the journalist may feel are the least offensive contentions. These and other themes are examined in *Ethics, Morality and the Media*, a formidable collection of essays from 27 contributors, including Newman, Sander Vanocur, Raymond Rubicam (of Young & Rubicam), Ben Bagdikian, and pollster George Gallup.

This is an ambitious and ultimately successful book. The editor and compiler (Thayer) went to enormous lengths to ensure that his book did not replicate standard fare. Newman's entry, for example, contends that while the press has undeniable responsibilities in the grand scheme of things, the *public* bears a certain amount of responsibility, too: They, collectively, must cultivate some understanding of the media and become more sophisticated users (i.e., do not read sinister implications into teddy bear retrospectives).

Bagdikian sounds a similarly unusual theme; he contends that the information overload—and this was 18 years ago—has "stripped meaning from symbols," a sensible and intriguing notion. Thayer, in his prologue, speaks to the interconnectedness of all media and *all culture*, something all too often ignored by the critics turned statisticians who attempt to analyze media entirely out of their cultural contexts.

RELATED WORKS

Borgatta, E. F., & Crook, K., eds. (1988). *The Future of Sociology*. Newbury Park, CA: Sage. By the editors' admission, a work on the future of sociology is an ambitious project, and that is true; for the nonsociologist, reading the work requires some ambition, too.

However, media scholars with a fundamental understanding of sociology will find several sections of the book comprehensible and functional. Of specific interest is an article titled "American Media Inquiry of the Last Quarter-Century: A Pattern of Decline" by S. J. Ball-Rokeach. In essence, Ball-Rokeach argues that the "weak media-powerful audience" position which was popular in the 1960s is an "overgeneralized and outdated" view.

The author also maintains that research into media effects has been weakened through lack of funding and an essential lack of interest among sociologists. The argument is far from conclusive, but it does provide a perspective on how sociologists view the media and its role in social processes.

Crick, M. (1976). *Explorations in Language and Meaning*. New York: Wiley. Crick attempts to bridge some of the gulf between anthropology, which he defines as the "reflection of human beings on themselves," and semantics. He devotes a great deal of the work to refuting the work of British anthropologists, whom he claims have long ignored the link between language and anthropology.

Crick's book can be distilled (and it *does* need distillation) to one main ingredient: That we must understand meaning in order to understand culture; the study of meaning is a jumping-off point for evaluating links between culture and language.

A point of particular interest to the journalist is the idea that language is a shared possession, a point originally stressed by Wittgenstein (see Appendix A). This relates to the notion that studying language can lead to a greater understanding of the public that utilizes it. Unfortunately, Crick has entombed his own ideas in ponderous and meandering prose which offers only a few relevant insights.

Galbraith, J. K. (1975). *Money: Whence It Came, Where It Went*. Boston: Houghton Mifflin. An understanding of money is, of course, a useful commodity for the journalist; after all, we're taught to "follow the money" when following a story.

On the surface, Galbraith's book is a guide to following the money from a historical perspective. But on a deeper level, it presents a useful perspective for the student of journalism ethics: the frequent inaccuracy and irrationality of "conventional wisdom." Galbraith challenges some ideas we have accepted as conventional wisdom, including our perceptions about inflation, tariffs, and the various standards which stabilize our money supply.

The history of money is, in some ways, history itself, and to an extent it is an *ethical* history. Galbraith notes that the pursuit of money illuminates "human behavior and human folly." And while the contention that the love of money is the root of all evil "can be disputed, what is not in doubt is that the pursuit of money, or any enduring association with it, is capable of inducing not alone bizarre but ripely perverse behavior."

That is a good lesson for those interested in the ethics and morals of people and business.

Graubard, S. R. (1973). *Kissinger: Portrait of a Mind*. New York: Norton. To slip into book-review parlance, this is a must-read for journalists, for several reasons.

- First, this is a study which includes details of how Kissinger researched and wrote *A World Restored*. It is not often that anyone in the business of stringing words together is offered this insight.
- Second, Graubard takes pains to point out that *A World Restored* (Kissinger's doctoral dissertation) was available in almost any large library at a time when reporters nationwide were guessing and groping for an idea of Kissinger's political philosophy. In point of fact, Graubard, a professor at Brown, notes that few people in public life have put their opinions into print so extensively as Kissinger—and it is remarkable that the American press corps largely overlooked this fact.

Do not expect a balanced evaluation of Kissinger or his politics; Graubard is a friend and admirer and makes no pretensions to objectivity. However, the book still points out—graphically—the way in which many journalists have an aversion to the library.

To digress, journalists and other observers have characterized Kissinger as Metternichian, and even broadly hinted that Metternich was Kissinger's hero. Irrespective of anyone's view of Kissinger, it is obvious from a cursory reading of *A World Restored* that Kissinger was not an admirer of Metternich (nor Castlereagh, for that matter). Instead, he (Kissinger) chose to study the Napoleonic era because it resembled his own: The problems of Austria, Great Britain, Russia, Prussia, and France seemed to offer a perspective from which to study the twentieth-century instabilities among the United States, Soviet Union, Great Britain, France, and Germany.

The two volumes, read as a companion set, provide a valuable perspective into the methodology of gathering information and relating it to another situation.

One other point, perhaps relevant, perhaps peripheral: Graubard notes that it was the *nontraditional* aspects of a Harvard education which allowed Kissinger to produce what is obviously a nontraditional dissertation. Harvard, according to Graubard's account, allowed its scholars free run when attacking an idea, and did not seek to limit their creative approaches.

Hayakawa, S. I. (1941). *Language in Action*. New York: Harcourt, Brace & Co. Journalists are all too familiar with the ways in which words and concepts become skewed in their meaning, whether by accident or by intent. Hayakawa argues that words are as often a *barrier* to communication as they are an *aid*—and few people who make their livings with words would argue that point.

Intuitively, we know that words can slant, reports can mislead, and classifications can confuse. And those of us interested in words typically have an idea of what we know, verbiage-wise, but are mystified by how we know it.

The people who have some of the answers are semanticists, but semantics and its related disciplines are often tough sledding for those not trained in the field. Hayakawa provides a layperson's guide through the world of words, and offers a readable framework for linguistic analysis. He challenges some of the assumptions we take for granted and analyzes ways in which clear language structure can aid clear thought.

Henry, Jules (1963). *Culture Against Man.* New York: Random House. Henry, a professor of anthropology, investigates human values and finds them lacking—in part, because of the intrusion of institutions into personal relations, along with the pervasiveness of greed and materialism. Of particular import for the scholar of mass communications is Henry's chapter titled "Advertising as a Philosophical System."

Henry invents his own lexicon to describe the language of advertising: He describes an entire taxonomy of misleading verbiage, and makes a convincing case for critical thinking about the mass media.

The book is good-natured but the outlook is gloomy; in sum, it alleges that institutions (including but not limited to the media) are destroying the culture. More than a quarter decade later, the culture appears more or less intact—but if one subscribes to Henry's observations, a case could be made that the culture is eroding along the lines he predicted.

Jones, M. O. (1988). *Inside Organizations: Understanding the Human Dimension.* Newbury Park, CA: Sage. Here is an odd literary duck, indeed: a collection of studies of organizational workings from specialists in a variety of fields—history, communications theory, folklore, and, of course, standard "organizational theory."

Readers who expect a standard helping of organizational theory will be disappointed (but how many people could that really be?). This work presents an interdisciplinary approach which, while not of immediate interest to the journalist, presents some situations that present compelling parallels.

For example, *Inside Organizations* deals with "symbolic behavior"—the ways in which organization members act out their roles within the structure. While the studies are confined to such areas as health care, universities, and manufacturing, some useful insights are included. Also of some relevance is the discussion of "organizational folklore," that collection of (probably) apocryphal stories which survive and, to an extent, affect the workings of current organizational members.

Again, while journalism as such is not dealt with or even mentioned, some relevant articles do offer some insights. Refer to the section of *Inside Organizations* which deals with working in a "machine paced" environment—that is, a working situation where deadlines are imposed by the equipment. That strikes a responsive chord, no?

Kirkpatrick, J. J. (1972). *Political Woman*. New York: Basic Books. Of use to the journalist not so much in its prima facie purpose—to study why women have been held back in their pursuit of political office—but as a superb example of how a scholar identifies, attacks, and analyzes a broad problem.

Professor Kirkpatrick gathered dozens of women legislators, conducted interviews, and administered questionnaires. She examines the cultural constraints (which have changed dramatically since 1972) and explores the particular difficulties faced by women seeking election.

The methodology of Kirkpatrick's study is clearly explained throughout and should prove helpful for any journalist analyzing a broad and essentially amorphous social condition. A particular strength of the work is that it allows the participants to tell a good deal of the story in their own words, a particularly effective device in long-form journalism.

Kissinger, H. (1973). *A World Restored: Metternich, Castlereagh, and the Problems of Peace*. See Graubard, *Kissinger: Portrait of a Mind*.

Krause, E. (1971). *The Sociology of Occupations*. Boston: Little, Brown. "History," Krause maintains, "is a graveyard of occupations and professional groups." What he does not say, but which a journalist quickly infers, is that contemporary history (i.e., reporting) is the same graveyard with some life in the bones.

The Sociology of Occupations is a reasonably worthwhile reference for the student of journalism and journalism ethics, in that it provides some insight into the way occupations function; in particular, it includes a section on how codes of ethics affect occupations (though not journalism).

Also, it is a tool for the journalist who must pierce the corporate and professional veil and understand the workings of various occupations. That, of course, is the root of many charges of unfairness. Businesspeople, for example, frequently score journalists for not understanding the world of business or elevating minor details to overstated importance (a charge to which I have no choice but to plead guilty). While this work is not a primer into occupations as such, it does provide an overview of what the author terms "occupational ideologies" and "group actions."

Levantin, R. C. (1984). *Not in Our Genes: Biology, Ideology and Human Values*. New York: Pantheon. This work is of passing interest in that it reflects an intramural dispute among scientists which was begun, in effect, by publication of a controversial book titled *Sociobiology*. It is an attack on those who claim a genetic basis of "human nature" and a broadside against those that Levantin labels as "reductionists."

Lippmann, W. (1929). *A Preface to Morals*. New York: Harcourt Brace. As an author, columnist and political analyst, Lippmann wrote on an enormous variety of topics, but his book on morality is probably among his less known. It is, in essence, a reflection on the state of morals and religion in what he calls "the machine age." Because Lippmann's career was so long, it comes as something of a shock to remember that the same man who wrote about World War II and the Kennedy era produced this work in the aftermath *of the Scopes trial*.

In any event, Lippmann devotes a page or two in his work to a discussion of ethical codes—the sanction of what he calls a "human morality" and the inherent problems of codes based on the "opinion of a majority, or on the motion of wise men, or on an estimate of what is socially useful." It is an interesting interpretation of sanctions, expressed, of course, in an era when what Lippmann called "the acids of modernity" were beginning to eat away at the acceptance of divine sanctions and we began grappling with the effectiveness of human sanctions.

Masters, R. D. (1968). *The Political Philosophy of Rousseau*. Princeton, NJ: Princeton University Press. Although parenthetical to journalism and ethics per se, Masters's book provides some background into a name which appears whenever ideas of human nature and a "social contract" are discussed. Masters's commentary is welcome and worthwhile, and is presented in addition to, and not in lieu of, the original text.

Schlesinger, A. M., Jr. (1945). *The Age of Jackson*. Boston: Houghton Mifflin. The journalism scholar can gain an insightful understanding of the evolution of journalism by examining the Jackson era. While we're taught in American history that Jackson originated the concept of the kitchen cabinet, we're usually not told that the people who held informal power in the Jackson era included a sizable number of journalists (which raised the early question of co-opting journalists by bringing them into a circle of power, a problem which certainly has not gone away).

As Schlesinger points out, prior to Jackson the journalist had been regarded primarily as a servant of the ruling class, but never its equal. That changed when the election of Jackson "cracked the aristocracy." Newspapermen, such as Amos Kendall and Francis Preston Blair, filled vacancies in his kitchen cabinet.

Schlesinger recounts these and other details with his unique ability to relate history in a nonchronological order. *The Age of Jackson*, which won a Pulitzer in 1947, is episodic and groups events by context and content—eschewing the "one damn thing after another" complex which dogs so much historical writing.

Such a free-floating perspective is only possible when the writer has absolute, total command of the material. Witness the density and scope of just one passage (in this case, about Jefferson, not Jackson), which puts facts into an incisive historical perspective:

> [Jefferson], in whom keen sensitivity to national needs always overcame loyalty to abstractions, steadily revised his views on industrialism during his presidency. "As yet our manufacturers are as much at their ease, as independent and moral as our agricultural inhabitants," he exclaimed in 1805, apparently with surprise. Four years later he conceded that an equilibrium of agriculture, manufacturing and commerce had become essential to American independence. In 1813 he recanted explicitly: "events have settled my doubts." In 1816, at the first serious attempt to enact Hamilton's Report on Manufacturers, Jefferson remarked contritely, "Experience has taught me that manufacturers are now as necessary to our independence as to our comfort." Eight years of responsibility had made certain the triumph of the statesman over the philosopher.

A student of journalism could do well to examine not only the historical impact on the press related by Schlesinger, but also to the masterful way he recounts history of all varieties.

Schlesinger, A. M., Jr. (1957). *The Age of Roosevelt*. Boston: Houghton Mifflin. This multivolume work is a good illustration of how history interacts with what we call journalism. Reading *The Age of Roosevelt* was largely a measure of self-indulgence on the part of the author, since I had been involved in the research of a competing Roosevelt biography, and it was a matter of personal interest to note the differences between the two works (and, of course, among competing Roosevelt works which I've also read).

Many historical works use, as primary references, the journalistic accounts of the time. (*The New York Times*, for example, is available on microfilm in any major library.) Schlesinger's work is of particular profit in that it often steps back to analyze critically the press coverage itself, something missing in a great deal of history which *relies* on press accounts.

An example:

> Newspapermen were quick but wrong to ascribe the increase in spending in the summer of 1934 to Keynes. No doubt Keynes strengthened the President's inclination to do what he was going to do anyway, and no doubt he showed the younger men lower down in the administration how to convert an expedient into a policy. But it cannot be said either that spending would have taken place without his intervention or that it did take place for his reasons. In 1934 and 1935 the New Deal was spending in spite of itself.

Many historians cannot or will not take such a departure from the "record" provided by the news media. See also the entry on Schlesinger's autobiography *In Retrospect*.

Schlesinger, A. M., Sr. (1963). *In Retrospect: The History of an Historian*. New York: Harcourt, Brace & World. The elder Schlesinger offers a fascinating glimpse of the history-gathering process, along with some equally fascinating gossip about historical figures.

If one accepts the relationship between journalism and history (and there are many, I believe), *In Retrospect* is something of a course in basic news gathering. Schlesinger is not at all reluctant to explain the details and "angles" of producing works of history.

Two points are of particular interest to the ethicist: Schlesinger's recounting of his battles with textbook censors and his contention that things can only be fully understood when presented in complete context. The latter proposition puts forth the idea that few concepts or quandaries emerge from a vacuum; dilemmas are not created in and of themselves. This might be of particular interest to the student of journalism ethics who eschews the "cookbook" theories put forth to "solve" ethical puzzles.

Silk, L., and Vogel, D. (1978). *Ethics and Profits*. New York: Simon & Schuster. Silk, an economist and member of the editorial board of *The New York Times*, and Vogel, a faculty member at University of California, Berkeley, produced a work rather similar to Kirkpatrick's *Political Woman* (cf); they convened a group of subjects and probed for their responses.

In this case, the subjects were American business leaders, and while much of the specifics of the inquiry is dated, the dialogue is telling and many of the situations remain the same. (One of the oldest jokes defining news is that it is "the same things happening to different people"; remove the words "oil crisis" from this 1978 work and substitute "savings and loan crisis" and you'll find the same basic thrust.)

This is a must-read for journalists concerned with their own ethics and the ethics of those they cover. The book was based on a series of eight three-day meetings held in the mid-1970s; participants, among other things, consistently struck the theme that they were frustrated by their inability to communicate with the public.

Journalists, in the view of many of the businesspeople interviewed, comprised a virtual fourth branch of government, an entity which wields enormous power and uses the poor performance of a few to castigate the entire business community.

Silk and Vogel's exploration provides a fine insight into how "the other side" sees the press. It is not an apologia for the business community, but rather an investigative report into that community's motivations. While many journalists might contend they already know the answer—yes, we are aware that we are not held in particularly high esteem by the business community—this book offers a reasonably cogent explanation of *why*.

Tuchman, B. (1984). *The March of Folly*. New York: Knopf. An ethicist is often confronted with the question, "Why did this person act this way?"

Tuchman's thesis is a useful one for investigators of this dilemma. She proposes that governments, and by extension all human groups, sometimes perversely pursue policies contrary to their best interests.

This is of particular interest to a scholar investigating *coverage* of governments engaged in counterproductive policies. While the Trojan War and the Renaissance popes are a bit removed from this theme, coverage of the Vietnam War is highly germane; the section on the changing attitudes of the press is illuminating.

The late Ms. Tuchman was an assiduous researcher, and as such she added a valuable contribution to the history of press dissent by collecting *specifics*; the so-called press war is often related in generalities. Typically, she resisted the tendency to make broad and general reference to, for example, Walter Cronkite's gradual disaffection with government policies. Instead, she asked Cronkite for a transcript of his now famous broadcasts, and printed the remarks verbatim.

Appendix C
Methodology of the Pilot Study

As mentioned in the text, radio news directors were chosen for this initial investigation because they represented a relatively homogenous group. Also, the number of radio news directors is so large that a follow-up survey of major proportions could be undertaken with no duplication of respondents.

A systematic sample was produced, using a random number as a starting point from which to begin the count. Respondents were chosen at regular intervals, a method widely felt to produce a sample equally valid with a purely random sample (Wimmer & Dominick, 1987, p. 75).

An initial mailing was made to 249 news directors. In addition to a postage-paid envelope for return of the anonymous questionnaire, news directors were also mailed a postage-paid postcard which carried their station's call letters. They were instructed to mail the questionnaire and postcard under separate cover. This guaranteed their anonymity but enabled me to keep track of who had returned the questionnaire; a second mailing was made to those who did not return the postcard.

Eleven envelopes were returned as undeliverable. Of the remaining 238 news directors who received the questionnaire, 120 completed and returned it. The results were summarized in Figure 13.2 in Chapter 13. In addition to numerical data, it is also interesting to mention some of the verbal responses. (Respondents were invited to evaluate the questionnaire for purposes of this pilot study.) Three wrote that they found the issue too broad to respond to in questionnaire fashion, but in two cases wrote detailed narrative responses.

Two respondents wrote that they found the questionnaire "interesting" and "quite clear." Some wrote comments adjacent to the questionnaire comments themselves, including one respondent who admitted that he/she would probably not report on the transgressions of other reporters "out of self-preservation."

A discussion with one of the initial evaluators during the initial in-person testing of the questionnaire proved interesting. He expressed "deep suspicion" of my motives, primarily because I was "an academic," and doubted that "anyone would return a questionnaire on this subject." However, after I informed him that I had spent fifteen years as a journalist (in fact, we had worked in the same market at one point), he became not only cooperative but eager to provide me with "horror stories." This, and comments from other initial interviewees, prompted me to include details of my professional background in the cover letter. Perhaps this helped achieve a reasonable rate of return for a mailing dealing with a relatively controversial subject.

An Explanation of the Correlations

The r correlation (explained further in a moment) between Question 1 ("should learn to take it") and Question 9 ("have frequently observed journalists avoiding . . . ") is .48 ($p < .001$). The cross-tabulation of Question 2 ("prefer not to call attention to their sins") and Question 9 produces an $r = .46$ ($p < .001$).

For readers not familiar with the verbiage of social science research, r is a measure of how closely two responses correlate with each other. The highest r is 1.00, and would very rarely be seen in social science research, unless you chose a painfully obvious relationship such as the persons who failed to return the questionnaire and people who died before the questionnaire was mailed. The correlation (r) between questions 1 and 9 is, for example, .48, a reasonably strong correlation for survey research. We determine the strength, in part, by the probability that it could be reproduced by chance. The .48 r correlation between Questions 1 and 9 is described as being $p < .001$, meaning that the probability of that happening by chance is less than .001 percentage, meaning less than a one in a thousand chance. (In other words, if the correlations were done a thousand times, the result we achieved would probably happen, according to statistics, only once.) The correlation coefficient r is commonly used in survey research of this nature (Bainbridge, 1989, p. 167).

Now, back to the results: A modest correlation was exhibited among news directors who felt that "media self-censure would be an effective deterrent" and those who had professed to observing journalists avoiding stories about other journalists. For the cross-tabulation of questions 1 and 3, $r = .30$ ($p < .01$). Some negative correlation ($r = -0.25$, $p < .01$) was also exhibited among respondents who felt that concern over journalism ethics was "media bashing" (Question 4) and those who agreed with Clurman's contention in Question 1 that the press should "learn to take it." No significant negative correlations were found with Question 3.

Possible Interpretations and Need for Further Study

Perhaps the tendency to favor self-censure and vigorous reporting on press issues is rooted in observance of cover-ups; but since this is self-reported behavior—and "avoiding stories" is a rather vague description—the relationship is circumstantial.

Respondents did report greater reluctance to pursue negative stories on rival reporters and news co-workers, but whether that has any significance beyond the norms of typical human interaction needs further study. Indeed, the 14 percent of respondents who strongly agreed and the 39 percent who agreed that they would pursue a negative story on a member of their own news department seems to indicate a rather high degree of willingness to "rock the boat," so to speak. But that is speculation and needs further research, perhaps in comparison with figures from other occupational groups. Further research is also needed into:

1. The attitudes of news executives from other media, including television and newspapers.
2. Data and comparison of the attitudes of news workers and news executives.
3. More specific, quantifiable details of instances where journalists avoided negative coverage of other journalists.

References

Alter, J. (1990, January 22). The art of the profile. *Newsweek*, p. 54.
American Society of Newspaper Editors (1986). Newsroom ethics: How tough is enforcement? *Journal of Mass Media Ethics*, 2(1), 7–16.
Anderson, D. (1987). How managing editors view and deal with ethical issues. *Journalism Quarterly*, 64(2), 341–345.
Atwater, T. (1986). Consonance in local television news. *Journal of Broadcasting and Electronic Media*, 30(4), 462–472.
Bagdikian, B. (1972). *The effete conspiracy*. New York: Harper & Row.
Bainbridge, W. S. (1989). *Survey research*. Belmont, CA: Wadsworth.
Ball-Rokeach, S. J. (1988). Media systems and mass communications: American media inquiry of the last quarter-century: A pattern of decline. In Borgatta, E. F., & Cook, K. (eds.), *The future of sociology* (pp. 317–332). Newbury Park, CA: Sage.
Baumhard, R. (1968). *An honest profit: What businessmen say about ethics in business*. New York: Holt, Rhinehart & Winston.
Bennett, W. Lance (1988). *News: The politics of illusion*. New York: Longman.
Benson, B. (1989, April). So we want to be better managers, do we? *Communicator*, pp. 13–15.
Biagi, S. (1987). *NewsTalk II: State-of-the-art conversations with today's broadcast journalists*. Belmont, CA: Wadsworth.
Bloch, M. (1964). *The historian's craft*. New York: Random House.
Boccardi, L. D. (1987). Press responsibility: The journalist's view. *Mass Communications Review*, 14(3), 11–13, 35.
Bogart, L. (1972). *The age of television*. New York: Ungar.
Bok, S. (1982). *Secrets*. New York: Pantheon.
Boot, W. (1989, May/June). Getting high on Tower. *Columbia Journalism Review*, pp. 18–20.
Boylan, J. (1986, November/December). Declaration of independence: A historian reflects on an era in which reporters rose up to challenge—and change—the rules of the game. *Columbia Journalism Review*, pp. 30–45.

Braden, M. (1989, March 11). Shop talk at thirty: Reporters should not deceive. *Editor & Publisher*, p. 68.
Bukro, C. (1985). The SPJ code's double-edged sword: Accountability, credibility. *Journal of Mass Media Ethics*, 1(1), 10–13.
Burke, J. (1978). *Connections*. Boston: Little, Brown.
Campbell, R., & Reeves, J. L. (1989). Covering the homeless: The Joyce Brown story. *Critical Studies in Mass Communications*, 6(1), 21–42.
Christians, C. G. (1985). Enforcing media codes. *Journal of Mass Media Ethics*, 1, 27–36.
Christians, C. G., Rotzoll, K. B., & Fackler, M. (1987). *Media ethics: Cases and moral reasoning* (2nd ed.). New York: Longman.
Clurman, R. M. (1988, July/August). Recipe for a gutsier press. *The Quill*, pp. 30–36.
Cohen, J. (1989). Propaganda from the middle-of-the-road: the centrist ideology of the news media. *Extra!* 3(1), 12.
Compaigne, B. (ed.) (1979). *Who owns the media?* White Plains, NY: Knowledge Industry Publications.
Cooper, T. W. (1986). Communications and ethics: The informal and formal curricula. *Journal of Mass Media Ethics*, 2(1), 71–79.
Coser, L. A., Kadushin, C., & Powell, W. W. (1982). *Books: The culture and commerce of publishing*. New York: Basic Books.
Cunningham, R. (1988, June). Re-examining the ombudsman's role. *The Quill*, p. 12.
Curcio, D. (1988, June 14). [Correspondence].
Curcio, D. (1988, June 19). [Interview].
Davenport, L. D., & Izard, R. S. (1985). Restrictive policies of the mass media. *Journal of Mass Media Ethics*, 1(1), pp. 4–9.
Davis, K. (1989, April 4). [Interview].
Denniston, L. (1988, September 26). [Remarks made during September 26 taping of PBS television program]. *The Politics of Privacy*.
Dershowitz, A. (1989, April 10). [Interview].
Dewey, J. (1969). *Outline of a critical theory of ethics*. New York: Greenwood.
Dill, B. (1986). *The journalist's handbook of libel and privacy*. New York: Free Press.
Elliott, D. (ed.) (1986). *Responsible journalism*. Newbury Park, CA: Sage.
Ephron, N. (1989, July/August). Quoted by M. Gottlieb. Dangerous liaisons: Journalists and their sources. *Columbia Journalism Review*, pp. 21–35.
Fink, C. (1988). *Media ethics in the newsroom and beyond*. New York: McGraw-Hill.
Fishman, M. (1988). *Manufacturing the news*. Austin: University of Texas Press.
Flew, A. (1979). *A dictionary of philosophy* (2nd ed.). New York: St. Martin's.
Forer, L. (1987, December 14). [Comments on libel laws made during interview program] *Sonia live in L.A.*, Cable News Network.
Friendly, F. (1987, March 3) [Interview following] *The second conference on TV & ethics*, Emerson College.
Friendly, F. (1987, November 1). [PBS television series]. *Ethics in America*.
Gans, H. J. (1985, November/December). Are U.S. journalists dangerously liberal? *Columbia Journalism Review*, 24(4): 29–37.
Gates, D. (1989, June 12). It's almost impossible to get it right. *Time*, p. 65.
Geertz, C. (1980). Blurred genres: The reconfiguration of social thought. *American Scholar*, 49(2), 165–174.
Gillmor, D. M., Barron, J. A., Simon, T., & Terry, H. (1990). *Mass communication law: Cases and comment* (5th ed.). St. Paul: West.
Gomery, D. (1989). Media economics: Terms of analysis. *Critical Studies in Mass Communication*, 6(1), 43–60.
Goodwin, H. E. (1983). *Groping for ethics in journalism*. Ames: Iowa State University Press
Griffith, T. (1986, January 27). The trouble with being fair. *Time*, p. 61.
Gustafson, J. (1990, January 4). [Interview].

Hanson, K. A., Ward, J., & McLeod, N. (1987). Role of the newspaper library in the production of news. *Journalism Quarterly*, 64(1), 714–720.
Hayakawa, S. I. (1941). *Language in action: A guide to accurate thinking*. New York: Harcourt.
Hazard, J. W. (1985, March 4). How private are your records? *U.S. News & World Report*, p. 93.
Hentoff, N. (1979, July 21). Privacy and the press: Is nothing sacred? *Saturday Review*, pp. 22–23.
Hentoff, N. (1988). *The first freedom: The tumultuous history of free speech in America*. New York: Delacorte.
Hesterman, V. (1987). Consumer magazines and ethical guidelines. *Journal of Mass Media Ethics*, 2(2), 93–101.
Hewitt, D. (1985). *Minute by minute*. New York: Random House.
Hiebert, R., Ungurait, D., & Bohn, T. (1986). *Mass media IV*. New York: Longman.
Hodges, L. W. (1986). The journalist and professionalism. *Journal of Mass Media Ethics*, 1(2), 32–36.
Hodges, L. W. (1987). Press responsibility: An introduction. *Mass Communications Review*, 14(3), 2–5, 22.
Hohenberg, J. (1978). *A crisis for the American press*. New York: Columbia University Press.
Hulteng, J. L. (1976). *The messenger's motives: Ethical problems of the news media*. Englewood Cliffs, NJ: Prentice-Hall.
Jankowitz, M. (1990, January 12). [Television interview] *This week with Connie Chung*.
Kelley, Kitty. (1989, July/August) Quoted by M. Gottlieb. Dangerous liaisons: Journalists and their sources. *Columbia Journalism Review*, pp. 22–35.
Kelly, A. H., Harbison, W. A., & Belz, H. (1983). *The American Constitution: The origin and development*. New York: Norton.
Klaidman, S., & Beauchamp, T. L. (1987). *The virtuous journalist*. New York: McGraw-Hill.
Klapper, J. T. (1960). *The effects of mass communication*. Glencoe, IL: Free Press.
Krause, E. A. (1971). *The sociology of occupations*. Boston: Little, Brown.
Labunski, R. E., & Pavlik, J. V. (1986). The legal environment of investigative reporters: A pilot study. *Media Asia*, 13 (1), 43–45.
Leslie, J. (1986, September). The anonymous source: Second thoughts on deep throat. *Columbia Journalism Review*, pp. 33–35.
Lippmann, W. (1922). *Public opinion*. New York: Harcourt Brace.
Logan, R. A. (1985). Jefferson's & Madison's legacy: The death of the national news council. *Journal of Mass Media Ethics*, 1(1), 68–77.
McGinniss, J. (1989, April 3). My critic's cloudy vision. *The New York Times*. p. A-23.
McGinniss, MacDonald & Malcolm: The '3M' controversy cont. (1990, February 25). *The Boston Globe*, pp. B-43, B45.
Malcolm, J. (1989, March 13). Reflections: the journalist and the murderer. *The New Yorker*, pp. 38–73.
Matson, W. I. (1970). *Sentience*. Berkeley: University of California Press.
Merrill, J. C., & Odell, J. S. (1983). *Philosophy and journalism*. New York: Longman.
Meyer, P. (1983). *Editors, publishers and newspaper ethics*. Washington, DC: American Society of Newspaper Editors.
Miller, A. (1982). *Miller's court*. Boston: Houghton Mifflin.
Mollenhoff, C. R. (1989, March). 25 Years of Times v. Sullivan. *The Quill*, pp. 27–31.
Mort, J. (1987, November 21). The Vanishing Labor Beat. *The Nation*, pp. 588–590.
Moyers, B. (1969). The press and government: Who's telling the truth? In W. K. Agee (ed.). *Mass media in a free society*, pp. 16–24. Lawrence: University of Kansas Press.
News Media and the Law (1987, Winter). pp. 25, 26.

Newton, L. H. (1989). *Ethics in America study guide*. Englewood Cliffs, NJ: Prentice-Hall.

New York Times manual of style and usage (1976). New York: Times Books.

O'Donnell, L., Benoit, P., & Hausman, C. (1990). *Modern radio production*. Belmont, CA: Wadsworth.

O'Donnell, L., Hausman, C., & Benoit, P. (1989). *Radio station operations* (2nd ed). Belmont, CA: Wadsworth.

Palmer, N. D. (1987, November). Going after the truth—in disguise: The ethics of deception. *Washington Journalism Review*, pp. 20–23.

Peterson, T. (1966). Social responsibility—theory and practice. In G. Gross (ed.), *The responsibility of the press* (pp. 33–49), New York: Fleet.

Petrow, R. (1987, December 3). [Interview].

Picard, R. G. (1988, Spring). Measures of concentration in the daily newspaper industry. *Journal of Mass Media Economics*, pp. 61–74.

Plato (1981). *Gorgias* (W. Hamilton, translator). New York: Penguin.

Postman, N., & Wiengartner, C. (1966). *Linguistics: A revolution in teaching*. New York: Delacorte.

Project Censored: 12-year old national media research effort selects its choice of significant stories not widely publicized by the national news media (1988, June 11). *Editor & Publisher*, pp. 80, 166.

Prosser, W. L. (1960) Privacy. *California Law Review*, 48, 338–423.

Ramer, M. A. (1987, August/September). The news dilemma: Public servant or profit slave? *The Professional Communicator*, pp. 24, 25.

Rand, Ayn (1971). *The new left: The anti-industrial revolution*. New York: Signet.

Riffe, D. (1986). Gatekeeping and the network news mix. *Journalism Quarterly*, 63(2), 315–321.

Rivers, W., & Schramm, W. (1969). *Responsibility in mass communication*. New York: Harper & Row.

Rivers, W., & Schramm W. (1986). The impact of mass communications. In R. Atwan, B. Orton, & W. Vesterman (eds.), *American mass media: Industries and issues* (3rd ed.) (pp. 5–16). New York: Random House.

Rooney, E. (1989, October). Once upon a time, reporters would use trickery to get story. *Solutions Today for Problems Tomorrow: A Special Report by the Ethics Committee of the Society of Professional Journalists*, pp. 10, 18.

Rowe, C. (1989). Judge story sparks aggressive competition. *1988–89 Journalism ethics report*, Washington, DC: Society of Professional Journalists, p. 8.

Sarault: Journal-Bulletin should adopt code of ethics. (1990, February 24). *Providence Journal-Bulletin*, p. A-4.

Schoeman, F. D. (1984). *Philosophical dimensions of privacy*. Cambridge: Cambridge University Press.

Schramm, W. (1966). Who is responsible for the quality of mass communications? In G. Gross (ed.), *The responsibility of the press* (pp. 348–361). New York: Fleet.

Schulte, H. (1987, December 8). [Interview].

Searl, J. R. (1980). Prima facie obligations. In Zak van Straaten (ed.), *Philosophical subjects* (pp. 238–259). Oxford: Clarendon.

Second Conference on TV & Ethics (1987, March 7). Symposium sponsored by Emerson College.

Siebert, F., Peterson, T., & Schramm, W. (1964). *Four theories of the press: The authoritarian, libertarian, social responsibility and Soviet Communist concepts of what the press should be*. Salem, NH: Ayer.

Sigma Delta Chi, The Society of Professional Journalists (1989). *1988–89 Journalism Ethics Report*.

Smith, J. (1986). Legal historians and the press clause. *Communications and the Law* 8(4): 69–80.

Sommers, C., & Sommers, F. (1985). *Vice and virtue in everyday life: Introductory readings in ethics* (2nd ed.). San Diego: Harcourt Brace Jovanovich.

Spinoza, B. (1964). In H. A. Joachin. *A study of the ethics of Spinoza.* New York: Russell & Russell.

Stein, M. L. (1989, March 18). Bee ombudsman tracks his paper's mistakes. *Editor & Publisher,* pp. 20, 39.

Stensaas, H. S. (1986). Development of the objectivity ethic in U.S. daily newspapers. *Journal of Mass Media Ethics,* 2(1): 50–60.

Stephens, M. (1988). *A history of news: From drum to satellite.* New York: Viking.

Stepp, C. S. (1986, December). Tough calls: When a public figure's private life is news. *Washington Journalism Review,* pp. 39–41.

Tuchman, B. (1984). *The march of folly.* New York: Knopf.

Vanslyke Turk, J. (1986, December). Information subsidies and media content: A study of PR influence on the news. *Journalism Monographs,* 100.

Wallace, M., & Gates, G. P. (1984). *Close encounters.* New York: Berkeley.

Warren, J. (1989). To tell the honest truth, has the court given journalists a right to lie? *Solutions Today for Problems Tomorrow: A Special Report by the Ethics Committee of the Society of Professional Journalists,* pp. 10, 18.

Warren, S. D., & Brandeis, L. D. (1890). The right to privacy. *Harvard Law Review,* 4, 193–220.

Wells, H. G. (1940). *The outline of history.* Garden City, NY: Garden City Publishing.

White, T., Meppen, A. J., & Young, S. (1984). *Broadcast news writing, reporting and production.* New York: Macmillan.

Wimmer, R. D., & Dominick, J. R. (1987). *Mass media research.* Belmont, CA: Wadsworth.

Wulfmeyer, K. T. (1989). What's ethical and what's not in electronic journalism: Perceptions of news directors. *Media Ethics Update,* 2(2).

Wyman, J. V. (1989, March 19). The balance between public interest and the right to privacy. Providence, RI, *Evening Bulletin,* p. B-11.

Credits

Text

Page 60: From Richard Campbell and Jimmie Reeves (1989). Covering the homeless: The Joyce Brown story. *Critical Studies in Mass Communications,* 6(1), 21–42. Reprinted by permission of the Speech Communication Association.

Pages 78–79: Courtesy of ABC News, "This Week with David Brinkley."

Page 107: From Robert Picard (Spring 1988). Measures of concentration in the daily newspaper industry. *Journal of Mass Media Economics,* 61–74.

Page 116: From Judy VanSlyke Turk (December 1986). Information subsidies and media content: A study of public relations influence on the news. *Journalism Monographs,* 100, 3. Reprinted by permission of the Association for Education in Journalism and Mass Communication.

Photographs

Figure 1.1: Irving Haberman/Eye Witness Photos.

Figure 7.1: Courtesy of ABC Television.

Figure 7.2: Courtesy of *The Providence Journal-Bulletin.*

Figure 10.1: AP/Wide World Photos. Figure 10.2: AP/Wide World Photos.

Index

Aaron, Betsy, 27
Abelson, Raziel, 162
Accountability, 133–134
    censorship and, 9–10, 143–144
    dimensions of, 133–137
    internal discipline and, 137–138
    libel law and, 141–143
    ombudsman, 138–140
    press council concept in, 140–141
    self-criticism/self-censure and, 145–152
Accuracy. *See* Objectivity
Accusation, power of, 90
Advertising, 111, 134
Agee, Warren K., 173–174
Age of Jackson, The (Schlesinger), 191–192
Age of Roosevelt, The (Schlesinger), 192
Alter, Jonathan, 103
American Society of Newspaper Editors, 137
    code of ethics of, 125, 128, 129, 180
Ames (Iowa) *Tribune*, 131
Anderson, D., 126
Anonymous sources, 126, 135, 136–137
Aquinas, Thomas, 165
Archival material, 120
Areopagitica (Milton), 16

Aristotle, 15, 19, 22, 40, 163
Associated Press, 5
Associated Press Managing Editors Association, code of ethics of, 125, 128, 129
Atwater, T., 107
Augustine, St., 164–165
Authoritarian theory, 16

Bacon, Francis, 166
Baerelson, Bernard, 44
Bagdikian, Ben, 98, 107, 108–109, 145, 174–175, 186
Baker, Russell, 62
Ball-Rokeach, S. J., 44–45
Barron, J. A., 135
Baumhart, Raymond, 15
Beauchamp, T. L., 10, 133–134, 138, 145, 180–181
Behar, Richard, 104
Bennett, W. Lance, 34, 116, 119
Benoit, P., 105, 106
Benson, Bob, 112
Bentham, Jeremy, 18, 169
Biagi, Shirley, 23, 44, 104, 109
Biden, Joe, 90
Bidney, David, 167
Bill of Rights, 10

207

208 INDEX

Bitter Years, The (Petrow), 39
Bloch, Marc, 38, 39
Bly, Nellie, 98
Boccardi, Louis D., 47, 50
Bogart, Leo, 7
Bohn, T., 82
Boilerplate copy, 120
Bok, Sissela, 82, 99
Book publishing, 109–111
Books: The Culture and Commerce of Publishing (Coser, Kadushin, Powell), 109
Boorstin, Daniel, 116, 119
Boot, William, 77–78
Borgatta, E.F., 186–187
Boylan, James, 11, 12, 146
Braden, Maria, 100–101
Bradlee, Benjamin, 98, 99, 100
Brandeis, Louis, 79, 80
Breal, Michel, 31
Broadcast News, 130
Buckley, William F., 102
Budner, Lawrence, 64
Buffalo Evening News, 98
Bukro, Casey, 146, 151
Bureaucracy, news, 120–121
Burke, James, 4
Bush, George, 90

Cairns, Huntington, 163
Calgary Herald, 139
Campbell, Richard, 58, 60
Carter, Jimmy, 10
Casebier, A., 175
Casebier, J. J., 175
Castillo, Julio, 118
Categorical imperative, 13, 15–16
CBS News, 27–29, 63, 93–94, 126
Censorship, 9–10, 143–144
Centrist ideology, 62
Chicago Daily News, 95
Chicago Sun-Times, 98
Chicago Tribune, 98, 101
Child abuse coverage, fairness and, 55–58, 59–60
Christians, C.G., 15, 82–83, 176, 182
City of God, The (St. Augustine), 165
Civil War, 5, 34
Close Encounters (Wallace), 63
Clurman, Richard M., 145, 146, 151
Codes of ethics. *See* Ethics in journalism, codes of
Cohen, Jeff, 62
Columbia Journalism Review, 77

Columbia University Seminar, 29, 33
Columbus, Christopher, 4–5
Commentary, codes of ethics on, 129
Communication Ethics: Methods of Analysis (Jaska and Pritchard), 178–179
Compaigne, Benjamin, 108, 109, 175
Complaint-handling process, 139–140
Confessions (St. Augustine), 165
Confidential sources, 129, 135–136
Conflict of interests, 67, 71, 128
Consequentialist theory, 18–22, 23, 87–89
Consonance, 107
Constitutional Convention of 1787, 10
Constitutional privilege, in codes of ethics, 128–129
Constitution, U.S., 80
Context
  codes of ethics on, 129
  word choice and, 58, 60–61
Controls. *See also* Accountability; Ethic in journalism, codes of; Government controls social responsibility and, 46, 47–48
Cooke, Janet, 113–114
Cooper, Kent, 81
Cooper, Thomas W., 17
Copleston, Frederick, 161–162
Corrections, 140
Cosby, William, 10
Coser, Lewis A., 109, 110–111
Crawford, N. A., 176–177
Credit information, 91
Crick, M., 187
Crisis for the American Press, A (Hohenberg), 178
Crook, K., 186–187
Crowd size, estimating, 37, 48–49
Culture Against Man (Henry), 189
Cunningham, Richard, 139
Curcio, Diane, 55–58, 59–60
Cutaways, 63

Davenport, L. D., 126
Davis, K., 81
Denniston, Lyle, 72
Deontological theory, 18
Dershowitz, Alan, 90
Descartes, Rene, 166–167
Dewey, John, 11, 14, 162, 170
Dialect, rendering, 102
Dialogues (Plato), 162–163
Dill, B., 83

Discourses of Epictetus, The, 164
Donaldson, Sam, 78
Dos Passos, John, 105
Douglas, William O., 79
Dukakis, Michael, 90
Durant, Will, 167, 166, 163, 167*n*
Dwyer, R. Budd, 115

Economy of scale, 105–106
Editor and Publisher, 66, 73, 100, 140, 145
Edwards, Douglas, 6–7
Effete Conspiracy, The (Bagdikian), 108, 174–175
Element selection, fairness and, 62–64
Elizabeth I, Queen of England, 3
Elliott, Deni, 43, 52–53
Embarrassment complaints, 83
Emerson College Conference on TV and Ethics (1987), 135
Employers, accountability to, 134
Ends versus means, 93–103
Enquiry Concerning the Principles of Morals (Hume), 168
Entman, R., 181–182
Ephron, Nora, 72
Epictetus, 164
Epicurus, 164
Epistemology, 30
Errors
  accountability for, 140
  codes of ethics on, 129
Essay de Semantique (Breal), 31
Essays (Bacon), 166
Ethics: Theory and Practice (Thiroux), 162
Ethics in journalism, 13–24. *See also* Fairness; Objectivity; Profesionalism; Social responsibility
  codes of, 125–132 basic tenets of, 126–129 enforcement issue and, 132 memo-and-meeting approach to, 126 opposition to, 131–132 prevalence of, 125–126 self-censure and, 146 technology and, 129–130
  consequentialist/non-consequentionalist, 18–22, 23, 87–89
  defined, 14–16
  economics and. *See* Media business
  ends versus means and, 93–103
  of golden mean, 15, 18, 19, 20, 22, 23
Ethics in journalism (*Continued*)
  logical versus temporal priorities and, 22–23
  personal judgment and, 11–12
  philosophic constructs for, 16–18
  readings on, 173–194
  versus reason, 11*n*
  reconstruction of events and, 113–121
  violations. *See* Accountability
  virtue decisionmaker, qualifications of, 23–24
Ethics and philosophy, readings in, 165–171
Ethics and Profits: The Crisis of Conscience in American Business (Silk and Vogel), 162
Ethics and Profits (Silk and Vogel), 193
Ethics for Modern Life (Abelson and Friquegnon), 162
Ethics for the Media (Rivers and Mathews), 182
Ethics, Morality and the Media (Thayer), 186
Ethics of Journalism, The (Crawford), 176–177
Ethics (Spinoza), 167
Explorations in Language and Meaning (Crick), 187
Extensional meaning, 35–36

Fackler, M., 15, 82–83, 176
Fairness, 35, 36–37, 54–66
  element selection and, 62–64
  government regulation of, 66
  interpretations of, 56
  mechanical attempts at, 54, 55–58, 59–60
  news-gathering process and, 64–66
  perspective and, 61–62
  word choice and, 58, 60–61
Fairness Doctrine, 66
False light complaints, 83
Farr, William, 135
Fink, Conrad, 34, 81, 111–112, 131, 132
Finnegan, John R., 87
First Amendment, 10, 17, 81, 90
Fishman, Mark, 120
Flew, Anthony, 14
Forer, Louis G., 83
Four Theories of the Press (Siebert, Peterson, Schramm), 16, 46, 184–185
Francis, Fred, 144
Frankena, William K., 162
Franklin, James, 9

Freebies, 128, 186
Freedom of press, 10
Friendly, Fred, 6, 12, 13, 27, 50, 155
    on privacy rights, 90
    on Stuart case, 29–30, 34
Friquegnon, Marie-Louise, 162
Future of Sociology, The (Borgatta and Crook), 186–187

Galbraith, J.K., 187
Gannett Company, 106, 108, 109
Gans, Herbert J., 34
Gartner, Michael, 131
Gates, David, 62
Gaudet, Hazel, 44
Geertz, Clifford, 117
Gettysburg Address, 36
Ghiglione, Loren, 183
Gillmor, D.M., 9, 17, 135, 136
Golden mean, 15, 18, 19, 20, 22, 23
Goldstein, Tom, 95, 98, 114
Gomery, D., 106
Goodwin, H.E., 13, 81, 177
Government controls
    censorship, 9–10, 143–144
    ethic codes and, 131–132
    Fairness Doctrine, 66
    social responsibility and, 47–48
Government sources, 62
Grandose, John, 162
Graphic, 45
Graubard, S. R., 188
Greeley, Horace, 46
Greene, Bob, 98
Greenville News, 84
Griffith, Thomas, 54, 55
Groping for Ethics in Journalism (Goodwin), 177
Gross, G., 177–178
Gulf War, 143, 144
Gustafson, James, 23–24
Gutenberg, Johannes, 4, 5
Gutmann, Amy, 162

Hamilton, Andrew, 10
Hamilton, Edith, 163
Hansen, A., 120
Harper, Pat, 99–100
Harris, Benjamin, 9
Harris, Byron, 23
Harrison, Jonathan, 168
Hart, Gary, 78, 90
Harwood, Richard, 138–139
Hausman, C., 105, 106

Hayakawa, S. I., 31–32, 35, 36, 37, 52, 188–189
Headlines, 58
Hearst, William Randolph, 45
Hegel, G. W. F., 169
Henry, Jules, 189
Hentoff, Nat, 3, 9, 85
Hesterman, V., 134
Hewitt, Don, 6–7, 93–94, 100
Hiebert, R., 82
Historian's Craft, The (Bloch), 38
Historical method, 38
History of an Historian, The (Schlesinger), 193
History of News, A: From the Drum to the Satellite (Stephens), 5, 185
History of Philosophy, A (Copleston), 161–162
Hobbes, Thomas, 46, 166
Hodges, Louis W., 43, 68, 71
Hohenberg, J., 178
Homeless persons
    impersonation of, 99–100
    word choice and, 58, 60
Hulteng, John, 135, 180
Hume, David, 167–168

Imperative of Freedom, The (Merrill), 69
Impersonation, 96–97, 98–100
Individual rights, 8–9
Informed-public-accessible-press theory, 51–53, 66
Inside Organizations: Understanding the Human Dimension (Jones), 189–190
Insider information, 138
Intentional meaning, 35, 36
Introductory Readings in Ethics (Frankena and Grandose), 162
Investigative Reporters and Editors (IRE), 142
Izard, R. S., 126

Jankowitz, Mark, 29, 30
Jaska, A. A., 178–179
Jefferson, Thomas, 42
"Jimmy's World," 113
Johnson, Lyndon, 12
Jones, M. O., 189–190
Journalism, evolution of, 3–12
    communications media and, 5–8, 11
    governmental restraints and, 9–11
    individual rights and, 8–9
    personal ethics and, 11–12

printing press and, 4–5
Journalism ethics. *See* Ethics in journalism
Journalism Monographs, 116
Journal of Mass Media Ethics, 35
Judeo-Christian ethic, 16
Jump cuts, 63

Kadushin, Charles, 109, 111
Kafka, Franz, 110
Kant, Immanuel, 15–16, 19, 168
Kelley, Kitty, 72–73
Kilgallen, Dorothy, 98
Kirkpatrick, J.J., 190
Kissinger: Portrait of a Mind (Graubard), 188
Klaidman, S., 10, 133–134, 138, 145, 180–181
Klapper, Joseph T., 44, 45
Knight-Ridder, 108
Korzybski, Alfred, 31
Kovach, Bill, 29
Krause, E., 190
Krause, Elliott A., 70, 190

Language in Action: A Guide to Accurate Thinking (Hayakawa), 31, 188–189
Lanson, Gerald, 146
Lapham, Lewis, 69, 70
Lasher, William, 105–106
Lazarsfeld, Paul, 44, 45
Leslie, J., 137
Levantin, R. C., 190
Lewis, Will, 135
Lexington (Kentucky) *Herald-Leader*, 100
Libel laws, 10, 47, 83, 103, 114, 141–143
Libertarian theory, 16, 46, 48, 51–52
Licensing, 9
Lichter, L. S., 179–180
Lichter, S. R., 179–180
Lippman, Walter, 12, 52, 132, 155, 183–184, 191
Little, Gary, 89
Locke, John, 46, 80
Logan, Robert A., 140
Louisville *Courier-Journal*, 126, 138
Lubunski, R. E., 142
Lucretius, 164

McCarthy, Joseph, 7, 12, 155
McClure, Robert, 44
MacDonald, Jeffrey, 72, 101

McGinniss, Joe, 72, 101
Machiavelli, Niccolo, 165–166
McLeod, N., 120
Magna Charta, 8
Malcolm, Janet, 72, 73, 101–102, 103
Manhood of Humanity, The (Korzybski), 31
Manufacturing the News (Fishman), 120
March of Folly, The (Tuchman), 193–194
Martin, Mary, 7
Mass Media in a Free Society (Agee), 173–174
Masson, Jeffrey M., 73, 101–102
Mass opinion, 7
Masters, R.D., 191
Mathews, C., 182
Matson, Wallace, 61
Media business, 104–112
    advertiser pressure and, 134
    book publishing, 109–111
    economy of scale in, 105–106
    effects of oligopoly, 106–111
    as investment commodity, 104–105
    newspapers, 108–109, 111
    profit *vs* responsibility in, 111–112
    radio, 104–105
    television, 107
Media-effects research, 43–45
Media Elite, The: America's New Power brokers (Lichter), 179–180
Media Ethics: Cases and Moral Reasoning (Christians, Rotzoll, Fackler), 15, 176
Media Monopoly, The (Bagdikian), 107
Media Power Politics (Paletz and Entman), 181–182
Merrill, John, 17–18, 47–48, 51–52, 69, 70, 156, 181
Meyer, Philip, 125
Mill, John Stuart, 15, 16–17, 18, 43, 169–170
Milton, John, 16, 17
Minneapolis Star and Tribune, 87
Misappropriation complaints, 83
Misrepresentation, 96–97, 98–101
Missoulian, 82
Mollenhoff, Clark R., 142, 143
Money: Where It Came, Where It Went (Galbraith), 187
Moore, G.E., 162, 170
Morality, versus ethics, 14–15
Mort, Jo-Ann, 65
Mounce, H. O., 171
Moyers, Bill, 35, 36, 37, 48

Murrow, Edward R., 5, 6, 7, 12, 55, 145, 155
Mythologization, 94–95

Nauman, Art, 140
NBC News, 94, 99–100
New England Courant, 9
News: The Politics of Illusion (Bennett), 34, 116
News at Any Cost, The: How Journalists Compromise Their Ethics to Shape the News (Goldstein), 95
Newsday, 98
News Media and the Law, 84
News services, 5
Newton, Lisa, 80
New World, discovery of, 4–5
New York Daily News, 95, 98, 114
New Yorker, 72, 73, 103
New York Times, 72, 102, 145, 146. *See also Times versus Sullvan*
  centrist ideology and, 62
  fairness principle of, 55, 61–62
New York Weekly Journal, 10
Nicomachean Ethics (Aristotle), 163
Nietzsche, Friedrich, 170
Nonconsequentialist theory, 18, 19–22, 23
Not in Our Genes (Levantin), 190

Objectivity, 5, 27–41
  attainability of, 34, 35
  codes of ethics on, 128
  evolution of ideal, 35
  extensional/intentional meaning and, 35–36
  fairness and, 36–37, 62
  market-influenced, 34
  semantic confusion and, 31–34
  in Stuart case, 27–30, 33–34, 40–41
  and truth, determining, 37–41
Occupational ideology, 70
Odell, J. S., 17–18
Odell, S. J., 181
O'Donnell, L., 105, 106
Oldfield, Barney, 144
Oligopoly, 106–109
Ombudsman, 138–140
"On Liberty of Thought and Discussion" (Mill), 17
On the Nature of Things (Lucretius), 164
Other Side of the News, The, 29

Paletz, D. A., 181–182

Palmer, N. D., 100
Pantheon, 110
Patterson, Thomas, 44
Pavlick, J. V., 142
Perry, John L., 54, 55
Personal ethics, 11–12
Perspective, word choice and, 61–62
Peterson, Theodore, 16, 45–46, 178, 184
Petition of Right, 8–9
Petrow, Richard, 39
Philadelphia Inquirer, 108
Philosophy and Journalism (Merrill and Odell), 181
Picard, Robert, 107
Pipe artist, 113
Pittsburgh Press, 137
Plagiarism, 138
Plato, 43, 45, 162–163
Playing It Straight (Hulteng), 180
Police, policy on turning over tapes/photos to, 97
Police information, privacy issues in, 84
Political Philosophy of Rousseau, The (Masters), 191
Politician Woman (Kirkpatrick), 190
Postman, N., 30, 31
Powell, Walter, 109, 111
Power
  of accusation, 90
  of media effects, 43–45
  obligations of, 43, 45–46
Preface to Morals (Lippmann), 191
Press and the Decline of Democracy, The (Picard), 107
Press councils, 140–141
Prince, The (Machiavelli), 166
Principia Ethica (Moore), 162, 170
Printing press, 4–5
Prior restraint, 9
Pritchard, M. S., 178–179
Privacy rights, 10, 77–92
  codes of ethics on, 129
  deterrence concept and, 19–22, 87–89
  in information age, 90–91
  legal foundations for, 79–80
  philosophical foundations for, 80–81
  power of accusation and, 90
  public attitude toward, 84–85
  public information and, 84
  public persons and, 77–79, 90
  versus "right to know," 81–83
  rule change regarding, 79, 81, 85–86
  state laws on, 83–84

Process and Effects of Mass Communication, The (Schramm), 183–184
Professionalism, 12, 67–73
　acceptable/unacceptable behavior, 67
　fabrication of quotes and, 73
　freebies and, 67, 71
　journalism and, 67–71
　social/professional relationships and, 71–73
Prosser, W. L., 80
Providence *Evening Bulletin*, 87–88
Providence *Journal-Bulletin*, 131–132
Pseudo-events, 116, 119
Publick Occurrences Both Foreign and Domestick, 9
Public Opinion (Lippmann), 52, 183
Pulitzer, Joseph, 45
Pulitzer Prize
　Cooke affair and, 113–114
　to undercover stories, 98

Quest for Truth, The: An Introduction to Philosophy (Gustafson), 23
Questioning Media Ethics (Rubin), 182–183
Quill, The, 139, 146
Quotes, of dialect, 102
Quotes, fabrication of, 73, 101–102, 103

Radio, 5, 11, 49, 104–105
Radio-television News Directors Association, code of ethics of, 125, 127–128, 129
Ramer, Mary Anne, 108
Rand, Ayn, 156
Random House, 110
Rashomon effect, 62, 66
Rawls, John, 15
Raymond, Henry, 46
Reader's Digest, 145–146
Reeves, Jimmie, 58, 60
Reporters' Ethics (Swain), 185–186
Responsibility in Mass Communications (Rivers, Schramm and Christians), 182
Responsibility of the Press, The (Gross), 177
Reversals, 63
Richards, D. A. J., 11*n*
Riffe, D., 107
"Right to be let alone" concept, 79–80
"Right to know" concept, 81–83, 129
Rivers, William, 45
Rivers, W. L., 1
Roberts, Cokie, 78, 86

Rooney, Ed, 95
Roosevelt, Franklin Delano, 81
Rosenthal, A. M., 146
Ross, W. D., 19
Rothman, S., 179–180
Rotwein, Eugene, 168
Rotzoll, K. B., 15, 82–83, 176
Rousseau, Jean-Jacques, 46
Rubin, B., 182–183
Rumor, 77, 90

Sacramento Bee, 136, 140
St. Paul Pioneer Press and Dispatch, 87
Sarault, Brian, 131
Schanberg, Sydney, 145
Schlesinger, Arthur M., Jr., 191–193
Schlesinger, Arthur M., Sr., 119, 193
Schneider, Andrew, 137
Schoeman, F.D., 80
Schramm, Wilbur, 16, 45, 46, 51, 52, 177–178, 182, 183–184
Schulte, Henry, 135
Science and Sanity (Korzybski), 31
Searle, John R., 56
Seattle Post-Intelligencer, 89
Secrets (Bok), 82, 99
Sedition laws, 9–10
"See It Now," 12
Seib, Charles, 125
Seigenthaler, John, 66
Self-examination, critical, 145–152
Semantics, 31–34
Sentience (Matson), 61
Sex crimes coverage
　fairness and, 54–58, 59–60
　privacy rights and, 90
Shield laws, 135–136
Siebert, F.S., 16, 46, 184
Silk, Leonard, 162, 193
Silvers, Anita, 175
Simon, T., 135, 136
Simulation, codes of ethics on, 129, 130, 131
"60 Minutes," 100
Smith, Russell F. W., 30
Social contract theory, 46–47
Social Responsibilities of the Mass Media (Casebier), 175
Social responsibility, 16, 42–53
　government controls and, 47–48
　informed-public-accessible-press theory of, 51–53
　media effects and, 43–45
　obligations of power and, 43, 45–46

public misunderstanding and, 48–51
social contract theory of, 46–47
Society of Professional Journalists, 101, 146
code of ethics of, 125, 126–127
Sociology of Occupations, The (Krause), 70, 190
Socolow, Sanford, 63
Sources, accountability to, 135–137
Soviet Communist theory, 16
Spinoza, Benedict de, 167, 132
Stand-up, 22–23
Star Chamber, 9
Stein, M. L., 140
Stensaas, H. S., 35
Stephens, Mitchell, 4, 5, 146, 185
Stepp, C. S., 87
Stewart, John B., 168
Stimson, Henry, 162
Story of Philosophy, The (Durant), 167
Stott, Jim, 139
Stout, Anthony, 144
Strike coverage, fairness and, 64–66
Stuart case, objectivity of coverage in, 27–30, 33–34, 40–41
Stubbs, John, 3, 5, 8
Subjects, accountability to, 135
Suicide coverage, privacy rights and, 19–22, 87
Supreme Court, U.S., 16, 84, 141
Swain, B. M., 185–186
Swayze, John Cameron, 7

Technology
codes of ethics on, 129–130
privacy rights and, 90–91
Telegraph, 5
Teleological theory, 18
Television news
consonance in, 107
early, 6–7
element selection in, 62–64, 117
ends versus means in, 93–94, 99–100
logical versus temporal priorities in, 22–23
mass opinion and, 7–8
Terry, H., 135, 136
Thayer, L., 186
Theory of Ethics, A (Dewey), 162
Thiroux, Jaques P., 162
Thompson, Dennis, 162
Time, 146
Times versus *Sullivan*, 16, 141, 142–143
Tisch, Lawrence, 108

Tomlin, Lily, 113
Tommerup, Peter, 94–95
Tower, John, 77–78, 90
Tractatus Logico Philosophicus (Wittgenstein), 171
Tremblay, Mark, 139
Truth
as defense against libel, 10
determining, 37–40
Tuchman, B., 156, 193–194
Tufts, James H., 170
Turk, Judy Vanslyke, 116

Undercover operations, 96, 98–100
Ungurait, D., 82
Unofficial charges, responding to, 55
Utilitarianism (Mill), 169

Virtue decision, 23–24
Virtuous Journalist, The (Klaidman and Beauchamp), 10, 180–181
Vogel, David, 162, 193
Voting behavior, media effect on, 44

Wallace, Mike, 63, 115, 117
Ward, J., 120
Warren, James, 73, 101–102
Warren, Samuel D., 80
Washington Journalism Review, The, 100, 137, 146
Washington Post, 113, 138–139
Weak-media-powerful-audience theory, 44
Weiss, Philip, 109
Wells, H. G., 8, 9
Whearley, Jay, 13
Who Owns the Media? (Compaigne), 108, 175
Wicker, Tom, 79
Wiengartner, C., 30, 31
Will, George, 30, 77, 78, 79, 90
Williams, Edward Bennett, 177
Wittgenstein, Ludwig, 30–31, 171
Word choice
fairness and, 58, 60–61
perception and, 31–34
World War II, 5, 144
Wulfemeyer, K. Tim, 67, 71
Wyman, James V., 88

Yellow journalism, 45–46
York, Michael, 100, 101

Zenger, John Peter, 9–10